A GYPSY IN

OUR SOULS

EXPLORING ARIZONA

BY

MARIE J. LEMAY

&

SUZANNE T. POIRIER

For Katherine Watson
and
Jack Lasseter

Thank you for sharing your knowledge and love of Arizona,
and for awakening in us the desire to continue exploring

Courtney
Live Long and
Large and Enjoy
Love Midge 'Bud

A GYPSY IN OUR SOULS
EXPLORING ARIZONA

Copyright 2018
Marie J. Lemay and Suzanne T. Poirier

ISBN-13: 978-1986178815
ISBN-10: 1986178811

Photo Credits
Front Cover: Marie J. Lemay, Suzanne T. Poirier,, authors
Back Cover: Marie J. Lemay, Suzanne T. Poirier, authors

Printed in the United States

Toughnut Press, Tucson, Arizona
Cynthia Roedig
Editor-Publisher

Table of Contents

INTRODUCTION

Welcome! If you have opened the cover to peruse this introduction, you must be as curious as we are. We believe that curiosity is the core quality for the adventurer and explorer.

We arrived in Arizona in November 2010. Our goal was to stay six months to see the spring flowers and cactus in bloom. Heading back to the Northeast, we planned to explore all of the Canadian parks but that plan did not work out. Seven days after arriving in Arizona, all plans shifted to making this our permanent home.

We were thrilled about the decision to adopt a new state (with no snow and ice) but it was an environment which was very different. It was obvious that the learning curve in this new place would be long, painful, and sometimes difficult. Being adventurers and explorers, the eagerness to learn about this state was intense.

A friend had recently shared with us a quote that highlights the position of being a new resident in this state. The words of wisdom from Vicki Sullivan: "Newcomers to Arizona are often stymied by the different microclimates, geology, history, food, flora, fauna and cultures they discover. Often they feel out of place, not sure where they fit in. I tell them, when you start experimenting and exploring, your job is to collect the dots. After about a year, you will begin to connect the dots. At that point, you'll feel as if you belong as the dots begin to make sense. Don't worry, just have fun collecting the dots." Our friend is a wise woman.

For over five years, the collection of dots has been a primary focus as we attempt to piece together the history of Arizona. We have collected hundreds of dots in the process and we have enjoyed our journey of learning, doing, seeing, and exploring.

In this book, we will share with you some of the methods we used to assist us in our process of learning. We will also share with you many of the historical places, ghost towns, activities, cultural events and educational events we have participated in.

It has been a wonderful journey learning about Arizona. Come with us and become the adventurers and explorers you have always dreamed of.

CAST OF CHARACTERS

There are numerous characters appearing in the adventures described in this book. To increase the enjoyment of the reader, we decided that an introduction of those mentioned would be helpful.

Sue is the plotter, planner and researcher. Main jobs include giving Gypsy her directions, staying on the road, controlling Gypsy's speed, verifying the direction we are heading in, watching for ice on road (per the road signs), photographing and recording all adventures.

Midge is the navigator and spotter. Main jobs include spotting police, spotting animals of all kinds, watching for rocks (per the road signs), pointing out the beauty of the area, providing snacks, taking pictures of clouds, landscapes and oddities. An additional responsibility is singing "Blue Skies smiling at me…" whenever clouds become threatening. Note: singing the song often produces sunny results.

"Gypsy" is a 2006 Honda CRV who is currently ten years old and believes she is still a youngster. When we fell in love with her, she was new with only six miles. She was a brilliant burgundy and it was love at first sight. We still love her as much, but today she has well over two hundred thousand miles and tons of desert striping from the years of adventures. She still loves to go up, down and around hills and mountains. Regardless of the numerous scratches on both sides from the thorny branches, her preferences remain the same: driving on dirt roads and going through streams and rivers. She always loves having happy adventurers in the back seat.

We have met some fellow adventurers and explorers and

they willingly join us on many of our adventures. They have enhanced the fun and enjoyment of exploring this beautiful state of ours.

Mary Newman is a fellow adventurer who enjoys the great outdoors. She often joins us in visiting canyons, ghost towns and other varied adventures. Mary accompanied us on a road trip to Bisbee, Douglas and Naco. We stayed at the Copper Queen Hotel in Bisbee and at the Gadsden Hotel in Douglas, that are reportedly haunted. We all survived to finish the road trip. Together, we have explored Garden Canyon, Brown Canyon and Ramsey Canyon.

Bernadette Cardwell is our artist friend who exposed us to the artistic side of life in Arizona. We often spend time in the Tucson area, exploring the different neighborhoods, taking pictures of doors in the Barrio, searching for murals, and exploring the oddities of Tucson. She has accompanied us on trips to ghost towns and varied attractions. Bernadette will participate in any activity that does not include hiking. She is also a valuable asset to the group because she has the ability to read street signs from three blocks away.

Irma Thibault is our musical friend who has introduced us to the wide variety of music that exists in this state. She also loves to travel on any adventure. She enjoys seeing Native American sites, ghost towns, dry lakes and a wide variety of attractions. She loves to explore and often wanders in hopes in finding something exciting. One day she stubbed her toe on a piece of petrified wood. A great experience was sharing the chocolate soufflé at the La Posada Hotel in Winslow.

Dotty Brack is a fellow adventurer who has traveled far and wide. She loves adventures and will accompany us whenever possible. Her pursuit of knowledge is infectious and she even laughs when we arrive at a dry lake. Dotty was present at the La Posada Hotel in Winslow for the sharing of the chocolate soufflé. She also accompanied us on the journey to find Pearce Ferry (a ghost town) that happens to be at the bottom of the

Grand Canyon. In Seligman, she had the opportunity to sleep in a Harley Davidson-themed room.

Betty Nolan loves reading about Arizona and loves to explore the places she has read about. She is our pioneer who loves adventures in the wilderness and loves to cross rivers and streams. Her love of the pioneer women who settled this state adds a new dimension to an adventure. After reading the books written by Eulalia Bourne (schoolteacher, rancher, author), we took road trips to the ranches where she taught and we found her grave site in Oracle. Betty also loves soaking her feet in thermal springs.

Sue Smith started participating in adventures about three years ago. She is eager to learn and explore and willing to go on any adventure. She was even willing to sleep on a blow-up mattress in Portal. She also participated on a trip to Sasabe to see the Rancho de la Osa and to ride on the dirt road along the border fence looking for the historical border markers. In Gila Bend, she even helped us search for the crabs.

Jacqui Harrold currently lives in Scotland and visits Arizona about once a year. She is always happy to participate in a yearly road trip. She loves seeing any part of Arizona that is new and exciting. We always meet new people when we are with Jacqui. I think people are drawn to her because of her endearing accent.

Mike & Carolyn Flynn were our neighbors when we first arrived in Green Valley and we have remained friends. Together we participated in some fun and exciting adventures: hot air balloon ride, fossil hunting, Las Vegas trip, Laughlin trip, Route 66 International Festival, Barnum & Bailey circus, Cirque de Soleil in Tucson and a variety of musical venues.

This cast of characters (our friends and fellow travelers) have added fun, laughter and enjoyment to our adventures and lives. Together, we have created some unforgettable memories. As a group, we have also learned how to embellish some of the adventures and some of those details have not been shared in this book!

LEARNING ABOUT ARIZONA

*"Anyone who stops learning is old,
whether at 20 or 80. Anyone
who keeps learning stays young."*

- Henry Ford

In December 2010, the decision was made to make Arizona our permanent residence. Endless blue skies for days on end, warm winter temperatures, the cactus, the big sky country, affordable living, the anticipation of cactus blooming in the spring and the nakedness of the mountains made our decision very easy. Coming from New England where all of the mountains are covered with trees, the Arizona mountains were intriguing and pleasurable to look at.

We were so excited to be here for our first winter. We could wear shorts during the day, have the windows open, eat our lunches outdoors and look at the blue sky every day. We spent a lot of time checking out the new plants, trees and shrubs and admired all the winter flowers we encountered. Everyone in our neighborhood knew we were new to the area: we carried our camera everywhere and took pictures of everything. People would look at us, smile and say "Hello." We think they were remembering what it was like to be a new resident in this beautiful environment.

We also spent a lot of time checking out the wildlife. Early on, we had already seen a roadrunner, all sizes of bunnies and some strange looking birds with a crest on top of their heads.

It took us a while to find out the name of that bird: a Gambel's quail. We had many questions during the first six months, location of the car wash, the town center and references for places to get an oil change.

Then, we began to get the sense that becoming a part of our new environment was going to take a lot more education than we thought. We realized we were on a long learning curve that would prove to be fun, embarrassing, and memorable. And some of the areas we needed to learn in a hurry.

Everything in the desert picks, pricks or sticks. We heard that several times, but it took a long time to grasp the significance of that advice. One of us is a visual learner and the other is tactile. A lot of band aids were required that first year to cover up the holes inflicted by cactus thorns, mesquite thorns and flower stems. By golly, almost everything has thorns! To be prepared for the inevitable, we put plenty of band aids and tweezers in our first aid kit.

One day, we left for an adventure to the Willcox Playa. We felt secure having our band aids, tweezers and first aid cream. We were prepared for the next disaster involving things that prick, stick or pick. That day, we discovered that overconfidence can be dangerous. Driving around the playa, we discovered some sand dunes and decided to stop and explore. We were hoping to look for sea shells when disaster struck. Walking through the grass, we missed seeing the bush with "prickers." The round pricky balls were stuck from the shoes to the inseam. On the side of the road, one of us stood still, while the other was extracting the prickers. The cars driving by slowed down and the passengers smiled and waved. We learned the lesson about bushes that day.

The concept of cactus thorns, however, is a little harder to grasp. Let us explain. Sometimes you cannot see the danger. One day, we were walking around the neighborhood with Jacqui (our friend from Scotland) and we spotted a prickly pear cactus full of huge, red fruit. We knew that Mary makes prickly pear juice, so we decided to pick some. We had checked the big, red, ripe fruit and there were no visible thorns. After collecting about twenty fruits, the feeling was unanimous. No more picking fruit. Every finger of both hands had invisible thorns. We used a lot of scotch tape that night in the process of removing dozens of annoying baby thorns. Took a long time to learn that lesson and even today unexpected disasters still happen to the tactile resident.

In New England, the air smells "earthy" and fresh after a cleansing rain. It's the time when everyone opens their windows to let in the "fresh air." In Arizona, the rain is always welcome but, in the desert areas of the state, the odor is unfamiliar and disturbing to new residents. The first time we smelled the desert after a rain, we thought there was an electrical fire in the neighborhood and we were prepared to call 911.

It was a transforming experience when all of a sudden we began to enjoy the desert smell. After a rain, we always open the door and the windows. We have since learned that the smell comes from the creosote bush and it happens every time it gets wet. We have read in many books and articles that the main thing people miss when they move away is the smell of the desert after a rain. Want to know if it rained last night? Just smell the air and the creosote will tell you.

Want to find out if someone is new to the area? Just ask them to list the five "Cs." The list of the Cs is reportedly important to know. When we were new to southern Arizona, we heard that question many times. Over time, we learned that Cattle, Citrus, Cotton, Copper and Climate (five Cs) represent the main industries in the state. Driving around the state, it is easy to find examples of all of them.

And speaking of climate, due to the intensity of the sun and the extreme heat in the summer, maintenance of Gypsy is different than if we were living in New England. Windshield wipers dry out in about eighteen months, batteries last about two years and the sidewalls of tires begin to crack at about four years. Different vehicle maintenance requirements, but cars do not rust and exhaust systems last forever. Gypsy does not mind living in the desert.

Another interesting thing we discovered was that all of the people we were meeting were from other states, just like us. All of the people were friendly and loved being in Green Valley; however, we wondered where all the native Arizonans were! It took us almost six months to meet a native Arizonan. Since then, we have met many people born in this wonderful state and they have taught us many lessons.

One big area of difficulty for us was the pronunciation of street names, places, foods etc. We have shown significant growth in this area, but this requires continuing improvement. Some of the places in the area assist visitors in the correct pronunciation. We went to Chiricahua National Monument and we found a sign that spelled out the name for us: Cheer-ah-cow-wah. Standing in front of the sign, we practiced for a few minutes and we still remember it.

On some occasions, our pronunciation difficulties have produced some moments of embarrassment. One such moment occurred at Tumacacori National Monument. We were talking to the ranger on duty and we were sharing with her how happy we were to be living in southern Arizona because we loved seeing the Saguaros (pronounced Cigaros). The ranger did not succeed in controlling her laughter. It took her some time to be able to tell us the correct pronunciation. She had us practice Sah-war-oh: over and over again. When we left the visitor center, we were still having problems but now we say it properly. Today, we sound like Arizonans when we call them Sah-war-ohs. We are on friendly terms with the park ranger and see her often. I wonder if she remembers our first encounter as vividly as we do.

There are many Spanish names and words in the area and we are still working hard to acquire the proper pronunciations of places, things and people. It is a challenge for newcomers who do not realize "LL" sounds like a "y" and that a "j" is pronounced like an "h". Still a work in progress, but improving.

During our first year, the embarrassing moments went beyond the improper pronunciation of words, names or places. One beautiful morning, we decided to go to the Tucson Rodeo Parade. What a fine, warm, sunny day it was and we were thrilled to be there. Sitting in the stands, the view of the parade was fantastic. We loved seeing the cowboys, the horses, the floats, the carriages, and the bands. On one float, we saw a creature with ears like Mickey Mouse. Wow! Look at that. They even included Mickey Mouse in their parade. Unfortunately, we shared that knowledge out loud and it was overheard by two children about six or seven years old, sitting directly in front of us. The children sighed, turned around and said "That's Truly Nolen." We remember that day very well. We said nothing. Later, we looked at each other and asked: "What's Truly Nolen?" Today, we know that it is a pest control company and every time we see their yellow vehicles with mouse ears and a tail, we remember that day at the parade.

Our first spring in southern Arizona was exciting. The flowers were starting to bloom and we were going from place to place is search of the natural beauties. One afternoon, in early March, we were driving down La Canada on our way home. On the right side of the road, the rocks were all painted green. We thought that was so neat. Painting the rocks green for St. Patrick's Day. That night, we shared with Mary how excited we were to see the rocks being painted for St. Patrick's Day. Mary got very quiet and took some time before she informed us that the green spray was weed control. We felt the pain of being new.

After about six months, we were beginning to use fewer

band aids and we were finally beginning to pronounce words correctly. We took water with us on all trips, kept our fingers off cactus and their fruit, but we were still feeling the need to learn more about the state of Arizona. The wanting to learn has taken us on an adventure that has been exciting, educational and life-changing for the both of us.

Our quest was to learn about and understand the people and places in Arizona. We have worked toward this goal by using a variety of available resources. We visited the Green Valley Chamber of Commerce on many occasions. We would gather up any magazine about exploring southern Arizona, seeing the Southwest and things to see in Arizona. We also chose a number of pamphlets on sites we wanted to explore.

In the grocery store, we saw a magazine that caught our attention. We bought the *Arizona Highways* magazine on that day and we were impressed by the quality of the magazine. We thought it would be an asset to get an annual subscription. For months, we used this magazine as a resource for places to see in this great state. After five years of exploring most of the areas in Arizona, we still find interesting places to see.

We have also used TV shows as a resource. When we first arrived, we regularly watched *Tucson Treasures* with Gina Trunzo. The program profiled people and places in southern Arizona. We would document every place we wanted to research. Today, we enjoy the information gathered from *The Desert Speaks* with David Yetman and *AZ Illustrated* with Tom McNamara. Over time, we have gathered a lot of valuable information from these sources.

Gathering information from a variety of sources increased our knowledge about places to explore, but also helped us to locate cultural activities we wanted to participate in. The *Green Valley News*, the *Arizona Daily Star,* the *Tucson Weekly*, the *Arivaca Connection* and the *Tubac Villager* have been reliable, on-going sources of information.

For gathering historical information we used lectures for gathering dots. We attended lectures on the Historical Border Markers, the History of Rio Rico, Buffalo Soldiers, Apache War Tactics, Arizona Outlaws, Ghost Towns in the Santa Rita Mountains, in Search of Water, the Navajo Code Talkers, and many others.

Our main source of historical information, however, came from books. We have read books detailing the history of mining, the camel experience, the ghost towns, the Spanish expeditions but we have also read several others which gave us a different perspective on other parts of Arizona history. Here is a short list of some books we have enjoyed: *The Secret Knowledge of Water* by Craig Childs, *The Trunk Murderess: Winnie Ruth Judd* by Jana Bommersbach, *The Oatman Massacre* by Brian McGinty, *Going Back to Bisbee* by Richard Shelton, *Fire in the Sky* by Travis Walton, *I Am the Grand Canyon* by Stephen Hirst and *With Their Own Blood* by Virginia Culin Roberts. These are some of the tools we have used in building our collage of Arizona.

There were other topics that needed our attention and we chose to enroll as members of OLLI (Osher Lifelong Learning Institute). This would enable us to choose what classes we wanted to attend and we could choose as many classes as we wanted per semester. This provided us with a never-ending source of information. The classes we chose were varied and included topics such as: geology, identifying rocks, national parks, flora, fauna, weather, water, history of Arizona, western art, Indian art, Kachinas, Arizona places to see, and many more. We learned about the lumbering industry in this state, about the largest contiguous ponderosa pine forest in the country, and about the little red tadpoles that hatch in the desert puddles during the monsoon season.

We were rapidly learning about all of the places to see in this big state of ours and our recording system became obsolete. Using the list system, we were continuously adding on, crossing off, adding on, rewriting, etc. We changed to a new system that involved a shoe box. Whenever we find a new and interesting site, we research it, print out the information and put it in the box for future use. This system has assisted us in preparing longer trips to see a variety of sites. We have grown from doing day trips to see one place, to "bundling."

We have explored many places in Arizona and have participated in several local and cultural activities. The search, however, goes on. We are continually looking for new and exciting places to visit. The search is becoming harder but we have not yet reached our goal: to see every inch of Arizona.

CULTURE

Culture is defined as the sum of attitudes, customs and beliefs that distinguishes one group of people from another. Culture is transmitted through language, objects, rituals, institutions and art from one generation to another.

When we moved to Green Valley, in the southern part of Arizona, we were unaware of the cultural differences that existed in this part of the country. This area belonged to Mexico until 1853 when the United States signed the Gadsden Purchase with Mexico. The culture of this area is a beautiful blend of many groups who have lived here: the Native Americans, the Spaniards who arrived in the 1600s, the Chinese who came to build the railroad and work in the mines, the miners who came from many different countries, those of Mexican ancestry who stayed after the Gadsden Purchase, the dust bowl refugees, and the retirees who come from every state in the US.

All of the individuals who have come here, along with the Native Americans, have created a culturally diverse community which is very different from the area where we were born and raised. Here, we have been introduced to many customs, rituals, foods, traditions and beliefs we had never encountered before.

We reside about twenty miles from Tucson, the largest city in Southern Arizona, and this has offered us the opportunity to participate in many cultural events and traditions. Historically, Tucson offers many glimpses into its past and diversity through its architecture and neighborhoods. In the barrios, some of the earliest residences can be seen. It is an area that attracts many photographers and tourists because of its bright colors, famous doors, courtyards and the architectural style influenced by the Spanish. Pictures of the barrio doors can be found in magazines, tourist booklets and in many gift shops across the state. In the Sam Hughes historical neighborhood, houses from many time periods sit side-by-side and the eclectic nature of the area is charming. The brightly colored houses, walls and doors in this neighborhood is what caught our attention. We took pictures of every colored structure we could find.

We have explored the architectural diversity that exists in Tucson, from the mission churches to the modern skyscrapers. We have also taken the time and effort to research and participate in some of the traditions and customs that were new to us. We cannot possibly share with you all of the events, but we will share with you some of the experiences.

Musical Events in Arizona have introduced us to a variety of music we were not familiar with. It did not take us long to discover that we loved cowboy and Latin music. We have attended performances by Dolan Ellis, Marshall Trimble, Rex Allen Jr., Ted Ramirez, the Ronstadt Generation, Kristyn Harris, Juni Fisher, Devon & the Outlaw, The Tumbling Tumbleweeds, Gabriel Ayala, Domingo DeGrazia, Tony Duncan, Robert Mirabal and R. Carlos Nakai. What a treat to experience such a variety of musical talent.

Roadside Shrines and crosses are a Spanish-Catholic tradition brought to the New World by the early missionaries. They mark the site of a fatal accident or other tragedy. They appear throughout southern Arizona and in Sonora Mexico.

It did not take us long to discover the shrines or elaborate crosses that exist along the sides of the roads. We have seen them on the edges of interstates and on rural roads. These miniature places of worship are usually beautifully adorned and contain at least one statue of a saint. Worshipers will stop and leave candles, plastic flowers and a variety of objects including pictures of a loved one. We have seen a variety of sizes, colors and shapes. A six-foot shrine is readily visible and accessible on Arivaca Road near the Sopori Ranch. It was erected in memory of Arthur Lee, the nephew of the Confederate General Robert E. Lee, who accidentally died at the ranch. This shrine contains a statue of Santa Teresa, but statues of other saints share her space. Some of the sites contain benches or chairs so visitors can sit and pray or remember. We have stopped at the Santa Teresa shrine on many occasions and have shared this tradition with family and visitors.

La Fiesta de Los Vaqueros (Celebration of the Cowboy) is an event that celebrates the western and cowboy culture. This event occurs in Tucson every February, but the rodeo tradition exists in many cities in Arizona. Here in Tucson, the event last for nine days and schools are closed during the fiesta to allow the children to participate. This is a significant event and it draws many participants and visitors. During this event, one can fulfill their wish to be a cowboy or cowgirl - you can buy a cowboy hat, dress in western wear, sit by a rancher, pet a horse and dream about riding a bull.

This event includes: nightly barn dances, a junior rodeo, a pro rodeo, mutton bustin' (young children riding sheep) and the rodeo parade. The rodeo parade contains two hundred, non-motorized floats and holds the distinction of being the longest non-motorized parade in the United States. The parade is exciting and offers lots of opportunities to mingle with a variety of people. Great place to meet Arizonans and to hear the history of the parade. Whenever available, movie stars will join the parade if they are in the area filming. At one parade, we sat next to a man who listed for us all the movie stars he has seen. We have not seen any movie stars. Maybe next year.

We went to the pro rodeo because we wanted to experience this cultural event. We were apprehensive and feared we would not enjoy the tradition. That day, we did plenty of clapping to the music, eating junk food, cheering for the participants, and stomping our feet in appreciation of a great performance. We came home tired and hoarse, but well fed, happy, excited and quite sure that we would see another pro rodeo. We even bought a cowboy hat. Great tradition and great fun to participate.

Traveling around the state, we have encountered hundreds of **murals** in multiple locations. We have seen them in small communities, on tribal lands and in large cities. It is estimated that in Tucson alone, there are more than five hundred visible murals. The City of Tucson Mural Arts Program seeks to create a city-wide outdoor gallery of original artwork. There are websites from which we download walking, hiking or driving tours that assist in finding these art treasures. There are also websites with pictures of many of the current murals and mosaics found around the city. On several Sunday mornings, we we've taken off with Bernadette in search of the murals and, currently, we have located and photographed three hundred and twenty-five beautiful pieces of art. Recently, eight new murals were added in the downtown area. Of course, we found them. In 2016, the city undertook a new project. The Tucson Arts Brigade began placing murals on downtown dumpsters in an attempt to decrease the graffiti in the area. The pilot project involved the selection of five dumpsters. On our search for the newest murals, we found one of the five dumpsters. How cool is that! For those interested in murals, Benson, Flagstaff and Douglas are other locations to explore. Benson has a wide variety of murals depicting the significance of the railroad in the area.

Dia de los Muertos (translated to Day of the Dead) is a Mexican holiday celebrated throughout Mexico and by people of Mexican ancestry living in other places. This multi-day holiday, with its origins in pre-Colombian cultures, is celebrated by some individuals in Arizona. The dates coincide with All Saints Eve, All Saints Day and All Souls Day: October thirty-first, November first and November second. The tradition involves gatherings of friends and family to remember and pray for deceased family and friends. In 2008, the tradition was placed on the Representative List of the Intangible Cultural Heritage of Humanity by UNESCO. The significance of this annual tradition is observable and tangible. In the United States, there are several components which include the building of altars, the Procession of the Little Angels, the visits to the cemetery, and the All Souls Procession.

We have seen a variety of altars built in remembrance of a deceased friend or loved one. The majority of the altars contained sugar skulls, marigolds (thought to attract the souls of the dead), cardboard skeletons, statues of skeletons, tissue paper decorations, fruits and nuts, photos of the deceased, muertos (considered to be the bread of the dead) and other memorabilia. The altars vary in size and color, but many of the items listed above are found on every altar. We have seen them in several places including the Tucson Museum of Art, the Mercado and in Tubac.

In Tucson, the Procession of the Little Angels and the All Souls Procession occur on the weekend closest to the traditional dates. At the children's event, it is the time that the children build altars to invite the spirits of the dead children to come back for a visit. A very touching event.

On November second, the tradition continues with a visit to the cemetery. Family and friends gather to clean and decorate the graves and tombs of the deceased. Some families will build altars near the grave that will include favorite foods and beverages of the deceased, photos of the departed, and other personal memorabilia. Chairs and food are brought to the cemetery so the living can spend time remembering and praying for the deceased loved ones. The intent of the altars and the offerings is to encourage visits by the souls of the departed. We visited the cemetery in Tubac the day after and the cemetery was beautiful with all of the decorations and flowers.

The All Souls Procession is an annual tradition that can be observed in southern Arizona. We know that processions occur in Arivaca, Tubac and Tucson. The procession in Tucson started in 1990 when a young artist, having returned from a trip to Mexico, walked down the street in Tucson with a memorial to her deceased father. The year after, she was joined by others. The years have gone by and in 2015, one hundred thousand people of all ages and ethnicities participated in the All Souls Procession that marched through the streets of Tucson. Bernadette introduced us to this event in November, 2011.

Off we went with our chairs to observe the procession through the streets. The procession consisted of music, floats, people with their faces painted white, some individuals with skeleton suits, families with matching t-shirts to honor their deceased family member, individuals carrying memorials of their loved ones, people on bicycles, children in strollers, and thousands and thousands of people. On the edges of the procession, some participants carry bowls to collect the lists of names of the deceased to be remembered. At the end of the procession, there is a closing ceremony that includes fire spinners, dancers and music.

In 2011, there was also an individual who chanted as part of the ceremony. From our location in the crowd, all we could see was a man in a white robe surrounded by the night sky. His chanting was heard for miles and felt haunting. Behind him was a large cauldron that contained the lists of the deceased, which was lifted up and set ablaze. The crowd cheered and clapped, and then everyone dispersed. It is hard to express all the emotions that we experienced on this first All Souls Procession; it was amazing, awesome, overwhelming, sad, inspirational and touching. We will always remember participating in this event and we still get goose bumps when we recall the chanting at the closing ceremony. This is a tradition unlike anything we have ever seen or participated in. It is a tradition of celebration and remembrance, an honor to life and death.

A family-friendly music festival is held in downtown Tucson on the **2nd Saturday** of every month. The event includes vendors, a variety of food purveyors, living statues, street performers and a variety of entertainment in multiple venues. We have frequented this event on many occasions and we believe that it is an example of the diversity of Tucson. On one occasion, a bagpipe band was marching up Congress Street while the drumming group was playing on the corner of Congress and Stone. The stage entertainment can include Taiko drummers, Latin guitarists (such as Domingo DeGrazia), belly dancers, rock bands, the Irish/indie Dusty Buskers, and/or jazz bands. The combination of the street performers with their guitars and horns, the drummers, the stage entertainment and the bagpipes attest to the blending of many talents and interests. This is a great event and there is no admission fee. Enjoy!

Mariachi bands and music was a new musical style for us and it has become a favorite. Mariachi music has its origins as far back as the 1700s and has evolved into the type of music we hear today. Mariachi bands can have as many as eight violins, two trumpets and at least one guitar. The music is often heard at family gatherings and in religious celebrations. In Mexico, this style of music may also be included in the Catholic mass. We have seen many groups at different events and the resemblance is striking. The costumes are similar, the positioning of the members is identical and the music is familiar and distinguishable. In 2011, UNESCO recognized Mariachi as an Intangible Cultural Heritage. We love mariachi music and we often dance to it.

Arriving at a festival, we always listen for the music that indicates the **Folklore dancers** are performing. In Mexico, the folklore dances are a blend of indigenous, African and European heritage. There is a wide variety of folk dances and they can vary greatly from region to region. The dances we have observed express the rhythm of Mexican music and the beautiful, colorful dresses the dancers wear reflects the vibrant colors of their culture. We always stop to listen and observe.

Arizona is the only place in the United States where the centuries-old **Yaqui Easter Ceremonies** can be observed. When the Yaquis came into contact with the Europeans, they blended their ancient rituals with Catholicism to form an independent religious blend. The Easter Ceremony is a five-day ritual that dramatizes the capture, torture, and crucifixion of Christ. Blended into the ceremony is the Deer Dance, the maypole, all-night vigils, processions and the burning of an effigy. Elaborate costumes, ancient rituals and colorful flowers are also blended into the event. We chose to observe some of the Holy Saturday ceremony at the Pascua Pueblo in Tucson. The ceremony on that day was "La Gloria," which involves two groups of individuals. The church group (and allies) ritually kill the men who killed Jesus. This is a renewal ceremony in which goodness triumphs over evil. We did not fully understand many parts of the ceremony, but the significance of the event was apparent. Family groups sat together with all ages present; from the elderly to tiny babies. Young girls were dressed in beautiful white dresses for the occasion. This is a ceremony we may return to someday. The book *A Yaqui Easter* by Muriel Thayer Painter, describes the elements of the ceremony and is a good source of information.

In Arizona, we found **food** items we had never eaten on the east coast. Mexican restaurants abound in this area and they have Sopaipillas on their dessert menu. We ordered some and, suddenly, these cute oval fried pastries appeared on our table with a bottle of honey. They have become one of our favorite

Mexican treats. Another delicious item is the fry bread, a specialty of the Tohono O'odham. It looks like east-coast fried dough but it tastes much better. We never pass one by. The Sonoran Hot Dog, however, took us some time to order. Then, one day, we decided it was time to try this highly-acclaimed food item. A Sonoran dog comes with a large, long and deep bun that looks like a boat. The contents can include a hot dog wrapped in bacon, caramelized onions, raw onions, tomatoes, mustard, mayonnaise, avocado, pinto beans, cheese, Pico de Gallo and a jalapeño pepper. Does not sound appealing when you order it for the first time, but this food item has become one of our favorites and we share the experience with our family and friends. There is a saying that you cannot be an Arizonan until you have eaten a Sonoran Hot Dog. An interesting note: one of our family members took a picture of the Sonoran Dog and sent the picture to their friends in Vermont.

Since 1974, Tucson has hosted an annual event called **Tucson Meet Yourself.** It is a yearly celebration of the diversity, traditions and culture of this area. The focus is on presenting artists and communities that carry on living traditions. Crafts, food vendors and performances are ongoing throughout the event. In 2015, it is estimated that one hundred thousand people participated in this event.

Going to a festival, a parade, Walmart, the grocery store or a restaurant can be an exciting adventure in southern Arizona. There is no doubt that the **cowboy culture** still exists in this area and we see evidence of that regularly. A love of the cowboy is a throwback to the multitude of western movies and TV shows that existed in our formative years. We can always spot a rancher in a store with the cowboy hat, the worn heels on the boots, the dungarees, and sometimes a gun in the holster. It is always tempting to approach and just say "Hi". It is always a treat to know that the traditions of cattle ranching, horseback riding, and tending to a ranch still exist not far from where we live. On one occasion, we also saw a female rancher with her long braid, cowgirl hat, boots and dusty jeans. Yeah! When the winter visitors arrive in southern Arizona, some of them love to don their cowboy hats and boots but we can always tell the real cowboy from the visitor.

We have observed **Tohono O'odham** women performing the **Basket Dance** at festivals and Indian Art fairs. The women hold tribal-made baskets and perform dance patterns to the rhythmic and pleasing music. The age range of the participants varies and at the last dance we observed a four-year old also participating, holding her tiny basket. On one occasion, they invited members from the audience to come onto the stage and dance with the group. It was our pleasure to join them and we look forward to spending more time with the dancing group.

One day we drove by the **cemetery on the Tohono O'odham** reservation near the San Xavier del Bac Mission. We stopped to explore. The cemetery was fenced with No Trespassing and No Photography signs posted. There were many graves in the cemetery and the majority of the graves were marked with white crosses with no names. There were some gravestones that displayed the names of the deceased. The cemetery was well tended. We observed and did not take pictures. It was apparent that this was sacred ground and we did not want to disrespect their beliefs and traditions.

We have spent a lot of time participating in and gathering information on many of the cultural traditions in this borderland area in which we live. Besides the activities we mentioned above, we have participated in or observed the following: the Harvest Dance on the Hopi reservation, basket making by the Tohono O'odham, preparation of the materials prior to making baskets, swaying to Waila music, a Pow-Wow at St. Xavier del Bac, Navajo woman preparing yarn prior to weaving, Tony Duncan doing the Hoop Dance, performances by the White Mountain Apache Crown dancers, and the process of traditional Hopi pottery firing. On the Hopi reservation, we purchased a sifter basket (usually given as a wedding present), a round ceremonial basket (given by a young lady to a young man she likes) and two wall-hanging Kachinas (would have been given to children to teach them about the Kachina spirits). At other occasions, we have also purchased some Kachina dolls that were carved for the purpose of selling to tourists.

We feel privileged to have participated in the various activities and we are grateful for the time and information that people have been willing to share with us. It has been exciting, stimulating and educational to live in a diverse environment.

FLORA

Flowers. Flowers. Everywhere. That was our dream when we arrived in Arizona. We were here because a hotel desk clerk in Tombstone told us that we had not seen anything until we had seen the desert in bloom. We were prepared to wait for two to three months for the flowers to appear and we anticipated spending a peaceful winter in a warm climate. Little did we know the adventures that would follow in the coming months (and years).

From the time we arrived, the camera was always in our pocket and pictures were taken of all the new cactus, bushes, plants and trees that were found. Currently, we can tell the newcomers by the photos they take of all the plants. In many cases, the names of the plants and winter flowers were unknown to us, but pictures were taken for later identification. In the beginning, the identification of each species of cactus seemed important, so an effort was made to distinguish between the kinds of prickly pear and cholla cactus. That goal was abandoned in the first three months.

During the first three months, we had no idea how much learning was in store for us. We thought that the Texas Mountain Laurel seed pods were pistachios and we were waiting for the fruit of the barrel cactus to bloom. We were unaware of the thorns on the mesquite trees and on their branches, that fell on the sidewalk. Beautiful ocotillos were viewed as dead plants.

Time passed and spring finally arrived; a lot earlier than we anticipated. The trees turned pink, white, red, purple and

yellow. The cactus formed bud after bud and the show we had
been waiting for was beginning. To our amazement, the cactus
flowers bloomed in a large variety of colors: pink, pink with
yellow centers, pink with green centers, yellow, yellow with
red centers, yellow with green centers, red, red with yellow
centers, translucent green, green, orange with green centers
and orange with yellow centers. We even found some prickly
pear cactus with pink and yellow blooms on the same plant.
Pictures were taken of everything that looked like a flower or
bud. Excitement was in the air. Mother Nature was exploding
with beauty. Wow!

Most of the excitement was happening in our own
neighborhood. Then, we started noticing some yellow flowers
and pink flowers on the sides of the road. What a novel idea
it was to branch out and see what we could find in other
areas. The variety of flowers that were found in the first few
months was amazing and overwhelming. We needed help in
the identification of the beautiful flowers.

We found a website called **www.desertusa.com** that
assisted us in identifying and locating wildflowers in our area.
We use the Tucson and southern Arizona sector. The website
includes desert flower reports and information as to the
exact location of the blooms. It has been a useful tool for us
in the identification and location of spring, summer and fall
wildflowers.

The purchase of flower books was the next step in our
educational process. The following books have proved
invaluable to us in the identification of the various flowers we
have photographed: *Plants of Arizona* by Anne Orth Epple,
Wildflowers of the Mountain Southwest by Meg Quinn and the
*National Audubon Society, Field Guide to Wildflowers, Western
Region*. Lately, we have also purchased the book *Wildflowers - A
Field Guide to Flowering Plants of Southern Arizona* by Maggie
Moe Milinovitch. To this date, these books have been used on
many occasions to identify new varieties of flora.

To increase our knowledge of the flora in the area, a decision was also made to use local resources that would assist us in the accomplishment of our goals. We started by visiting the **Tucson Botanical Gardens.** A beautiful environment to wander through and enjoy all of the flowers, bushes and trees that grow in this climate. There are distinct areas exhibiting different types of plants. This garden is a welcome place for newcomers to explore because a lot of the flora is identified. We have returned to this site on numerous occasions for their special events and exhibits and at different times of the year to see the different blooms.

Another valuable resource is **Tohono Chul Park** located in a suburb of Tucson. It is a botanical garden and nature preserve with paths that wander through a large variety of trees, bushes and flowering plants. A large portion of the flora is clearly identified. Tohono Chul also has special exhibits and events throughout the year.

The **Phoenix Botanical Garden** was another useful local resource. This site also has special exhibits and events throughout the year. In 2014, the Phoenix Botanical Garden featured an exhibit of Dale Chihuly's Glass Artwork. There are some pieces that remain in the garden for the public to enjoy.

In Globe, the **Boyce Thompson Arboretum** is a garden to be enjoyed. With the mixture of beautiful rock formations, a pond, historical structures and beautiful flora, it is hard to remember that the area is educational as well as enjoyable.

One day, we wandered into the **Reid Park Rose Garden** and we were totally surprised. It was the beginning of November and the number of rose bushes in bloom was astonishing. We had no idea that roses could grow profusely in the Arizona climate. We spent a long time looking at the many varieties of flowers. When we were leaving, a lady working in the garden told us to come back during the week of Thanksgiving. Visitors who come during that week are given a bouquet of flowers for their Thanksgiving table. What a nice thought.

Purchasing books, visiting a variety of local resources, taking pictures of every new flower and driving from location to location did prove beneficial. We learned that Arizona has many different varieties of flora in the desert environments, in the mountain areas and in the higher elevations of the White Mountains. We had started the process of identifying some the wildflowers and our ability to identify varieties of cactus was increasing.

The need to continue learning, however, prompted us to enroll in a class on flora through the Osher Lifelong Learning Institute. Our instructor, Meg Quinn, was an invaluable resource for us. We were exposed to a large variety of flora and to the process of germination and survival in a desert environment. We learned that cactus survive by storing water during the monsoon season and can survive up to eighteen months from the stored water. Wildflower seeds remain dormant in the soil awaiting the right amount of rain at the right time of year. The "Great Spring Blooms" that occur every five to seven years only occur if it rains at specific times during the winter months. This class opened our eyes to the process of producing blooms in this environment.

Today, we are more informed and educated than we were five years ago. In the process, we have taken pictures of three hundred and fifty-four different flowers and have smelled many of them. We have seen flowers and trees bloom several times a year. What? Trees bloom more than once? Yes. The Texas Ranger (sometimes called the Texas Sage) blooms in the spring with brilliant blue or purple flowers, then the flowers drop off producing a purple carpet around the bush. About two weeks after the next rain, the Texas Ranger will bloom again. Some summers, they can bloom up to four times. This also occurs with some of the cactus, the Oleander tree and the Desert Willow.

Another amazing phenomenon is the change that occurs

in the tubular cacti. In the spring, before the monsoon storms start, the Saguaro cactus and many other varieties are thin. Once the rains begin, the cacti get "fatter." They are storing water for their survival. It is amazing to witness the process.

Sometimes, we stumble upon beautiful displays of flowers. On our way to Yuma, both sides of the road were lined with the brilliant yellow flowers of the brittlebush in full bloom. On our way to Springerville, The Devil's Highway was lined with yellow summer flowers for miles and miles. The median was covered with bright orange Arizona poppies on Interstate 19, between Green Valley and Sahuarita. North of Safford, the median was covered with bright pink Penstemon. Passing through Flagstaff in the fall, there were fields of bright yellow and pink flowers (unidentified) for miles. Driving through Sonoita in the fall, the road is lined with sunflowers. At other times, we also find them while exploring ghost towns, looking for petroglyphs, visiting Native American sites or rock hounding. We are always appreciative of the beauty wherever we find it.

At other times, we take off on "Flower Chasing" adventures. These trips are always fun and exciting, but not always productive. Ruby Road is usually a great place to see spring wildflowers. We have found Mariposa lilies, Arizona rainbow cacti, gold Mexican poppies and phacelia along this stretch of road. Spring blooms vary according to rainfall, but can be magnificent in this area. One spring, we brought Mary and Bernadette to show them the beautiful spring flowers. No flowers were found on that day, but we sure had many laughs. Bernadette's puppy (Jaxs) had accompanied us on this trip. We drove through the area where the white cows are always seen and he had the opportunity to see one. Never knew a puppy could growl so long and so loud.

One day, we were in search of petroglyphs in the Picacho Mountains and admired the beautiful brittlebush in full bloom. Upon leaving, Sue Smith suggested that we stop at Red Rock. She had heard on the radio that the lupines were in bloom and could be seen along Sasco road. We took the road in search of the lupine. We did find a few of the small purple flowers, but the spectacular flower show on the other side of the road stopped us in our tracks. For miles, we saw brilliant Orange Globe Mallows. The spectacle was the most impressive we had seen to date. Many pictures were taken that day, but they did not capture the brilliance of the color and the emotions of viewing such a magnificent event. We hope to have the occasion to see this again.

Route 86 near Kitt Peak is well known for its spring flowers. In 2015, the website we use stated that the poppies were in bloom, so we called Sue Smith and told her we were going to see "Millions of Poppies." She agreed to join us on the adventure. At the time, we were hoping we could easily find the blooming beauties. Driving along, the scenery turned into a sea of yellow. Millions of poppies were seen. We drove about three miles and all you could see were poppies. The number of flowers was incredible. Lupines and Parry penstemon added an occasional blue and pink to the ongoing sea of yellow. Incredible poppy bloom that year.

People frequently ask us about our favorite flowers. We have seen so many different flowers and we have enjoyed them all. There are some, however, that remain exciting to see. Therefore, we have created this list: the white majestic bloom of the Saguaro cactus, the yellow flowers of the prickly pear blooming in the desert, the dinner-plate size flower of the Trichocereus cactus, the grape smell of the Texas Mountain Laurel flower, the red or pink penstemon bloom, the brilliant yellow poppies, the golden summer poppies, the barrel cactus blooms in a desert environment, the green translucent flower on a teddy bear cholla and the bloom of a bluestem poppy which looks like a fried egg.

The list of our favorites was so difficult to make because

so many varieties of flowers make us smile. The flower of the wild onion is so small, yet so incredibly beautiful. The lupine's tiny blooms glow in the sunshine and light up the sides of the road. There is such beauty in Arizona's blooms.

Have we met our goal of seeing the Desert in Bloom? We have seen some beautiful displays of wildflowers since our arrival and we have learned about the blooming process. Every spring is different depending on the amount and timing of the rainfall. Some years you can have magnificent poppies and another year the poppies are hard to find. The magnificent Orange Globe Mallow blooms were seen one time. We will stay and continue to watch Mother Nature as she impresses and surprises us.

WILDLIFE

Both of us love animals of all kinds: the feathery variety, the furry ones, the prickly kind and the scaly types. Living in Arizona has provided us with moments of laughter, times of wonder and moments of excitement. We will share with you many of the wildlife we have encountered and some of the funny moments they have created.

Southern Arizona is one of the birding meccas of the United States and thousands of visitors come to this state to view the large variety of birds that exist here. In this state, there are more than a dozen different species of hummingbirds. In Madera Canyon, there is a bird watching site that feeds a variety of birds, including the beautiful hummingbirds. Great place to sit and enjoy them. Living here, we have seen the beautiful, brightly-colored birds on a daily basis. On the way to the pool, on our morning walks, on the way to the car, it is common that the little green, red and blue bombers cross our path and buzz by our heads. They are a common sight here and we always stop to admire them and watch them feed. Makes us smile.

Sandhill cranes, golden eagles, bald eagles, falcons, hawks and snow geese winter in southern Arizona. Here in the Sonoran desert area, we notice an increase in the population of hawks during the winter months. On one of our favorite roads, we love to count the number of hawks sitting on the top of telephone poles and we count a much larger number from November through March.

Not far from our residence, we have a pair of large ravens who love to make their nest in the large pine trees. They always sound the alarm when the hawks and owls enter their territory. It alerts us of the intruders' presence and we can sometimes spot them flying by. The ravens have successfully raised their families in our neighborhood and it is enjoyable listening to the different sounds they make when communicating.

In 2015, we had a pair of Great Horned owls that built a nest about five hundred feet from us. Oh, what fun that was! The entire neighborhood would check on the status of the nest building with great anticipation. We waited and waited and then someone heard a small, squeaky sound in the nest. From then on, the neighborhood watched the growth and development of the four young ones on a daily basis. The babies were photographed, filmed and examined through the lenses of binoculars until the day they flew away. The next year, we all hoped they would return. They did not. Instead, they took up housekeeping two streets west of us. We bet they thought we would not notice. We did.

On one of our trips to the Buenos Aires National Wildlife Refuge, we noticed some huge, flat mounds in the desert. We stopped to examine the mounds and found several entrances and exits. We were confused so we stopped at the visitor center to inquire about our discovery. Apparently, kangaroo rats will build an earthen house, and when an uninvited guest arrives, the kangaroo rat expands the house by adding another exit and this process continues until the mound becomes huge. We were told that burrowing owls, tortoises and snakes will gladly move in without invitation. Interesting factoid.

One of our favorites little critters is the prairie dog. We have seen several of our beloved critters in this state. Near Seligman, there are large colonies and they are easy to spot from the road. We had stopped on Crookton Road to take a picture of a Burma Shave sign when a prairie dog popped out of his hole and looked in our direction. He was only about five feet away from us so we got a great picture. We also love to stop at the Empire Ranch near Sonoita so we can monitor the growth of the colonies. We love watching them scamper around and hearing the sentry bark an alarm to alert others of our presence. They make us laugh and we are happy that this state believes they should be protected for future generations to see and enjoy.

Some people often mistake ground squirrels for prairie dogs. They do have similar shapes and they also build mounds when digging their residences. One big difference is their size. Ground squirrels are about one-fifth the size of prairie dogs. There are several colonies around Green Valley and we always slow down to see them. We have learned that if we stay still for a little while we will see a little head pop out of the ground. One funny characteristic: when they run, their tails stick up straight into the air. Cute.

At the Arizona Sonora Desert Museum, the Coatimundi always captivates us. What a beautiful and interesting animal, with its elongated nose and elegant tail. They reportedly roam around areas of southern Arizona. We have not seen one in the wild, but there is hope. Our friend, Mary, saw the tail of a coati moving in the golden grass in Madera Canyon. Maybe someday, one will bless us with its presence.

One day, there was an article in the daily newspaper about "El Jefe" (The Boss). El Jefe, the only jaguar known to be living in the United States, lives in the mountain range we can see out of our living room window. Jaguars have been known to come north from Mexico in search of mates or food, but this male lives here. The article contained a picture of the beautiful, big cat. Hopefully, someday a beautiful female will visit our mountains and the population will grow. How exciting to see such a beautiful specimen.

Breaking News: In December 2016, a camera in the

Huachuca Mountains, near Sierra Vista, captured a picture of another male jaguar. Examination of the photograph verified that El Jefe is not the only jaguar that resides in Arizona. Great news. We say "Welcome" to the new resident.

Desert Dogs (coyotes, foxes and wolves) roam wild in the expanse of southern Arizona. The coyote is a familiar site in this area and we have had many opportunities to see this beautiful animal. Traveling around Arizona, it is not uncommon to spot a coyote running across the street, walking across a field, or even leisurely walking down the street. One night we were coming home after a concert and it took us a long time to get to our parking spot. In front of us, a coyote was walking down the middle of the street so we had to wait our turn. As the day turns to night, we can hear them yipping and howling from our patio. The sounds of the coyote are pleasurable and haunting.

On the way home one afternoon, we spotted a large animal in a dry wash and turned around to investigate. At first, we thought it was a mountain lion, but it turned out to be a beautiful bobcat. It was in pursuit of a mourning dove (for lunch, we assumed), so we had the opportunity to take great photos. It was not particularly concerned that we were watching and slowly moved away when the hunt was unsuccessful. We have seen teenage bobcats in our neighborhood and we were informed by a neighbor that a baby one walked by the side of our house. They sometimes hunt in our area, so the opportunity to see one always exist.

Since becoming residents, we have been introduced to a new variety of wildlife that are elongated with long tails and short legs. We have seen iguanas, lizards of all sizes and colors, and geckos. At first, there was a fear that they would enter the house. We thought "Yuck." We have learned to enjoy them. We love watching them show off for us: some of them do push-ups, some of them pose, and some seem to be playing. They are all beautiful little creatures who help us keep the insect population at a tolerable level and we always welcome the new arrivals when we see them. Sometimes we spot some that are only about an inch long. On one of our trips to Northern Arizona we fell in love with a fluorescent green and tan lizard with a double-banded collar around its neck. We took its picture and later discovered that it was a collared lizard. The park ranger informed us that it loves to get its picture taken and runs to the side of the path whenever guests walk by. We knew there was something special about that one.

The first time we saw wild burros in Arizona was in Oatman. There is a herd of burros that occupy this town in hopes of getting food from the tourists. There are other herds throughout the state. We have seen them at Lake Pleasant and near Monument Valley. On one occasion, we decided to get closer to get better pictures, so we decided to drive through the desert. We thought it looked like a road, but we think we were driving along the burro paths. We will never forget the look of the burros' faces when they saw us approaching! We captured their surprised and alarmed faces in the photo. Every year, the herds of wild burros are culled and they are put up for adoption. We have seen many adopted burros throughout this state: they can be seen among the horses or cows in many pastures.

Spiders are not our preferred wildlife and, usually, they do not live long lives in our residence. There was a day, however, when a big, beautiful spider captivated us. At a demonstration at the Tubac Presidio State Historic Park, we were introduced to a beautiful female tarantula. We were told not to touch her (because she becomes stressed) but we had the opportunity to closely examine her. The coloring and pattern was spectacular. On that day, we also learned that the female spends the majority of her life in her burrow. The male, smaller and black in color, is the one that is usually seen wandering for food and for a mate. On one occasion, we did see a male. Having gathered more information about this specimen, the fear level has decreased significantly.

We love driving along Route 82 and Route 83 in the Sonoita area. While there, we spend a lot of time and energy looking for white rumps. That is how we spot the Pronghorn antelope. We frequently spot some in that area and the last time we saw the herd, it contained several youngsters. It is encouraging to see that their population is growing. They are also visible at the Buenos Aires Wildlife Refuge and on the Mogollon Rim near the Sunset Point rest area on Interstate 17.

Think Arizona is still the wild west? Come with us and we will show you herds of wild burros left behind by the miners and we will show you herds of wild horses left behind by the Spanish. Wild horses? Yes, we have found some Spanish mustangs that are reportedly still ninety-seven percent pure. We discovered the horses when we went on a tour of the ASARCO copper mine in Green Valley. The guide told about the number of horses that live on the property and their origin. Over the years, we have checked on the horses, have seen their babies and watched them grow into big, beautiful adults. We have also seen the movement of the herds to new territories. On one occasion, we were approached by a teenager who had apparently been ostracized by the herd because he was a young male. He looked sad and lonely and we think he wanted us to become his mothers. We took a picture of him and we have thought about him many times. Two years later, we saw a big, gorgeous male with the same markings of the sad youngster. Oh! We bet that's him all grown up. Lately, a friend of ours saw a teenage male, all alone and sad. He had the same markings as our lonely youngster that had grown up to be a beautiful mustang. Maybe this young one was his son. How great would that be!

Little walnuts with legs is what we call them. Gambel's

quails are gregarious birds that live in coveys along dry washes and amongst low shrubbery. In the spring, we start noticing that the quail are now in pairs, rather than in groups. This means the coming of nesting, eggs, then babies. Everyone in the neighborhood looks forward to seeing the little quail and shares information about where and when they were spotted. We have seen many young quail since our arrival, but we will never forget the group of eighteen. One day, we heard loud calls from the adults as some youngsters were locked in one patio and the rest of the group were on another patio. The adults were screaming and everyone was frantic, including us. We opened the gates, thereby, rescuing the stranded youngsters and had the opportunity to watch as they walked down the sidewalk: one adult in front, eighteen furry walnuts with legs in the middle and one adult in back. What a sight to see. It warms your heart and brightens your day.

Every summer, we participate in an eagerly-awaited event. We pack up our water and bring our chairs to sit by the Campbell Street bridge to await a great spectacle. At dusk, twenty thousand Mexican Free-tailed bats will drop from the bottom of the bridge, form into a wide line and head towards Tucson in pursuit of a meal. The first time we went, we were totally amazed to see the number of bats. Every year, we have the same feeling. We have introduced family and friends to the event. It is a spectacle to experience at least once.

Javelinas kind of look like a pig with modifications. At the Arizona Sonora Desert Museum, there is a sign that clearly states that they are NOT pigs. They are peccary. They migrated from South America and are believed to be the descendants of ancient hippos. They are seen throughout southern Arizona and are frequently seen in our neighborhood. They love rummaging through garbage cans when the opportunity presents itself, they dig holes in the lawns to make mud bogs, they eat plants on patios, eat succulents in gardens, eat prickly pear cactus and will eat the beloved blooms of the Trichocereus cactus. People complain about their odor, their behaviors and their antics, but we believe that southern Arizona would miss them if they disappeared. People love to see them and photograph them, love to share stories about the new babies in the herd, and enjoy watching them take baths in their mud holes.

Coming west, seeing a roadrunner was high on the list of priorities. The first day we arrived in Arizona, we stood within ten feet of a beautiful roadrunner. He was standing there and we believed that he wanted us to photograph him. For some reason, the camera would not work and he wandered away. Later, we discovered that the battery was at the villa being charged. Since that first encounter, we have seen hundreds of the legendary bird in many locations throughout the state. Their markings are spectacular and intricate. It is no wonder that wood carvers do not try to carve the roadrunners. One day, we were walking along a dry wash and we became the observers of a courtship ceremony. The male would chase the female around the tree, they would stop, face each other, puff up their feathers and the sequence would repeat itself. All of a sudden, another male appeared and everything changed. The female flew to the top of a patio wall and the male was trying to make up his mind whether to chase the female or fight the other male. We walked on so we are unaware how the story ended. It was definitely an opportunity of a lifetime and we appreciated the dance.

Now, let us share a story about the rabbits. When we arrived, we fell in love with the beautiful, furry, gray rabbits in the area. They were so cute and cuddly and we reluctantly believed the information that they are at the bottom of the food chain. We still love seeing the rabbits in the neighborhood and have accepted that the population increases and decreases according to the number of predators in the immediate area.

About six months after we settled here, we began taking OLLI classes on Flora, Fauna and many other topics. It became easy for us to share some of the information we were learning with our friends and neighbors. We told the others that we could tell the sex of a rabbit by looking at them. How? Easy. If the tail is on the left side, it is a male; if the tail is on the right side, the rabbit is a female. On a few occasions, some people would share with us that they had seen two "boys" that morning. Eventually, we confessed our sins and many laughs were had. Today, we still do not know how to differentiate between one sex or the other, but it doesn't matter. We enjoy seeing them hopping along the sidewalks and standing perfectly still thinking we do not see them. They are a great addition to the neighborhood.

Wildlife is a daily part of life in this area and is readily visible in this wide-open environment. We have been introduced to a variety of animals, birds and insects that we never knew existed. We have seen many others that we have not listed in this chapter and we have an on-going list of those remaining to be seen. We will continue to be on the lookout for buffalo, black widow spiders, Gila monsters, trogons, bighorn sheep, mountain lions, black bears and Mexican wolves.

SNAKES

In November 2010, enjoying the sunshine, the big blue skies, the occasional beautiful cloud formations, the winter flowers, the green grass in the parks, the rose gardens, the Gambel's quail, the roadrunners and hummingbirds, we were unaware of the following information. On the list of known snakes in the state of Arizona, there are thirty-nine different kinds of snakes listed: seventeen non-venomous and twenty-two venomous. According to Arizona Game and Fish, there are thirteen species of rattlesnakes in this state, more than any other state.

Watching the news in February 2011, the reality hit us when the newscaster announced, "The snakes are out," and they listed the precautions that should be taken. We did not hear much of the precautions, the only thought was "Yikes!" Being new to this area, there is the expectation that snakes are everywhere and they are sitting there waiting for you to walk by. At that time, we delayed going to some places due to the danger of snakes. At other times, we would be heading out on an adventure and people would remind us to watch for snakes. During the first year, we were more uncomfortable than alert.

Some learning about snakes took place that first year. We learned that snakes are not everywhere, but can be anywhere. The saying, "Do not put your hands or feet anywhere your eyes have not been," was engraved into our brains and we still operate in accordance to that motto. This advice makes sense when you learn that most bites occur on the arms and lower legs. We also learned that the large majority of those bitten by snakes are white males between the ages of eighteen to twenty-five under the influence of a few drinks.

To enhance our knowledge about the snakes who share this environment with us, we enrolled in a class on snakes through the Osher Lifelong Learning Institute. Our instructor was a reptile expert and the class was very interesting. For sure, we listened carefully to everything he said. We learned a lot in that class including: snakes live where there is a reliable food source, they can be active all year, they are more afraid of humans than we are of them, given the occasion they will retreat and they will only attack when threatened. Venomous snakes use the venom to disable their prey. Humans are too large to be prey, therefore, a snake prefers to save his venom for an edible target. Fifteen percent of snake bites are dry bites with no venom being delivered. Snakes are part of the natural balance of this environment we live in. We left that class feeling more comfortable and educated.

In our community, Green Valley, there is a procedure for assisting residents in dealing with their fear of snakes. There is a snake removal number we can call if we see a snake in our area. The Fire Department volunteers come, catch the snake, calm down the resident who called, and relocate the snake. Unfortunately, the snake will not survive if it is relocated more than one mile from its territory.

Being new to the area, another prominent fear is the fear of death if bitten by a snake. According to the Arizona Venom and Poison Centers, during a recent ten-year period, over nineteen hundred snake bites were reported but resulted in only four deaths. There have been no recent deaths reported in Southern Arizona. Medical personnel in this area are well prepared in the event of a snake bite. We spoke to a lady at Tohono Chul Park, in Tucson, who survived a rattlesnake bite. Her story was very interesting and educational. By the way, she was relating her story while we were watching a rattlesnake!

Have we seen any snakes? Yes, we have seen some snakes. According to our instructor, however, many more snakes have seen us and we missed them because of their ability to blend into their environment. The first snake we encountered was slithering across the road in Tubac. At that time, it helped re-enforce the thinking that snakes were everywhere. Since that unnerving first encounter, the spotting of snakes has become a curiosity and sometimes even a bit exciting.

One afternoon, we were driving around on the dirt roads at the Empire Ranch looking for the prairie dog colonies. All of a sudden, a large, long and salmon-colored snake darted across the dirt road and disappeared very quickly. Wow! Was our initial thought. We researched for months and eventually spoke with a snake expert; it was a coachwhip snake whose color blended in with the color of its environment. How cool is that?

One morning, we were approaching Walgreens on Esperanza in Green Valley when we spotted a dead coral snake. We had the opportunity to examine its beautiful, colorful pattern. It was exciting to see one. By the way, during our class on snakes, we learned that coral snakes are no danger to humans unless they are picked up. Their mouths are too small to bite a finger, an arm, or a leg. The only option is for them to bite a human on the webbing between the fingers. The one we saw was definitely too small to be a threat.

Visiting *Los Morteros*, a historical site, we saw a snake on the dirt road ahead of us. We stopped walking, threw a rock in its direction, and approached cautiously when he remained stationary. What a beautiful snake. We had the chance to examine it from head to tail and to take pictures so we could identify it when we returned home. The snake was about four feet long with gorgeous markings and colors. Upon researching, it was a gopher snake and would not have posed a threat to us. His favorite prey is rattlesnakes, so it is a friend. The gopher snakes look similar to rattlesnakes, coils when threatened, and will shake its tail pretending to be a rattlesnake. We bet that his behavior helps him survive encounters with humans.

About two years ago, we had an encounter with a snake that verified a reduction in our fear factor. We went to Tohono Chul park for an evening event and were sitting there (with a large crowd) listening to a speaker. A child behind us yelled, "Snake!" The crowd stood and the docents came running. The docents said, "Gopher," the crowd sat down and the speaker continued. Three years earlier, we would have left. We stayed for the rest of the event.

Over the years, we have remained cautious and alert, but the fear factor has diminished. Going to the Grasslands Fair at the Buenos Aires National Wildlife Refuge is a treat for us. Besides watching for the Pronghorn antelope, we get to see many varieties of snakes that live amongst us. The snake experts are also available to answer any question we may have about their behavior, their habitat, the area of the state in which they reside and their preferred foods.

The Arizona Game & Fish department does not use the terms Threatened or Endangered in their classification of species that need to be protected. They are identified as "No Open Season." Eight snakes have been classified as No Open Season: Sonoran Shovel-nosed snake, Milksnake, Mexican garter snake, Narrow-headed garter snake, Twin-spotted rattlesnake, Rock rattlesnake, Ridge-nosed rattlesnake and Massasauga rattlesnake. Hunting and killing a snake, therefore, would require the ability to distinguish one species from another. This is not one of our skills. To us, a snake is a snake.

For those who love snake crafts, we have seen necklaces made from rattlesnake vertebrae, keys chains with rattles, change purses made from snake skin and complete skeletons of snakes for sale. Vendors were seen at the Grasslands Fair in the Buenos Aires National Wildlife Refuge near Sasabe.

We remain alert to their presence and we are aware that we live and play in the environment in which they live. We currently have one that resides in our neighborhood and it has been spotted by some of our neighbors. The only sign we have seen is the skin that it shed about two months ago. Someday we will meet our resident snake and we are hopeful it will be a good experience for us all.

ARIZONA SEASONS

We live in the Sonoran Desert. We are thrilled to live here, and it's the only place where the mighty and extraordinary saguaro cactus lives. Standing in the museum at the Tumacacori National Historical Park, we read carefully the information panel on the Sonoran Desert.

We finished the first panel and moved on to the next section. Wow! A panel on Arizona's seasons. What? There are five seasons in this state? We had never heard of a place that had five seasons. We read on and this is what we learned. In Arizona, there is winter, spring, dry summer, wet summer, and fall. We were surprised by the information but pleased to learn that we lived in a different and unique place.

In the state of Arizona, the temperatures vary according to elevation. The higher the elevation, the cooler the temperatures. Many people flock to the mountain areas in the summer time for a relief from the triple-digit heat. In the winter time, many residents and tourists flock to the mountains for skiing and other outdoor activities.

Winter is a time when the beauty of the red rocks, mountains, desert and saguaros are sometimes coated by a brilliant white coat of snow. Yes, it does snow here. We saw snow in Tombstone when we were on our journey across the lower forty-eight states.

In Green Valley, the elevation is twenty-nine hundred feet and we have seen snow twice in five years. On both occasions, the snow was less than one inch and was melted by ten am. In the higher elevations, snow occurs frequently. The Santa Rita

Mountains are across the valley from our villa and we see snow on that mountain range frequently. The highest peak is Mount Wrightson at ninety-four hundred feet. On the Colorado Plateau, with an elevation of five to seven thousand feet, and mountain elevations up to twelve thousand feet, heavy snow occurs and skiing is available near Flagstaff and Pinetop.

When we miss seeing snow, we can go to Madera Canyon and throw snowballs at each other. We are not very accurate, so neither of us has been hurt in the process. One Christmas, we went to Mount Lemmon to have a picnic in the snow and to watch the children sledding. We even brought along Christmas plates and napkins!

In the Sonoran Desert, rainfall occurs in the winter and during the summer monsoon season. The winter rains are milder than the summer rains, but they are extremely beneficial. The amount and timing of the winter rains determines the number of wildflowers we will enjoy in the spring.

The winter temperatures in southern Arizona are warmer than New England, but we have seen some nights with freezing temperatures. In Green Valley, we have seen three consecutive nights of seventeen degrees Fahrenheit. One winter, however, there were zero nights of freezing temperatures. In the daytime, the lowest high we have seen was forty-seven degrees and that is rare. Those of us who live here full-time find that below seventy-five degrees Fahrenheit is "freezing". The part-time residents (who blood has not thinned) spend the entire winter in shorts in comparison to us in jackets and long pants. We are sure that we stand out!

All of a sudden, the temperatures rise, the sky remains blue for days on end, and we start seeing a hint of color. **Spring** is a time of unending magic in the desert. Excitement and anticipation is in the air. It is the time to take inventory as to which plants have buds, which trees are in bloom, and where the poppies are popping out of the ground.

Everybody spends more time walking their dog, reading on their patios, and spending outdoor time with neighbors and friends. The windows are open, the allergies have started and we all sleep well at night after running around checking the status of all the blooming trees, bushes and cacti. Our experience has been that the average spring temperature ranges from high seventies to lower nineties.

During the late spring, one local television station runs a very interesting contest called "Ice Break." Contestants get to guess the date and time when the "ice" will break on the Santa Cruz river - one of the few rivers that flows north, and whose water flows underground, except when it's monsoon season. The "ice break" is actually when Tucson will break the hundred-degree mark. We laughed the first time we saw this. In New England, the contest involves guessing when the ice breaks on a designated lake. Cute contest.

In New England, there is a saying that people use when it rains the whole month of April: April showers bring May flowers. In Arizona, there is usually no rain in April, but the spring flowers come out anyway. The winter rains prompt their bloom.

There is an interesting event that occurs during the spring in Green Valley. The white-winged mourning doves return to nest and to pollinate the blooms of the great Saguaro cactus. We can always tell they have arrived by the song they love to sing that sounds like cuckoo-to-you. A pleasant sound that we miss when they leave in the fall.

Dry Summer usually starts in May and encompasses all the month of June. Rain is rare at this time of year and temperatures range from high nineties and over one hundred degrees. Thirty consecutive days of triple-digit temperatures is not unusual during the dry summer.

In Lake Havasu City, the thermostat read one hundred and twenty-eight degrees in 1994. Here, in Green Valley, we have seen the thermostat reach one-hundred and thirteen degrees. Phoenix temperatures are always higher than ours because their elevation is lower.

Our daily schedule changes at this time of year. We do our errands early in the morning with the goal of being home about ten am. In the afternoons, we read all the books we purchased throughout the year, including the ones we found at the Festival of Books in Tucson. In the late afternoon, we spend time in the pool with our "pool buddies." It is a time of year to relax, rest, rejuvenate the spirit and research the places we want to explore when the weather begins to cool.

The only relief during this time of year is the decrease in temperature that occurs during the evening and night hours. In the Sonoran Desert, the temperatures can vary by up to thirty degrees between day and night. Therefore, after a day of one hundred degrees, we can open up the windows to enjoy the nighttime temperature of seventy degrees.

Tiny houseflies arrive at this time of year and quickly become pests. They are always trying to land on bare skin so they can absorb the moisture. Sometimes they get into the house and can cause some funny moments. They are much smaller than the New England house fly, and they are quicker. We keep count of the attempts to kill it. Most of the time, we do get to assassinate it before it dies of starvation.

Due to the extreme heat, the low humidity, and the constant breeze, heat-related mortality is three times higher in Arizona than in any other state. Every year, hikers, bikers, runners, walkers, tourists, sports fans and others, are overcome by the heat. In Southern Arizona, several die every year. We have often heard the saying: "Two hours from health to death."

On June twenty-fourth, there is an annual festival in Tucson called "Dia de San Juan."

It is a fiesta in honor of St. John the Baptist who is believed to bring rain. The festival includes a procession, crafts, music, the sharing of food, vendors and children's activities. During the procession, a man named John carries the statue of St. John through the streets of the Mercado neighborhood. The festival is a plea to the saint to send us rain.

Wet summer, also known as the Monsoon season, is eagerly awaited by many full-time residents. The season technically lasts from June fifteenth through September thirtieth and the monsoon storms typically peak from mid July to mid August. The start of the summer storms is carefully watched by the local weather forecasters and they share their predictions on a daily basis. The rise of the dew point is the key indicator that determines the start of the rains. The first rain of the season generally falls around the Fourth of July holiday.

Half of the annual rainfall in Southern Arizona occurs during the monsoon rains. At this time of year, the gulf stream across the US shifts more northerly and the moisture is pulled up from the Gulf of Mexico. This pattern change influences our weather.

We love this time of year and we love watching the monsoon storms develop. In the morning, the sky is usually clear, but by mid-morning the storms clouds start appearing over the mountains across the valley. The clouds start off white, change to grey, thicken, change to dark grey and by the time they arrive in Green Valley, the clouds are black. The thunder starts, the lightning begins, and the huge, cold rain drops start to fall. Then, it pours! It can rain one to one and a half inches in twenty minutes. The clouds move on and the storm is gone.

However, the storms can be fickle. One area gets the wind, the rain, the lightning and thunder. Another area, one-half mile away sees the black clouds and gets no rain. We have seen times when the east side of our residence gets wet and the west side remains dry. We have been known to check both sides of the house when it rains.

The summer storms often include a lightning show that is phenomenal. We have seen horizontal lightning that makes all of the surrounding clouds appear white and we have seen forked lightning with a minimum of seven forks. A great spectacle to watch.

Flash flooding is a frequent occurrence in this state due to the amount of rain that falls in a short period of time. Dry washes and dry river beds fill up rapidly and can cause dangerous conditions as some of the washes flow across the roads. An average of six people per year are killed during the monsoon season in an attempt to cross the flooded roads.

The high winds created by the monsoon storms (and occasionally during other seasons) create conditions that are hazardous to drivers on the Interstates. Dust storms can develop and decrease the visibility to zero at times. Many car accidents and fatalities have occurred during these storms. These high winds are also responsible for the huge dust storms that occur in the city of Phoenix: they are referred to as *Haboobs*.

Monsoon season brings its share of rain, lightning, flash floods, refreshing breezes and many changes to our environment. The summer flowers bloom, the saguaros are getting fatter as they store the water, the golden fields have turned green, green grass is growing on the desert floor, the Texas Rangers are blooming again and the Datura are blooming in the medians. It is the time of year we check the river every time we drive by to see if there is water in the usually dry river bed. It is also the time of year when we stop and look at the puddle that has formed on the desert floor. We always wonder if there are tadpoles in that puddle.

When we first arrived, the mention of monsoon created a bit of apprehension. We heard about flash floods and people drowning. It all sounded dangerous and we often postponed a trip in fear of the upcoming storms. Today, we understand the precautions that need to be taken during this season, and it has become our favorite time of year. We love to see Mother Nature at it's grandest.

Finally, one morning, we take off on our walk to get the newspaper and it is apparent that the monsoon is gone. The rains have stopped, the humidity has decreased and the morning temperatures are cooler. The air feels clean and crisp. **Fall** has arrived. After the summer heat, everyone takes a breath and starts looking at the calendar of upcoming events.

It is time to look for the fall flowers, take scenic drives to see the sunflowers and to search for some of nature's colors. October is a great month to view the foliage. At higher altitudes, the aspen and the maples are showing off their reds and yellows. At lower elevations, the cottonwood trees that grow along any water source are renowned for their brilliant yellow displays.

This is also the time of year we love hunting for desert gourds. We love picking them for ourselves and our friends and we often dry them for a table display. This is also the time when we look through our shoe box and select the next places to explore. October and November are great months for explorers and adventurers.

After six years, we have become accustomed to the rhythms and flows of the Arizona seasons and we appreciate the wonders of all five seasons. Each season has its beauty, wonder and excitement and we live in a location with one additional season to enjoy.

BASIN AND RANGE

On our Grand Adventure, we spent twenty-one months traveling through the lower forty-eight states enjoying the diverse terrains, different landscapes, and the various cultures in this great country of ours.

In Nevada, the Loneliest Highway in America was high on our list of things to do. Route 50, the Loneliest Highway, runs east and west, and we loved the ride. Driving up a mountain range we would eventually descend on the other side and see a beautiful valley in front of us. At the end of the valley, we would drive up the mountain, descend, and cross another valley. This pattern repeated itself several times. We had never seen such terrain and it felt exciting as well as novel. We stopped in some of the valleys and listened to the absence of noise; the absence of trees, birds and vegetation was also noticeable. At one stop, we could hear a truck coming; it arrived at our location ten minutes later. At that time, the term "Basin and Range" was unknown to us.

During a visit to Vermont, Jonathan Kim Ph.D., Geologist and Environmental Scientist, exposed us to the books by John McPhee. In his book *Basin and Range*, the author explains the topography typical in that part of the country. Basin and Range consists of mountain chains that typically are oriented north and south with flat valleys, or basins, in between. It was exactly what we had seen and experienced on the Loneliest Highway in America. Education combined with experience can be an eye-opening event.

When the decision was made to settle down in Green

Valley, the fact that Southern Arizona lies in a Basin and Range complex was not known. How thrilling it was to discover this in the place where we chose to stay. The exploration of Arizona has included exploring the differences that exist in some of these valleys and we will share some of our adventures with you. Some sites will be discussed in other chapters, therefore, are not mentioned here. Sit back, relax and enjoy the adventure.

SAN SIMON VALLEY

Driving west on Interstate 10, the first valley visitors encounter in Arizona is the **San Simon Valley**. The sixty-five-mile broad valley runs primarily north and south from Safford to the Mexican border. It is bordered on the east by the Peloncillo and Whitlock Mountains and to the west lie the Chiricahuas, Dos Cabezas and the Piñaleno Mountains.

Traveling through the valley, there are huge agricultural fields, large expanses of golden grasses blowing in the wind, beautiful views of the mountains, numerous dirt roads to explore, ghost towns, ranches and a multitude of flowers in the springtime. We visited the valley in February and we saw fields of yellow poppies and yellow bladder pods.

In the southern part of the valley, the road passes through a section of the **Boot Heel Volcanic Field**. In the fields of golden or green grass, volcanic craters, cinder cones and numerous remnants of lava flows can be observed. It is always exciting to view the remains of geologic activity that occurred hundreds of thousands of years ago.

The town of **Safford**, at the northern edge of San Simon Valley, lies at the base of Mount Graham. Mining, agriculture, prisons, and schools are the main components of their economy. The main agricultural product is cotton and the city has its own cotton gin. Safford is well known for the Mount Graham International Observatory and for its thermal springs. Many spas, resorts and state parks offer opportunities to soak in the springs.

Thirty-five miles from Safford, sand dunes are available for public recreation in the **Hot Well Dunes Recreation Area**. This site is listed as a must-see attraction in the Safford area. The sand dunes are located in a remote area, surrounded by desert terrain. They appear out of place and this enhances their beauty. It is a playground for the camper, the fishermen (they have a small pond stocked with game fish), the picnickers, and the all-terrain vehicle lovers. It also invites the thermal spring lovers; there are two thermal spring hot tubs available for soaking and relaxing under the sun or the stars. We, along with Betty, left our footprints on one of the sand dunes. Wonder if the footprints are still there?

North of Safford, the **Gila Box Riparian National Conservation Area** focuses on the preservation of some wilderness area along the Gila River. It is a beautiful drive to the site with jagged cliffs, cottonwoods, blue sky, desert landscape and, at times, a view of the river. It is a remote area containing historic ranches, cliff dwellings and rock collecting sites. Bighorn sheep are numerous along the river. Recreational activities include canoeing, rafting, picnicking, camping, hiking, rock climbing, rock hounding and relaxing by the water. We took the opportunity to walk down to the river's edge. It was exciting to see the Gila River flowing.

Driving south on Highway 80, a large, beautiful monument is easily spotted by the side of the road. This is the Geronimo surrender monument. The actual site of the surrender is in **Skeleton Canyon** in the Peloncillo Mountains. To get to the actual surrender site, take the dirt road a few hundred feet south of the monument. There is signage to the canyon. In the canyon, there is a pile of rocks (used to be a cairn) that designates the place of the surrender. The dirt road is narrow in spots and some stream crossings are mandatory. For the less adventurous, the C.S. Fly photographs of the surrender site are an option.

Scanning the ridges of the Chiricahua Mountains, you can sometimes spot the **profile of Cochise**. Seen from the Chiricahua National Monument, a profile of the face is visible. From this valley, the profile of the entire body can be seen. Good luck in finding Cochise. It took us a while to spot it.

On the eastern flank of the Chiricahua Mountains, sits the tiny, unincorporated community of Portal. Thousands of birders flock to **Portal** annually due to its location at the mouth of Cave Creek Canyon. The hub of the community features a store, café, lodge, post office, and about a dozen other structures. Visiting this area, we made the Portal Peak Lodge our home. We will always remember this beautiful place with its good food and friendly people who made us feel at home. It was sad to leave after three days. The javelina are also missed. The first night we arrived, about twenty javelina were roaming around the settlement and they were quite willing to pose for pictures. The following day, they were spotted again and we saw some very young babies nursing while the mother was eating. We will always have fond memories of this area.

Called the gem of the Chiricahua Mountains, **Cave Creek Canyon** is impressive with its massive rhyolite cliffs, a running stream, bare stone walls amidst the green trees and the silence of mother nature. The oaks, pines, junipers, sycamores, walnuts, maples and willows provide a carpet of green for the massive rock formations and spires. Driving through this canyon is pleasurable and refreshing. Mother Nature at its best. Wild birds also have the same idea. Thousands of birders flock to this area in hopes of spotting a Trogon, a Montezuma Quail or dozens of other species. We did not spot a Trogon, but we did get a wonderful photo of a Montezuma Quail, who sat and smiled for us.

For Civilian Conservation Corps (CCC) fans, there are remains of a CCC camp in the canyon and information about the camp is available at the visitor center. For the adventurers and explorers, the road through the canyon continues over the mountains and ends up in the Sulphur Springs Valley. We did a portion of the road, but returned to Portal. There was ice on the road at the top.

San Simon Valley is fun, educational, relaxing, exciting, impressive and we will definitely return for another visit.

SULPHUR SPRINGS VALLEY

Proceeding west on Interstate 10, as you approach Willcox, you have arrived in **Sulphur Springs Valley**. The valley, one hundred and ten miles long and fifteen miles wide, runs north and south from the ghost town of Bonita to the Mexican border. It is bordered on the east by the Dos Cabezas and Chiricahua Mountains; on the west by the Dragoon and Mule Mountains. The large, flat valley contains agricultural fields, ghost towns, old cemeteries, mines, cattle ranches and wildlife areas. Pecan and pistachio trees, corn and cotton fields, and even golden grasses can be seen in the mountain foothills. This is one of our favorite playgrounds in Southern Arizona. We have spent five years gathering numerous dots in Sulphur Springs Valley and we have enjoyed all the sites we have explored and activities we have participated in.

Willcox, along Interstate 10, is a charming small town with a population of about four thousand. It was founded as a stop on the Southwestern Pacific Railroad and later adopted cattle and agriculture as it's economic base. Today, tourism also provides some of the town's revenue. The Willcox area produces seventy-four percent of all of the wine grapes grown in Arizona. For those who love to pick their own fruit, Apple Annie's may be the place for you. We love their peaches and their apple pies.

In the historical section of Willcox, the Marty Robbins Museum is a treat for all of the Robbins fans. Another museum on the same street pleases all of the Rex Allen Sr.

fans. **The Rex Allen Museum** has comprehensive exhibits on the life and career of Rex Sr. and some exhibits on Rex Jr. They allow photos in the museum, so bring your camera. For those who wish to reminisce about the good old days when we could listen to the "Arizona Cowboy," there is always an old movie playing. Great museum to explore. Rex Allen Sr. was born in the area and his ashes were scattered near the Rex Allen Museum. In the park across from the museum, there is a statue honoring Rex and the gravesite of his horse, Koko.

At the beginning of October, the town of Willcox host Rex Allen Days. The festivities, attended by thousands of residents and visitors, include a three-day rodeo, a lengthy and lively parade, concerts and entertainment, a country fair and a carnival. Rex Allen Jr. usually attends some of the festivities. The country fair is a great place to browse through and to get some pictures taken with some "cowboys" and "desperados."

In January, **Wings over Willcox** is the major event that occurs in southeastern Arizona and it attracts thousands of birders from around the world. The great event? Sandhill cranes, hawks, falcons and eagles. Every year, thousands of birds migrate to the Sulphur Springs Valley to spend the winter; thirty thousand of those birds are sand hill cranes. During the event, several tour options are available for visitors: tours of local ghost towns, tours to view the cranes, hawk-finding tours and tours to other popular local attractions. In 2013, we took the tour that included the geology of Texas Canyon, the Johnson mine, the Sulphur Springs Valley and the cranes. The event also includes lectures and entertainment. For birders, this event is fun, educational, and memorable.

There are several locations to view the sand hill cranes, such as the power plant on Route 191, Cochise Lake Bird Sanctuary, and along the road in Kansas Settlement. Our favorite place to view the magnificent and majestic birds is **Whitewater Draw Wildlife Area**, managed by the Arizona

Game and Fish Department. Available water is managed to provide marshland, mud flats and open water areas for migrating birds. It is the prime viewing area to see the sand hill cranes. There are restrooms, walking paths, benches, viewing decks and scopes to make the experience more memorable.

We look forward to seeing the cranes every year and our procedure is as follows: pack a cooler, pack a lunch, leave the house by eight am, arrive at Whitewater Draw by eleven am, unpack lunch, unpack cooler, place chairs near body of water and wait for the show to begin. All eyes are focused on the sky and someone eventually yells: "There!" A line of small black dots appears on the horizon and suddenly the noise of the incoming birds is heard. When the cranes prepare to land, the noise level is overwhelming as they seem to be communicating with each other. This pattern of small dots, increased noise and landing birds continues off and on from about eleven-thirty am to one pm. By the end of the loudest show in Arizona, about ten to fifteen thousand cranes have landed less that an quarter mile away from us. We try to prepare first-timers for the noise and beauty, but there is no way to describe this incredible spectacle. This is a must-see and must-do for nature lovers.

Cochise, the well-known Chiricahua Apache Chief, is well represented in Sulphur Springs Valley. His birthplace was in the Chiricahua Mountains and his burial site is in Cochise Stronghold located in the Dragoon Mountains. His profile can be seen from the top of the scenic drive in the Chiricahua National Monument. The dry lake bed is called Cochise Lake and the bird sanctuary is also named Cochise. A lot of history in this valley.

For the adventurers who love historical places and old forts, **Fort Bowie National Historic Site** is the place for you. The US Army Outpost, established in 1862, is located in Apache Pass at the base of the Chiricahua Mountains. Many remains of the fort still exist. This is an educational and historical site.

Douglas, near the Mexican border, is the southernmost city in the valley. It was founded as a smelter town to process the copper ore from Bisbee. The smelter operations have since terminated. Douglas is home to the historic Gadsden Hotel which is known as the last of the grand hotels. Other interesting sites in the city include: the El Paso and Southwestern railroad depot, the Douglas Grand Theatre, and the Slaughter Ranch (also known as the San Bernandino Ranch).

Chiricahua National Monument, located in the Chiricahua Mountains, is southwest of Willcox. The park was established to preserve and protect the remains of volcanic activity. The ash-filled valley has eroded and has produced extensive hoodoos and balancing rocks. The park contains many walking trails and an eight-mile paved scenic drive to the top of the mountain. The view is stunning and surreal. The hoodoos appear to be an army of men marching through the valley. It is hard to imagine how this was formed. There are many information kiosks available and many pull-offs from which to view the beautiful and varied rock formations. Some of our favorite rock formations are the ones that look like stone mushrooms. This park is sometimes referred to as the land of the standing-up rocks.

The most striking feature of this valley is the **Willcox Playa**. The playa is a large, dry lake bed which is the remnant of Lake Cochise. In the dry seasons, the playa appears to be dried up land which can sometimes contribute to dust storms that interfere with the traffic on Interstate 10. During the wet seasons, the playa can contain one to two inches of water produced by the drainage from the surrounding mountains and will look like a lake. The playa looks different every time depending on the amount of sunlight, the level of water and the viewing perspective. This dry lake bed distinguishes this valley from the others in southeastern Arizona.

Alongside the dry lake bed (playa), there is an area of

light tan **sand dunes**. We have explored this area on several occasions and we have often wondered if there were shells in the dunes. On our tour in 2013, with Wings over Willcox, we stopped at the sand dunes. The guide, a retired geologist, informed the group that the sand dunes contained shells and remnants of fish from the evaporated lake. We searched and searched and we were rewarded! We found one small shell and one tiny fish bone. Our guide estimates that they are about twenty thousand years old. Needless to say we were thrilled and excited.

This valley has been educational, fun, exciting, thrilling and amazing for us. It is a one-of-a-kind place in Arizona to be enjoyed by all.

SAN PEDRO VALLEY

Continuing west on Interstate 10, the sign notifies drivers that they have arrived in Texas Canyon. This is at the eastern edge of the **San Pedro Valley**. The valley is fifty miles long and runs mostly north and south. It is bordered on the east by the Dragoon and Mule Mountains and on the west by the Santa Rita and Pajarito Mountains. The San Pedro Valley is significantly different than Sulphur Springs Valley in numerous ways. The San Pedro river runs through the valley, and with its line of cottonwood trees, it gives the valley a colorful green stripe. Desert landscapes, golden grasses, prairies, rolling hills and small mountains ranges are also found in this large valley. With its ghost towns, lakes, mine sites, and several historical sites, this valley offers educational and recreational options to a large variety of visitors. There are several town and cities in this valley. Enjoy the sites we have chosen to share with you.

Texas Canyon, along Interstate 10, is a large granite area that has eroded over time to create a jumble of rocks. It is known for its giant granite boulders, balancing rocks and unique rock formations. The rocks capture the imagination and this unique area attracts rock hounds and photographers. Near the Amerind Museum, there is an area with picnic tables and restrooms. It is a magical environment to visit and wander through. On one of our visits, we spotted a grinding hole in a huge boulder. Newcomers to this area are often spotted looking at the sign near one of the boulders. The sign reads "Please respect the privacy of our rattlesnakes."

Next, we go south of Sierra Vista, to the **Coronado National Memorial**. The park is administered by the National Park Service and its goal is to commemorate the 1540 expedition by Francisco Vasquez de Coronado into the Southwest Territory. Entering the park, fields of golden grass welcome the visitors. In a short period of time, the scenery changes into a desert landscape. The visitor center has artifacts and information pertaining to the Coronado expedition. Leaving the center, the windy and narrow dirt road leads to the top of the mountain and the scenery on the drive is stunning. At least, we thought so. Bernadette, in the back seat, refused to look at the beautiful valley because she would have been looking at the edge of the road with no guardrails.

At the top, information kiosks are abundant and on one board there is a picture of an expedition going through the valley. We looked at the picture and then the valley. It was easy to see the huge expedition party crossing this magnificent valley. This site has been placed on the National Register of Historical Places. This is a park full of beauty and history.

Sierra Vista is a city with a population of about forty thousand which serves as the main commercial, cultural and recreational hub of Cochise County. Fort Huachuca lies at the northwest corner of the city. Sierra Vista has been nicknamed "The Hummingbird Capital of the World." This area has been known as a bird-lovers paradise for many years. Annually, there is the Hummingbird Banding Project which attracts bird-lovers and enthusiasts to the event. The city also hosts the annual Southwest Wings Bird and Nature Festival which consist of lectures and one-day or overnight field trips. Another popular event hosted by the city is the annual Cowboy Poetry and Music Gathering. Singers, poets and musicians gather for all those interested in a fun and exciting weekend. The music gathering is a popular event for us; it gives us another opportunity to support our favorite performers.

South of Sierra Vista, high up on the side of a mountain, the **Shrine of our Lady of the Sierras** greets visitors with its seventy-five-foot Celtic Cross. On the grounds of the shrine, there is a small rustic chapel, a visitor center, stations of the cross, a thirty-one-foot statue of the Blessed Virgin Mary, and a ten foot high "Angel of Revelation." The shrine is open for all who wish to enter and the history of the shrine is fascinating.

Mustang Corners, at the intersection of Route 82 and Route 90, is one of our favorite locations in San Pedro Valley. The corner got its name due to the herds of mustangs that used to run wild in the area. Today, there are no mustangs to be seen. At the corner, there is one gas station with a convenience store. There used to be two gas stations but one has closed; you can see the remains near the corner. During explorations of the San Pedro Valley we have come to rely on this corner for our gas, restrooms and snacks. It is a convenient location and the people are always friendly. Great place to rest, laugh and enjoy the company of fellow residents of Arizona.

A city of five thousand residents, **Benson**, is located at the junction of Interstate 10 and Route 80. The city was founded as a railroad town with the arrival of the Southern Pacific Railroad and continues to serve as a rail terminal. The city has numerous historical structures, both commercial and residential, and a walk through the downtown is like walking back in time. The railroad depot is currently the visitor center and a trip to the depot is well worth it. There are huge murals near the visitor center depicting the history of Benson as a railroad town. Murals are also visible in other parts of the town and we located some excellent murals of Indian dancers and desert flora at the Oasis Court, Benson's Historical Auto Court.

Driving east on Interstate 10, the rest area at Texas Canyon is a convenient and beautiful location to stop, stretch, use the restrooms and read the information sign. The sign says that **Council Rocks**, where Cochise and General Howard met in 1872 to discuss peace, is due south of the rest area. Sounds enticing and seems like a great place to visit. We have not visited the area described as a ruggedly beautiful place in Southern Arizona. We researched the directions and the area and we stopped the planning process when we read about the foot-holes in the rock to assist in the climbing. Adventurers should research the level of difficulty before the trip.

Elgin is located on Route 83 south of Sonoita where the scenery consists of fields with golden grasses and pronghorn antelope. The area is known for its vineyards and for the several wine festivals it hosts annually. Elgin is the location of nine vineyards that produce fifty thousand gallons of wine annually. One day we headed for the Sonoita Vineyards to taste and purchase some local wine. The wine tasting was definitely a happy event for Bernadette and Midge. The man pouring the wine was giving them very generous portions of wine to "taste." We thought that the man really liked Bernadette and maybe he wanted her to stay longer. Anyway, at the end of tasting seven different wines, two (out of three) of us left really "happy." Going to a second vineyard on that day was definitely not a good idea, but we did come home with some Arizona wine.

The **Murray Springs Mammoth Kill** site is located south of Sierra Vista on Route 90. This is a Paleo Indian site administered by the Bureau of Land Management to protect and preserve one of the oldest archaeological sites excavated in North America. During the excavation, a Clovis campsite, spear points, bison bones, bones of extinct horses and bones of mammoths were found. All of the information gathered indicates that thirteen thousand years ago human beings killed large numbers of game animals in this area. The largest of the animals was the mammoth; the archaeologists named one of the female mammoths Big Eloise. From the parking lot, there is a ¾ mile trail to the dig site that crosses a deep arroyo. The dig site can be viewed from the trail and there is an option to walk into the site. Several information signs are located along the trail and contain photos of some of the bones recovered from this area. Great historical place to visit.

Kartchner Caverns State Park, nine miles south of Benson, preserves a unique and pristine cave environment. The cave contains stalactites, stalagmites, ribbons and columns. The largest of the columns is named: Kubla Khan. Tours through the cave are offered and visitors are given the choice to visit the Rotunda Room or the Big Room. The path through the cave is paved, well-lit, and relatively flat with handrails. The first time, we saw the Rotunda room and we had to return to see the Big Room. During certain times of the year, bats occupy a section of the Big Room, so it is closed to the public. We found that Kartchner was one of the most beautiful and most accessible caves to tour. Glad to see that Arizona has preserved this natural treasure.

Patagonia, a town of about nine hundred residents, is located on Route 82. The town was formerly a supply center for all of the nearby mines and ranches. Today, it is a retirement community, an artists' center and is known for its birding habitats. The Patagonia-Sonoita Creek Preserve lies adjacent to Patagonia. The town is also the beginning of the scenic drive called "Patagonia Back Road Ghost Towns." This is a great scenic drive that will bring you through unpopulated areas with beautiful scenery. After exploring, hunger can be a problem. In this town, there is a restaurant called Velvet Elvis Pizza Co. which is capable of dealing with your need for tasty food. Their pizzas are *fantisimo.*

Route 83, from Interstate 10 to Parker Canyon Lake, is one of our favorite scenic drives in Southern Arizona. The northern part of the drive includes rolling hills with golden or green grasses, ranches and magnificent views of the Santa Rita Mountains. The southern part (from Sonoita to Parker Canyon Lake) includes rolling hills with desert landscape, shallow canyons and views of mountain ranges on both sides of the road. The road has many curves and hills, so taking your time and enjoying the scenery is mandatory. There are several sites to stop and explore if desired: a winery, Rosemont junction, Greaterville (where you can find gold nuggets in them thar' hills), Empire Ranch, Kentucky camp, Elgin wineries, Canelo cowboy church, Canelo cemetery, and Sunnyside. This is a great place to roam any time of year. In the fall, sunflowers line the edges of the road and make the drive magical.

Dolan Ellis, Arizona's Official State Balladeer, founded the **Arizona Folklore Preserve** in Hereford, in 1996. It is located at the mouth of Ramsey Canyon. The purpose of the preserve is to provide a place where the songs and stories of Arizona and the western culture can be preserved and performed. Performing artists provide entertainment to a small audience in an up-close-and-personal environment. It was great to be at one of Dolan's performances at the place he founded. This is a great place to hear talented performers. Country environment and western music at its best.

Whenever we are in need of magnificent Arizona scenery and a breath of crisp, clean air heading to **Sonoita** sounds like a great idea. This small town of eight hundred residents is located at the intersection of Routes 82 and 83 and is surrounded by fields of green or golden grasses. For years, it has been a popular place where the wealthy built vacation homes, retirement houses and ranches. Today, a new type of resident is moving in and thriving. Pronghorn antelope can frequently be seen in the area and sometimes the herd contains babies. At the latest count, it is estimated that three hundred pronghorns have made Sonoita home. We are glad they are there and we spend a lot of time and energy trying to spot them. On Labor Day weekend, Sonoita hosts a rodeo at the fairgrounds. Wild horse and burro adoptions have also drawn potential "parents" to Sonoita. We drove by one day during an "adoption" and we chose not to stop. Not pretty seeing two grown women crying because we can't fit the burro we love into Gypsy. We chose to drive home.

The **San Pedro Riparian National Conservation Are**a includes fifty-seven thousand acres of private land from the Mexican border to St. David. Its purpose is to protect a precious and fragile ecosystem along forty miles of the San Pedro River. The visitor center is at the San Pedro house in the southern section of the conservation area. A map of the area is available and highlights all of the attractions including an old fort, two archaeological sites, ghost towns and old cemeteries. Camping is allowed and hiking trails are abundant. This area protects green trees and flowing water in an otherwise desert environment. What a treasure to see and enjoy.

Naco is a small port of entry town along the Mexican Border. For some time, we had dreamed of going to Naco to see a garage that still remains. Why? We love Dolan Ellis and he sings this song about Patrick Murphy that always makes us laugh. The story goes as follows: Patrick Murphy was drinking in a bar. The more drinks he had, the more he wanted to help the Americans fight against the Mexicans. He got into his plane with some incendiary devices and flew over the border. He let go of the "bombs" over Naco. The only problem was that he hit Naco, AZ instead of Naco, Mexico. One of the buildings that was hit was a garage that contained the car of the Mexican

General who was a friend of the mayor of Naco, AZ. This was the only time that a US city was bombed. Patrick Murphy was never heard from again. Anyway, we went to Naco and sure enough - there was the garage that Patrick Murphy had bombed. One less curiosity item on the bucket list of things to see.

Tombstone is an historic western town that caters to children of all ages who love cowboys, *desperados*, and anything western. The dirt streets, the wooden sidewalks, the cowboys, the stagecoach, and the music from the saloons give this town an appearance of authenticity. So many things to see: shoot-outs in the street, the Bird Cage Theatre, the Boothill Cemetery, the biggest rose bush, the OK Corral, the diorama and the printing press. One can even spend time taking a mine tour, riding in a stagecoach, following the Earps walking down the street, stopping at Big Nose Kate's for a sarsaparilla, and posing for a picture with Doc Holliday. Tombstone hosts several annual events such as Wyatt Earp Days, the Rose Festival, Territorial Days, and Helldorado Days. This is a town that loves fun and treats its visitors like guests. This is a town very dear to our hearts. Tombstone is the reason we moved to Arizona. We visit the western town often and sometimes encounter people who remember us.

San Pedro Valley is filled with sites to please a large number of tourists. This is a valley we have frequented often and will continue to do so.

SAN RAFAEL VALLEY

San Rafael Valley is a small valley within the boundaries of the San Pedro Valley. San Rafael is bordered on the east by the Huachuca Mountains and on the west by the Patagonia Mountains. The valley is covered with miles of grasslands. The cattle are abundant and can be seen from the road that runs north and south through the valley.

At the southern end of the valley, explorers will find the **San Rafael Ranch** which gained recognition when it was selected as the filming location for the movie *Oklahoma*. Today, the ranch location is a State Park in an effort to preserve and protect the historical site.

The San Rafael Valley forms the headwaters of the Santa Cruz River which runs south into Mexico, veers north and re-enters Arizona in Nogales.

SANTA CRUZ VALLEY

Continuing west of Interstate 10, **Santa Cruz Valley** begins upon entering the city limits of Tucson. The valley is approximately seventy miles long, about thirty-five miles wide and runs mostly north and south. It is bordered on the east by the Santa Rita and Patagonia Mountains and on the west by the Sierrita and Pajarito Mountains. This valley is a major trade corridor due to the port of entry in Nogales and the several produce warehouses in Rio Rico.

This valley is a contrast to the San Pedro valley because of the number of mesquite trees that thrive in this area. Due to overgrazing in the past, the acres of prairies, although present, are few and far between. Through the center of the valley runs the Santa Cruz River which can be a raging torrent of brown water during the monsoon or a dry river bed in the dry season. In a few areas near Tubac and Tumacacori, some water may be present year-round.

The Santa Cruz Valley contains numerous ghost towns, cattle ranches, historic ranches, remnants of old forts, lakes, and a wide variety of recreational options. Sit back, relax and enjoy some of the places we have explored.

Nogales, AZ is the southernmost city in Santa Cruz Valley. Nogales, AZ and Nogales, Sonora were once united but were divided with the establishment of the new border after the Gadsden Purchase. With a population of twenty thousand,

Nogales, AZ is the smaller of the two cities although it is the largest border community with four ports of entry. The city has several historic attractions which include the historic Santa Cruz County Courthouse and the Old Nogales City Hall. In the old city hall, the Pimeria Alta Museum has several exhibits about the history of the surrounding area. The museum also has large murals by Corona, the famous Mexican muralist and bullfighter.

Some of the scenes in Hangover 3 were filmed in Nogales. We wanted to go audition for parts as extras, but we were not in town during the auditions. Oh well, our acting careers will have to wait for future filming sessions! A trip to Nogales, however, was planned for the filming dates. It was amazing to see how one section of Nogales was transformed to look like Tijuana, including an arch that says: Welcome to Tijuana. The movie set included temporary murals, street vendors in the park, sugar skulls on display and movie cameras. The historic shopping district sure looked different.

On Route 19, north of Nogales, lies a census-designated community of eighteen thousand residents. **Rio Rico** is home to numerous warehouses that receive and distribute produce and other goods imported from Mexico. Within the community, lies the remains of Calabasas, an historic settlement and ghost town. Several Native American sites have also existed in this area and arrowheads and spear points can still be found in the area. An old cemetery on the east frontage road (amidst the warehouses) is the final resting place of some of the settlers who helped establish this community. Rio Rico has no established "downtown" which added to our confusion when we attempted to explore. At the *Fiesta de Tumacacori*, we met Dwight Thibodeaux, amateur historian of Rio Rico, who informed us about an upcoming tour of the community and we immediately signed up. That tour exposed us to the Baca Float Ranch, Rancho Santa Cruz and the remains of Calabasas.

The book *Landscapes of Fraud* by Thomas E. Sheridan talks about the land grants and land deals in this area. Great read!

Tumacacori is an unincorporated community that abuts the community of Carmen. The two communities are joined in the 2010 census and, at that time, the population was three hundred and ninety-three people. The Wisdoms Café in Carmen is famous for its fruit burritos and Tumacacori is known for the Chili and Spice Co. which carries any spice that is desired. The biggest building in the area is the Mission San Jose de Tumacacori which is protected and preserved within the boundaries of the **Tumacacori National Historical Park**. The footprints of the church, built by the Jesuits in 1691 is still visible, but current visitors are looking at the mission church built by the Franciscans in 1757. Arriving at this site for the first time, it is easy to be awed by the beauty of this historical structure. Tours and guide books are available at the visitor center and explain the purpose of the mission and its history. A walk to the river and a walk to the orchard is also recommended. This park also protects two additional historic Jesuit sites: Mission Los Santos Angeles de Guevavi and Mission San Cayetano de Calabazas. Tours are offered to the satellite missions and reservations can be made at the National Park.

Tubac is a census-designated community of about twelve hundred residents with a long and interesting history. In this community, the Spanish built a Presidio (fort) in 1752 to protect their settlers. Once the Presidio was moved to Tucson, the community was abandoned. Tubac was deserted on several occasions due to the threat of danger from the raiding Apaches. The Pennington family, some of the first permanent white settlers in the area, lived in Tubac for some time and their residence still stands. Charles Poston, known as the "Father of Arizona," also resided in Tubac. Today, the community is an artists colony featuring numerous galleries and shops. The movie, *The Tin Cup*, starring Kevin Costner was filmed at the Tubac Golf course.

Juan Bautista de Anza National Historic Trail is a twelve-hundred-mile-long trail to honor the expedition by de Anza and his entourage. The trail runs from Nogales, AZ to San Francisco, CA. The maps of the trail and auto tour maps available at National Parks in southern Arizona highlight the historic sites that lie along the trail. The trails in Arizona are well marked and open to the public. During the De Anza Day festivities, the trail from Tumacacori to Tubac is used annually in a re-enactment of part of the expedition.

Nestled in the beautiful Santa Cruz Valley and near the Santa Rita Mountains, the little community of **Amado** is appealing to nature lovers and bird watchers. The community lies at the junction of Arivaca Road and can sometimes be bypassed by visitors heading west. Besides friendly people, beautiful horses and a new Wholesum Farms greenhouse, this area has some interesting attractions. The Longhorn Grill is listed as an Arizona Roadside Attraction and was used in the filming of *Alice Doesn't Live Here Anymore* featuring Ellen Burstyn and Kris Kristofferson. Exciting that a Martin Scorsese movie had a scene from Amado. Another interesting place is the Cow Palace Restaurant that has been serving customers since the 1920s. Going to the Cow Palace for dinner is always a big deal because, when you arrive and leave, time is needed to check out the photos and autographs on display. Would you believe that John Wayne ate here? And Whoopi Goldberg too! Driving by on Interstate 19, check out Amado's new cell tower; it is shaped like a water tower with AMADO on the side. Sure looks better than a palm tree or a pine tree.

The **Fred Lawrence Whipple Observatory** sits atop Mount Hopkins in the Santa Rita Mountains and on sunny days it appears to be a brilliant shiny white golf ball. The observatory is owned and operated by the Smithsonian

Astrophysical Observatory. The visitor center is at the base of the mountain and is open to the public; videos, photos and exhibits are available for viewing. Tours are available and depart from the visitor center. Explorers leave at nine am and return at three pm having completed the ride up the long, winding dirt road. The view of the valley from the top of Mount Hopkins is awesome. We went on a tour to the top and the experience was educational and the view was fantastic. On another occasion, we took Gypsy up the winding dirt road and she seemed to like that adventure as much as we did. For flower lovers, Mount Hopkins road from Elephant Head Road to the visitor center is a great place to see spring wild flowers and hundreds of ocotillo plants. They bloom along the road and can be easily seen and admired.

Green Valley is an unincorporated retirement community of about thirty thousand people; the number varies by season. It is located in the Sonoran Desert with stunning views of the Santa Rita Mountains, saguaro cactus, ocotillos, cholla, and other desert flora. The community is geared to retirees and provides a large variety of recreational and educational activities. Prior to becoming a retirement community, cotton fields were numerous in this area. During WWII, *guayale*, a Mexican shrub that produces a large amount of latex, which was used to make a type of rubber, was also grown here. Prisoners of war assisted in the harvesting process. This is the community where we chose to retire.

Sahuarita is a town of approximately twenty-five thousand residents that lies directly north of Green Valley. The Green Valley Pecan Co, the largest irrigated pecan orchard in the world, provides job opportunities and green trees to the Santa Cruz Valley. Another interesting feature is the ASARCO Mineral Discovery Center on West Pima Mine Road. The museum has a video and information about copper mining in Arizona. Mine tours are also available and allows guests the opportunity to see a large, open-pit copper mine. Sometimes, while on the tour, the group also spots some of the wild Spanish horses that live in the area. During WWII, a prisoner of war camp was located in the present-day boundaries of Sahuarita. Maps indicate that the camp was located across the street from the entrance to Quail Creek. The prisoners were used as labor in the surrounding fields.

The twenty-seven-mile scenic drive to the top of **Mount Lemmon** remains one of our favorite activities. The Sky Island Scenic Byway (also called the Catalina Highway) is the only paved road that reaches the top of the mountain. Adventurers climb six thousand feet on this scenic drive; from lowland desert to alpine forest. The viewpoints, the unique rock formations, the flowers and the cool, crisp air all add to the enjoyment of Mother Nature at its finest. Upon arriving at the top, hunger can be a problem; the Iron Door restaurant is our favorite with their outdoor seating and their home-made personal-size pies. Mount Lemmon was our selected site for a Christmas Day picnic (in the snow). In the fall, we head to the top during foliage season to see the radiant yellows and reds. Another place to explore on the way up (or down) the scenic drive is the Gordon Hirabayashi Site where the remains of a prison camp are visible. At the top, the community of Summerhaven is a great place to visit and also has an interesting history. Mount Lemmon is great place to explore, eat, hike, rest and just plain get away from the desert for a while.

Colossal Cave Mountain Park, located in Vail, is an underground cavern with almost four miles of mapped passageways. The cave is an ancient karst (dry cave) that was once used by the Hohokam Indians and later was used as a source for guano. Today, tours of the caves are available to the public. The Civilian Conservation Corps (CCC) was involved in the development of this park and their effort can be seen at the visitor center. A statue of a CCC worker is near the door of the gift shop. There is also a CCC museum located on the grounds of the park. Visitors can see the remains of the original ranch, take a horseback ride or picnic in the area. Hiking and camping are also optional activities.

At the base of the Rincon Mountains, **Saguaro National Park East** offers visitors the opportunity to view the Sonoran Desert landscape at its best. Located off of Old Spanish Trail Road in Tucson, the park contains a paved scenic drive and several viewpoints from which to stop and admire the beautiful mountains, the rock formations, the numerous saguaro cactus, yuccas, prickly pear and several other species of flora. The park also offers views of the city of Tucson, and wildlife are often spotted in the park. We spotted a deer grazing during our visit.

Tucson, a city with over five hundred thousand residents, has a long and interesting story. It has been continuously inhabited for over twelve thousand years and, at one time, was the capital of the Arizona Territory. Today, it is a vibrant, culturally diverse, accessible, fun, historical and artistic city. It offers a large variety of educational and recreational opportunities. Tucson has become our playground and we have participated in many events in this wonderful city such as: Dillinger Days at the Hotel Congress, Winterhaven's Christmas lights display, Parade of Lights, 2nd Saturday (musical events), the largest Gem and Mineral Show in the United States, the Tucson Festival of Books, the Greek Festival and many others. Tucson has also installed a light-rail streetcar that increases accessibility to some events. We rode the streetcar the first day it started! Tucson is also home to several places listed as Roadside Oddities such as the Diamondback rattlesnake pedestrian bridge that looks like and sounds like a rattlesnake and the El Tiradito (known as the Sinners Shrine). Tucson's zoo made the national news in 2014 with the birth of a baby elephant girl named "Nandi." What a joy to have watched her grow into the beautiful young lady she is today.

Tucson is a great city to live near and we always look forward to participating in new and different activities.

AVRA VALLEY

Avra Valley is a fifty-mile, northwest-to-southeast valley just west of Tucson. The valley is bordered by the Tucson, Silverbell, Sierrita, Roskruge and the Waterman Mountains. Desert landscapes, agricultural fields and spectacular views of mountain ranges abound in this valley. Interstate 10 is the main road through the valley. Recreational activities and options are numerous.

Driving west on Interstate 10, **Marana** is a city about ten miles west of Tucson. The city of about thirty-five thousand residents is one of the fastest growing communities in Arizona. This city has a long and interesting past, including several Native American sites and a Butterfield Stagecoach stop. Driving within the city limits, you can see large cotton fields. The fields are very noticeable when the cotton is ready to pick; with the sun shining on the fields, they appear to be very large, white, puffy clouds very close to the ground. When we drive on Interstate 10, we have often wondered how they harvest all of this cotton. Last year (2016), Marana hosted a Cotton Festival. You can guess that we went to this festival. There were food vendors, information booths, horse demonstrations, a petting zoo and a Mechanical Cotton Picker that demonstrated how the cotton was harvested. How cool was that to get an up-close and personal view of the process. Later, they dumped the cotton in a big pile so the children could play. We got our picture taken near the pile and near the huge cotton picker. Great fun.

Commercial airlines send their airplanes to **Pinal Air Park** for storage in the dry Arizona environment. Driving along Interstate 10, we've watched the number of planes increasing. The park is reportedly "open to the public," but when we arrived we discovered that access is strictly monitored and access is not permitted to "tourists." The park is fenced and a view of the planes is restricted. Seeing them from afar is more impressive. Another point of interest: in the 1970s and 1980s, the park was reportedly used as an airbase for the CIA. Interesting.

Saguaro National Park (West) in Avra Valley is one of our favorite National Parks in the area. We love bringing family and friends to the visitor center to view their magnificent introductory video. Every year, the blooming of the Saguaro cactus is a big event for us and a tour around the park is a treat. We also chase spring wildflowers alongside the dirt roads that meander through the desert. A special feature in the park are the remains of a CCC camp which contains partial walls and concrete slabs. Another place to explore is Signal Hill: a short trail leads to the top of a rocky hill where visitors can see some well-preserved petroglyphs. For outdoor lovers, hikers, picnickers, photographers, flower lovers and all adventurers, this is a great park to visit and enjoy.

Ironwood National Monument is located near Marana and can also be accessed by Sasco Road. The park is named after the longest living tree in the Arizona desert. In the park, beautiful Sonoran Desert landscapes and breathtaking views of mountain ranges are abundant. Driving on the dirt roads through the park, it is easy to feel that you are the only visitors. This is a primitive park with rock art, archaeological sites, bighorn sheep and abundant wildflowers in the spring. Visiting for the first time, we had one major concern. How were we going to know an Ironwood from a mesquite or another kind of tree? Going down the dirt road, we spotted a tree with beautiful pink buds. *Voila*! The Ironwood trees were in bloom. Thank you, Mother Nature. We got great pictures that day. Not far from the National Monument, the Silverbell Mine can be explored and an old cemetery is also in the area.

We (Midge, Carolyn, Betty and I) were talking one day

about our dream of going on a **Hot Air Balloon ride**. One day, the decision was made and the date was chosen. We were going to fly our balloon in Avra Valley where we could enjoy the beautiful landscape. On the morning of the balloon ride, the sunrise was exceptional: the sky was a golden yellow, the best sunrise we had ever seen. Great way to start our adventure. Taking pictures, stretching the balloon, watching the balloon grow bigger, climbing into the basket and waving goodbye were the first steps of our long-awaited dream ride. The scenery was unbelievable. We spotted jack rabbits, watched coyotes run through the desert, and thoroughly enjoyed being together on such a beautiful day. The wind was about five miles- per-hour and the flight was smooth. All good things must come to an end, and we had to descend. The wind nearer the ground was about ten miles-per-hour, so the balloon quickly accelerated. It did not take long for us to realize that a high-speed landing was about to come. We hit a dirt berm, narrowly missed an irrigation canal and fence, bounced three times in a plowed field (I wonder what the farmer was thinking) and finally landed and stayed put long enough for all of us to bail out of the basket. Funny how it had never dawned on us that hot air balloons do not have brakes. All of us landed in one piece and lived to hear the toast and the saying: A successful balloon trip is when you can walk away. How very true. Midge explains our sky adventure in Avra Valley in this manner - One and a half hours of peace, beauty, meditation, quiet and five minutes of terror. A bond was formed that day: Midge, Carolyn, Betty and I will always remember the morning we spent in Avra Valley.

ALTAR VALLEY

Altar Valley is fifty miles long and bordered by the Sierrita, Quinlan and Baboquivari Mountains. The valley runs north and south, from Robles Junctions to Sasabe, near the Mexican border, and merges with Avra Valley northeast of Robles Junction. Driving through this valley is like driving back in time. This is what Arizona must have looked like hundreds of years ago: desert landscapes, golden grass and large unpopulated areas. Ranches are scattered throughout the valley, but structures alongside the road are rare. Mother Nature rules in this valley!

Robles Junction (also called Three Points) is a community of about five thousand residents at the northern edge of Altar Valley. It is located at the junction of Route 86 and 286. Many visitors to the valley enter at this location. A restaurant named Cindy Lou's is located in this community; it has a good reputation.

Arivaca is an unincorporated community of about nine hundred residents nestled in the foothills of Southern Arizona and lies at the eastern edge of Altar Valley. The scenery surrounding the community is spectacular and the ground is rich with minerals. Mining has a long history in this area that dates back to the time of the Spanish expeditions. Mexican fire agates, opals, gold and silver can be found in this region. In the town, several historical structures remain and help tell the story of its beginning; visitors should check out the old schoolhouse and the historical stagecoach depot, to name a few. For the explorers, the mercantile has maps for a great scenic drive called "The Ruby Loop;" it is fun, beautiful and an adventure. After mining, shopping and walking around town, a great place to satisfy your hunger is the *La Gitana Cantina* on the main road. The cantina has delicious hamburgers, friendly people, and a great outdoor seating area.

Sasabe is a small unincorporated community on the Mexican border with a little-used port of entry. In 2010, the population of this community was fifty-four; in 2015, when we visited, the population was nine. The community has a small "downtown" with one general store still in operation.

The town is well known due to the *Rancho de la Osa*, a guest ranch that once catered to dignitaries and wealthy patrons. When we visited, the ranch was for sale. It was purchased and re-opened in February 2017 as a dude ranch. Driving into the center of Sasabe, it felt like we had entered a war zone. Barbed wire surrounds some of the structures and many of the buildings are boarded up and vacant. What a sad ending to a community once visited by Presidents and other famous people. It was sad to see.

Kitt Peak National Observatory is located on Kitt Peak in the Quinlan Mountains on the Tohono O'odham reservation. We chose not to take the night tours and drove up the mountain in the daytime. The road was paved and the driving was pleasant. There are pull-offs available on the road and Gypsy stopped at all of them. The scenery of the valley, the mountains, and the desert was breathtaking. Arriving at the top, you are greeted by a painting by Michael Chiago a world-class Tohono O'odham artist. At the visitor center, a video is available in the small museum. Information about the campus is also available for those who wish to do a self-guided tour. The walking tour is informative and interesting. At one point, we walked by some of the dormitories and the sign said: "Quiet please. Scientists sleeping." We chuckled (quietly). This was a great way to spend a day.

Heading south on Route 286 from Robles Junction, the entrance to the **Buenos Aires National Wildlife Refuge** is well marked. This one hundred and twenty-thousand-acre park preserves the semi-desert grasslands for the benefit of rare and endangered wildlife and is home to fifty-eight species of mammals. The bobwhite quail and the pronghorn antelope have been reintroduced and are sometimes spotted in the area near the visitor center. One day we visited the park with Mary and Danielle (Midge's grand-daughter) and we spotted a herd of seven pronghorn. The main section of the refuge contains a visitor center with an introductory video, a pond for bird viewing, and several dirt roads that allows visitors to see different sections of the park.

Other sections of the refuge include Brown Canyon, Arivaca Cienega and Arivaca Creek. All four sections of the park are worthy of exploration. In the spring time, this area is famous for its abundance of wildflowers. Annually, the refuge hosts the Grassland Fair that attracts several hundred nature lovers.

We have shared with you our excitement of living in the Basin and Range region of Southern Arizona. The six valleys described have brought much excitement, joy and laughter into our lives. We have enjoyed exploring each of them and hope you have been inspired to visit some of these places of interest.

CANYONS

In New England and the Midwest, there are numerous areas where evidence of glacial formation and melting can be found. You can find glacial scratches on rocks in Central Park, and on the Ice Age trail in Wisconsin, you can find moraines (ridges) and kettles (depressions) that were formed by the advancement and receding of the glaciers.

Here in Arizona, evidence of significant geological activity and erosion is readily apparent. You can see and touch the results of volcanic activity in the Springerville Volcanic Field, at Sunset Crater, at the Boot Heel Volcanic Field and at the caldera in Arivaca. You can see where the Colorado Plateau rose above the rest of the state when you stand below the Mogollon Rim. You can find evidence of the stretching of the earth's crust while driving through the Basin and Range complex in southern Arizona. Evidence of erosion can be seen in Texas Canyon and at Chiricahua National Monument. Mother Nature at its grandest is obvious in the land of big sky and majestic vistas.

The work of Mother Nature is also available for viewing in the magnificent canyons that exist in Arizona. Some of the canyons were formed in the mountains ranges, some are river-formed canyons, and Arizona also is home to some magnificent slot canyons produced by many years of erosion. We have seen some truly beautiful and stunning canyons and we will share some of them with you. Walnut Canyon, Cave Creek Canyon, Texas Canyon, Garden Canyon and Canyon de Chelly will not be included in this chapter as they have been included in other chapters.

Ramsey Canyon is part of the Nature Conservancy Project whose goal is to preserve and protect areas to be enjoyed by all. It is located south of Sierra Vista and is listed by Trip Advisor as the number one attraction in the Sierra Vista area. The cliff walls of the canyon provide a cool environment for birds, mammals and adventurers. The dirt path meanders up the canyon and the surrounding beauty makes the climb in elevation easy. Being surrounded by trees and listening to the small stream working its way down the canyon, give this canyon an air of peace and serenity. Along the path, remnants of the past can be seen: a lonely chimney, an abandoned cabin and an abandoned house. On our visit, we were told by other visitors that they had seen some deer by the abandoned house. When we arrived, the deer seemed pleased to have their pictures taken and were not alarmed by our presence. This canyon is frequented by bird watchers and is renowned for its natural beauty. We found this canyon to be a place where we could be one with nature and where we could hear the silence of the beauty. For the tired adventurers, at the bottom of the trail, there were two rocking chairs by the edge of the stream. This is where we found Irma by the time we got down to the bottom. This is a recommended place to explore.

Peppersauce Canyon is an Arizona hidden gem that sits at the base of the Mount Lemmon back road, just south of Oracle. It is a shallow, tree-filled canyon that is surprising the first time you visit. The enormous Arizona sycamore and walnut trees cannot be described in words. They provide shade to the entire canyon and provide a dramatic setting for camping, picnicking or hiking. We went to Peppersauce Canyon with Michael Flynn in pursuit of fossils. We did not find any fossils that day, but we couldn't stop looking at the big, big trees. We took lots of pictures that day.

Another hidden gem is **Coal Mine Canyon** on the Navajo Indian Reservation at the edge of the Painted Desert. It is located in a remote area near Tuba City. This multi-colored canyon is not listed on places of things to see, does not have signage and is difficult to find. The lack of visitors, however, does not decrease its natural beauty. The grey, white, pink, burgundy, and gold colors make the spires, unique rock formations and cliffs appear surreal. It is a magical place that offers visitors a place to dream, enjoy and be transformed by the sheer wonder of it all. There is a picnic table near the canyon's edge for those who wish to linger.

Brown Canyon is a beautiful sycamore canyon that is part of the Buenos Aires National Wildlife Refuge. It is located off Route 286 in the foothills of the Baboquivari Mountains. The narrow, dirt trail winds its way up the canyon, over foothills and through a stream. The trees provide shade in spots and add to the natural beauty with magnificent mountain views and the presence of Baboquivari watching over those who enter this peaceful place. The two-mile climb to the top ends at a natural rock arch. Climbing through the canyon, remnants indicate that settlers lived here. What a great place to live. The National Wildlife Refuge offers tours, nature walks and educational sessions at the lodge in the canyon.

Sabino Canyon is a beautiful, fun and exciting place to spend a day. Hiking, riding the tram, walking down the road or up the road, soaking your feet in the stream, sitting and admiring the rocks, chasing roadrunners to get a picture and just plain resting are activities one can participate in at this recreational site. This canyon is located in Tucson in the Santa Catalina Mountains and offers views of the Sonoran Desert landscape and majestic mountains cliffs. Riding or walking up the paved road, watch for the bridges; they were built by the CCC for the enjoyment of the public. Another feature to watch for are the small pools of water where you can soak your feet. The pools are easily located by following the sounds of children frolicking. On designated Thursdays, from October through April, volunteer naturalists will teach visitors how to pan for garnets. Enjoy, relax and have fun.

Want a shortcut from Green Valley to Route 83? Try traveling the **Box Canyon Scenic Drive**. This dirt road through the Santa Rita Mountains, accessed from Whitehouse Road, was built in the 1930s by the CCC as a shortcut for settlers and farmers. Evidence of the CCC is still present in the masonry retaining walls and the concrete culverts. The dirt road winds up and down and over the mountains and offers stunning views of the Santa Cruz Valley and the Santa Rita Mountains. Grasslands, wildflowers, views of the canyon, old mines and wild horses make the ride a treat. A great experience for the adventurer.

Rand McNally has designated **Oak Creek Canyon Scenic Drive** one of the top five scenic drives in America. The fourteen-mile scenic drive from Flagstaff to Sedona is one of our favorite adventures. The tall oaks, the majestic evergreen trees and the stream with a backdrop of red rocks and cliffs make this a scenic drive that makes visitors slow down and look. There are many pull-offs along the way and, on many occasions, there are no parking spaces available due to the large number of visitors who have the same idea. The rock formations are definitely worthy of being photographed and the colored cliffs beg to be climbed by the adventurous. Driving along this route, we often stop at "Midgie Bridge" to admire the rock formations. Another place to explore along this scenic drive is Slide Rock State Park that includes an historic homestead. Stopping at the park also includes watching the children (and some brave adults) slide down the smooth and slippery rock in Oak Creek. This drive allows us the opportunity to relax, slow down, admire Mother Nature at its finest and to breathe in the clean, crisp Arizona air. This canyon is also renowned for Mother Nature's colorful display in the fall.

Reliving the days of railroad travel is possible in Arizona.

Head for Clarkdale and jump aboard the **Verde Canyon Railroad** to enjoy a four-hour, forty-mile, round-trip ride from Clarkdale to Perkinsville. On the ride through Verde Canyon, visitors have the option of riding first class or coach, remaining indoors or riding on the open car. Regardless of the option chosen, this passage through the canyon is a treat. Rolling over trestles and through a tunnel adds to the fun of the ride but the real treat is the breathtaking views of mountain cliffs, the riparian area, and the red, grey and pink rocks that erosion has exposed for all of us to enjoy. In between admiring the scenery and looking for cliff dwellings, watch for animals; we spotted burros on the return trip. The Verde Canyon Railroad was named an Arizona Treasure. Justifiably so.

Madera Canyon, in the Santa Rita Mountains, is a hot-spot for bird lovers and photographers. In 2016, a nesting pair of trogons was spotted and the area is home to fifteen different species of hummingbirds. The landscape in the canyon ranges from desert landscape to aspen and pine forest. There are several picnic areas, hiking trails, benches to sit and rest, and a bird feeding area where you can sit and watch the birds. The stream flows most of the year and its sound sometimes echoes against the rocks; in the summer, the swimming hole is frequented by locals and the butterflies flock to the mud area. Wildlife is abundant in this canyon: we have seen turkeys, deer and some of our friends have seen bear and coatimundis. For flower lovers, this is a great place to explore. On the Proctor Trail, summer flowers are abundant and mimosas can be seen along the roads. In the spring, there are outdoor concerts at the gazebo. We often wonder if the wildlife enjoy the music as much as we do. For the true adventurers, a climb up Elephant Head might be a great experience; check out the little elephants at the top that were left by fellow climbers.

Driving from Globe to Show Low, you will eventually arrive at the **Salt River Canyon** scenic drive. With multiple turns, twists, and switchbacks the trip through the canyon takes some time: time to think how this beautiful canyon could have been formed. Every turn reveals a view more beautiful than the last one. The cliffs, the color, the glimpses of the river, the contrast with the blue sky provide an environment that is almost "too beautiful to be true." Pull-offs along the road offer different and unique views of this gorgeous canyon. Eventually, everyone arrives at the bottom. Whew! Getting out of the car, you begin to realize the depth of the canyon and its true beauty. A walking bridge provides an opportunity to get a close look at the beautiful Salt River, flowing rapidly to its destination. From the bottom, one can truly appreciate the power of water and erosion. We have traveled through this beautiful canyon several times and every time is a treat. It always seems more beautiful than we remember. For those who venture to this area, slow down, breathe and marvel at the wonder of it all. At the bottom of the canyon lies the border of the White Mountain Apache Indian Reservation and the San Carlos Apache Reservation - what a beautiful place for them to join.

Upper Antelope Canyon (also known as *The Crack*) is on the Navajo Indian Reservation near Page. It has been designated a Tribal Park and access is limited to guided tours. The slot canyon was formed by the erosion of the Navajo sandstone by monsoon rains and flash floods. As rains permeate the top of the sandstone, the cracks widen which allow direct sunlight to radiate down from the openings in the top of the canyon. The flash floods run through the bottom of the canyon and shape the unique rock formations. This tourist attraction is well-known to photographers and tourists alike.

Stopping at visitor centers, we often noticed pictures of people standing in a beautiful slot canyon. Again, the picture of the same canyon would appear in a museum. One day, our Arizona Highways magazine arrived and there it was! A picture of Upper Antelope Canyon. The decision was made: we had to go! The tour was scheduled, the cooler was packed, Gypsy was given her road directions and off we went. On the specified date and time, we arrived at the tour office for "our" tour and were surprised to see about one hundred other people there. We soon learned that there would be other tourists in the canyon at the same time as us. The ride to the entrance was exciting and cold - in the back of an open-air truck, driving through a river bed. Upon arrival, it was obvious why this canyon is known worldwide. The columns of beautiful pink sandstone greet you as you enter the largest part of the canyon. Progressing through the canyon, some areas get smaller and then the color starts changing. It is almost magic how the sandstone changes from pink to red then burgundy as the rays of the sun start radiating down into the eroded columns of sand. This was an adventure we will never forget and the beauty of the canyon cannot be described. The picture that hangs in our living room is an inadequate portrayal of the beauty we saw that day.

The grandest of Arizona's canyons is the **Grand Canyon**; it is truly special and remarkable in its own right. The canyon is two hundred and seventy-seven river miles long, up to eighteen miles wide and one mile deep. It is one of the Seven Wonders of the World and the only one located within the United States. In 1979, it was named a UNESCO World Heritage Site. We love exploring this area and have visited frequently.

The South Rim offers visitors the opportunity to view the canyon from many different perspectives. Heading west along the rim, a tram provides a ride as far as Hermit's Rest with multiple stops along the way for resting, admiring and picture taking. Heading east on the rim, the drive has several pull-offs that provide different views of the canyon and river. Features to explore along the South Rim include the Tusayan Ruins, the visitor center, Kolb Studio, the Bright Angel Trail, the historic El Tovar hotel and the Bright Angel Lodge. The Desert View

Tower, at the eastern edge of the canyon, was designed by Mary Jane Colter and is worthy of exploration. While visiting this structure, note the famous murals. The Hopi House is another structure designed by Colter and a great place to browse around looking for souvenirs. In the Bright Angel Lodge, note the fireplace: it is made from rocks gathered in the Grand Canyon and they are positioned in the same order as the canyon walls. When walking along and admiring this surreal canyon, it is easy to keep your eyes on the beauty. Once in a while, look up to the sky - you may be one of the lucky ones who sees a condor flying over. We have yet to see one.

The North Rim of the Grand Canyon offers visitors another perspective of the canyon in a calmer, more peaceful environment. The number of visitors is significantly less than the South Rim. At the South Rim, visitors are three-quarters of a mile from the river; on the North Rim, visitors are ten miles from the river so the views are dramatically different. Prior to arriving at the lodge, three viewpoints show the canyon at its best: Point Imperial, Cape Royal and Roosevelt Point. It is worth the time and effort to visit all three viewpoints. The rewards include beautiful flowers, unbelievable scenery and the Angels Arch. The Grand Canyon Lodge provides an exquisite place for guests to relax, eat and socialize. Western cabins are available for those who wish to stay overnight. For us, the North Rim was two days of peace, silence, beauty and adventure.

Going to the bottom of the Grand Canyon had been on our list of things to do for some time, so we booked a jeep tour to the bottom. At the beginning, the dirt road was well maintained but it became narrower and bumpier as we descended. The spectacular scenery changed from moment to moment and we could see long distances into some of the side canyons. It was exciting to be standing on a beach at the bottom of the canyon. Standing there, the depth of this huge canyon was apparent. Besides the incredible journey up and down the road, the majestic scenery and our knowledgeable guide, we will never forget the bighorn sheep, the pronghorn antelope, the Jerusalem burros and the whitewater rafters we waved to. What a great trip.

On another occasion, we returned to the bottom of the canyon. We drove Gypsy down a gravel road all the way to the bottom to see the ghost town of Pearce Ferry. This is reportedly where John Wesley Powell exited the Colorado River on his famous expedition. Gypsy seemed to enjoy the adventure.

The desire to see the Grand Canyon from another perspective prompted us to take a helicopter tour from the South Rim. We entered the cute, little, red helicopter, buckled up, put our headsets on and off we went. Heading to the canyon, the song "Chariots of Fire" was playing loudly. All of a sudden, the music stops, the helicopter drops about ten feet and the pilot cheerfully announces "Welcome to the Grand Canyon." Someone should tell this tour company that it is not nice to make their guests cry. It was an experience that gave us goose bumps and still does today when we recall the trip. From the air, miles of canyon walls and the river are visible. Our guide pointed out the beautiful rock formations and the buffalo herd that lives on the North Rim. What a great way to see the canyon. An adventure to be remembered forever.

Spending the day exploring a canyon is always a great way to enjoy the pleasures and beauty that Arizona offers. We will continue to explore these treasures.

MINING

The powerful forces of nature that created the dramatic canyons of Arizona, formed the basin and range complex, pushed up the Colorado Plateau and formed the Rocky Mountains also helped create an environment rich in minerals, metals and gemstones. As a result, mining has occurred in this state for thousands of years. From archaeological research, it is apparent that early native tribes mined both copper and turquoise for jewelry or trade. The Spaniards, arriving in the late 1500s, actively pursued the mining of silver in the southern part of the state. Miners flocked to Arizona in pursuit of gold, silver, copper and other precious minerals. The culture of Arizona was shaped, in part, by the miners and mine workers who arrived from various countries.

Mining continues to be a big industry in this state. According to the State Mining Office, in 2007 there were four hundred active mines in Arizona. Sixty-five percent of the copper mined in the United States comes from this state. The types of mines differ by location: the copper mines are primarily in the southern portion of the state and the uranium mines are in the northern portion.

Uranium mining was a big endeavor in the 1930s and 1940s. Today, there is reportedly one active uranium mine operating in Northern Arizona and there have been numerous newspaper articles talking about the possibility of re-opening the uranium mines near the Grand Canyon. In the book *Yellow Dirt* by Judy Pasternak, she describes the extent of the uranium mining and its aftermath in this state.

During our exploring and adventuring, it became obvious to us that mining operations were numerous. The majority of the ghost towns we visited are abandoned mining towns. Huge open-pit mines are visible in Bisbee, Green Valley, Morenci, Globe, Superior, and Winkelman, and old mine shafts are spotted in many of the areas we visited.

We wondered: four hundred active mines, but how many abandoned mines are there in this state We could not believe the estimate - the State Mining Inspectors office estimates there are about one hundred thousand abandoned mines in Arizona. Some are located in areas administered by the Bureau of Land Management and some are on private property. We have seen abandoned mines with horizontal shafts and some vertical shafts. Some of the mines we explored were fenced with warning signs and some were left as they were years ago.

Arizona is known for its gold, silver and copper production. It is also known worldwide for its specimens of Azurite and Malachite that are on exhibit in many museums throughout the world. How many minerals, metals and gemstones are mined in this state? Here are some: lead, zinc, manganese, tungsten, mercury, limestone, dolostone, pumice, diatomite, kyanite, peridot, potash, quartz, talc, marble, granite, basalt, cinders, agate, jade, onyx, calcite, chalcedony, uranium, magnesium, mica, lime, bentonite, zeolites, gypsum, turquoise, rhenium, tin, tourmaline, zircon, salt and several others. Impressive, isn't it?

When we think of mining, we think of big equipment, noise and tailing piles. In the northern part of Arizona, there is a silent army that mines some beautiful, tiny (less than a carat), brilliantly colored garnets. The ants excavate the gems in the process of digging their burrows and bring them to the surface. After a rain, they can be harvested on the shanks of the anthills. It is said that in the sunshine, one can see a pyramid of bright red "anthill garnets." We look for them every time we are in the area, but so far no luck.

North of Yuma, the Red Cloud Mine is well-known for its production of wulfenite. This orange-yellow mineral is found in only a few places on earth. Beautiful specimens can be seen at the Arizona Desert Museum, the Bisbee Mining and Historical Museum and the University of Arizona Mineral Museum.

Another gemstone mined in this state is amethyst. Want to go mine your own? The Four Peaks Amethyst mine, north of Phoenix, is a mining operation that requires a helicopter to bring supplies in and out. The workers access the mine via a nine-mile round-trip hike and live at the mine for one to two weeks at a time. Reservations can be made for a tour of this mine. The helicopter brings you to the mine, the miners (and the owner) give a guided tour of the mine and assist in the mining of your own personal amethyst. That would definitely be something to brag about.

Seeing several mines and reading about mines started to increase our interest in the process. Some mornings, we would put on our "mining" hats, fill up the cooler, pack the gloves and geology pick, give Gypsy her instructions and off we would go into the wilderness. We even bought the book *Roadside Geology of Arizona* by Halka Chronic to see if that would help in the pursuit of our fortune. We have not amassed a fortune but we have accumulated some beautiful stones that we put into our "Rock Garden."

On our first adventure, we went in search of selenite crystals in the hills near St. David. We had read about a place where you could dig for crystals so off we went with our geology pick, a small spade, gloves (because they are sharp) and an empty egg carton. The egg carton was needed to store the delicate crystals. Arriving at the place, the hills were visible but we saw no visible road to the bottom of the hills. We improvised and arrived at the parking area. Using the spade, I was having no success, but Midge was finding the crystals everywhere. The beautiful brownish crystals were laying on the surface, so digging was not required. The selection process went quickly and, soon, we headed home with an egg carton full of gorgeous specimens. We could not have been prouder! Success on our first attempt!

We have had many memorable "mining" experiences since our first success. One of the easiest involved harvesting jasper near Tuba City. On both sides of the road, thousands of pieces of jasper can be found by the explorer. Looking for the red, grey, and red/black stones requires no experience - if the rock feels waxy when touched, it is jasper. Jasper is a protection stone and is well-worth finding.

Other treasures we have found and collected include: a rock with a gold flake we found in Pearce, a chrysocolla we found in Green Valley, a piece of perlite and an Apache tear we harvested in Superior, a beautiful sample of hematite we found in the Cerro Colorado mine tailings, some Mexican fire agates from Arivaca, obsidian from the tailings at the Helvetia mine, and a piece of opal from Arivaca.

Being part-time "miners" gave us the opportunity to learn that we were not the only ones searching for fortunes in the Arizona wilderness. There are groups that gather occasionally to pan for gold in the Santa Rita Mountains and there are websites devoted to those who seek gold in Greaterville. Gold seekers with metal detectors reportedly still find gold nuggets in Southern Arizona. At one ghost town, south of Yarnell, we watched a man sluicing for gold in the stream. Some adventurers spend their vacations and weekends pursuing the golden rocks. Going up to Mount Lemmon, there is a pull-off that faces the San Pedro Valley. A sign at this stop states "There is gold in them thar hills." We bet there is!

Every so often, we come upon a sign "Gold Claim for sale" or we find a mine for sale online. This always raises the question: Rather than spending time in the wilderness with our book, geology pick and gloves, would we get richer quicker if we bought a mine? Still thinking about that. For the adventurers and explorers who believe in hard work to amass a small fortune, have fun "mining."

LAKES

Arriving in Arizona, it was immediately obvious that lakes are not as abundant in this state as they are in New England. However, in the process of exploring our newly adopted state, we found some beautiful lakes and reservoirs. We stopped at each lake, took photos and absorbed the beauty of blue water, blue skies and the spectacular views that are so common in this state.

Doing some research, we were surprised when we found a list of Arizona lakes and reservoirs. The numbers are as follows: one hundred and six lakes and reservoirs, eighteen urban lakes, four Tucson urban lakes and one Payson urban lake. Some of the lakes listed are intermittent lakes that do not necessarily contain water throughout the year. Some of the lakes contain game fish and are managed by the Department of Game and Fish.

In our travels, we have encountered twenty-five lakes and we have enjoyed every one of them. At times, we linger, watch people fishing and watch the egrets stalking the fishermen in the hopes of getting a treat. We will share some of these beautiful spots with you.

Near the downtown area of Payson, visitors will find a thirteen-acre lake which is part of a water reclamation project. **Green Valley Lake** provides the town with a recreation area containing green space, walking paths, shade and a quiet, peaceful space to rejuvenate the human spirit. Families, children, pets, egrets and retirees were taking advantage of the space dedicated to the enjoyment of the great outdoors. A must-see attraction for visitors.

Dankworth Pond State Park in Safford AZ is located on Route 191. The state park contains a ten-acre pond that currently contains game fish and provides trails for those who wish to walk around the pond. It is located in a beautiful natural setting. The pond is a man-made structure that was used for commercial catfish farming. An interesting feature at this state park is the thermal spring. Near the edge of the pond, there is an area where Betty sat and soaked her feet in the clear, warm waters bubbling from the ground. What a great place to relax.

North of Phoenix, explorers and adventurers will find a thirty-seven-hundred-acre reservoir located within the boundaries of Peoria. **Lake Pleasant** is a reservoir that was originally formed by the creation of an earthen dam along the Agua Fria River. Today, Central Arizona Project water is the primary source of water for this reservoir. This is an exciting lake to visit: fishermen hoping to get lucky, swimmers, boaters, campers and picnickers. Standing there, you hear the noise of people having fun, smell the scent of food cooking and a smile comes to our faces watching the children frolicking. This is an area of fun in a strikingly beautiful setting. If you visit this lake, watch for the wild burros that wander around the area. You might be lucky enough to spot one. We were!

South of Flagstaff, in the Coconino National Forest, lies **Marshall Lake**. It is a small marshy body of water that is usually full of coots and several other types of waterfowl. The scene is described as amusing and entertaining with all of the waterfowl bathing, splashing and quacking. Most years it is also stocked with trout and offers fisherman a quiet, peaceful environment for relaxation. The lake is on a dirt road, not far from the Lowell Observatory. When we arrived at the site, no coots or waterfowl were present. As a matter of fact, there was no water in the lake. We admired the incredible scenery: the mountains, the tall trees, the blue sky and the green grass. Irma, Dotty and Midge got their picture taken near the Marshall Lake sign with the green grass in the background.

Eighteen miles south of Tucson, **Sahuarita Lake** offers the public an area to relax, exercise and enjoy the great outdoors. The ten acre man-made lake is complete with green areas, several picnic areas, restrooms, a one-mile walking path, benches and the opportunity to try your luck at catching a fish. It is an enjoyable area to wander through or sit and meditate. Every time we spend time at the lake, we are always accompanied by several others who have the same idea.

Goldwater Lake is located four miles south of Prescott. The fifteen-acre lake is a reservoir formed by a dam on Bannon Creek. It is surrounded by pine forests and the water is stunningly blue due to the surrounding scenery. Hiking trails, picnicking, canoeing and camping are available at the beautiful recreational site. Goldwater Lake has the distinction of being at the beginning of a spectacular scenic drive. The dirt road from the lake arrives at Crown King after thirty-seven miles of ghost towns, incredible scenery and mining history. The road follows an old pony express and stagecoach road. Adventurers should read about this scenic drive before departing. We have not explored this area.

Becker Lake is a one hundred and seven-acre lake located two miles north of Springerville. It was built in 1880 and is one of the oldest reservoirs in the White Mountains. The average depth of ten feet provides a good environment for trout. Rainbow trout are stocked twice yearly and the lake also has brown trout who migrate from the Little Colorado River. The body of water is surrounded by the Becker Wildlife Area and is maintained by the Arizona Game and Fish Department. There is a boat ramp, restrooms, a dirt parking lot and hiking trails. The surrounding natural beauty adds an air of elegance to this small body of water.

Four miles north of Prescott, a bright blue body of water is located in the Granite Dells. **Watson Lake** is a seventy-acre reservoir that was created in the 1900s by the dam on Granite

Creek. The water was previously used for irrigation. Today, it is owned by the city of Prescott and used as a recreational site. The surreal beauty of this lake is created by the color of the water surrounded by huge granite boulders. Fishing, boating, hiking, camping, rock climbing and picnicking are available at this site. Truly a beauty to behold.

Mormon Lake is the largest natural lake in the state of Arizona. It is located in the Coconino National Forest, south of Flagstaff. The six-hundred-acre lake varies in size depending on the water level and in dry seasons it contains no water. When full, the deepest point of the lake can be ten feet deep. The lake is located in the largest continuous ponderosa pine forest in the United States. From the edge of the lake, the San Francisco Peaks can be seen in all of their beauty.

The lake was named in honor of the Mormon settlers who farmed the surrounding area. The farms no longer exist, but a settlement has grown up around the lake. Mormon Lake Village grew into a small settlement during the wetter years and Mormon Lake Lodge seasonally offers visitors food and lodging. Irma, Dotty, Midge, Gypsy and I were looking forward to seeing the largest natural lake in Arizona and seeing the well-known Mormon Lake Lodge. Our intentions had been to stay at the Lodge to be near the lake but we were unable to make a reservation. What a surprise when we arrived at Mormon Lake: it was empty. During our visit in May 2016, we took pictures of the San Francisco Peaks, the pine forest and the dry lake.

San Carlos Lake was created by the building of the Coolidge Dam as part of the San Carlos Irrigation Project. The lake is located on the San Carlos Indian Reservation and all activities are subject to tribal rules and regulation. The water level in this lake varies greatly by precipitation levels and irrigation needs. During years of average precipitation, San Carlos lake is one of the largest lakes in the state of Arizona and occasionally, the water has flowed over the top of the dam. During years of low precipitation and high irrigation needs, huge numbers of fish have died due to the low water levels.

San Carlos lake is surrounded by one hundred and fifty-eight miles of shoreline in a high desert environment. The blue water is an oasis that provides a wide variety of recreational activities to the surrounding area.

Visiting the Coolidge Dam was a priority on our list of things to see. At the end of a dirt road, a parking lot greets visitors who wish to explore this imposing structure. Visitors are allowed to walk on top of the multiple-dome dam and the lake can be seen from the viewing areas. On the front of the dam, large concrete eagles adorn the wall. We had to lean over the wall to see the eagles, so all of our pictures of the beautiful birds are profile shots. Beautiful architecture in a remote setting.

The drive to **Parker Canyon Lake** from Sonoita on route 83 is well worth the investment of time and effort. The backcountry drive takes you through rolling hills, areas of golden grass, old ranches and high desert terrain. On the way to the lake, visitors can stop to explore the Canelo Cowboy Church which is located in an historic one-room schoolhouse in the town of Canelo.

The one-hundred-and-twenty-acre lake is located amongst rolling hills and golden grass can be seen on the shoreline. Recreational activities at this site include fishing, camping, hiking, picnicking and paddle boats are available to rent. There is a Mercantile and Marina store on the premises. This is a peaceful, quiet environment.

In January 2013, we were driving south on Silverbell road in Tucson when someone in the car yelled, "Water!" This is how we found **Christopher Columbus Park**. This is an oasis in the desert. The man-made desert lake is surrounded by shade trees, palm trees, a walking path and everywhere you look you see egrets, herons, ducks, coots and several other species of birds.

Besides the large lake, the park also contains a playground, a smaller pond for model boat racing, picnic areas, a model airplane area and a duck pond. In this park, the egrets and herons keep a close watch on the fishermen hoping to get a free lunch. This urban park provides a respite and a welcome relief for all those who come and enjoy.

South of Safford lies a recreational gem - **Roper Lake State Park**. This park contains a thirty-acre lake on land purchased by the State for the purpose of creating a reservoir. This beautiful body of water is surrounded by desert landscaping and offers incredible views of Mount Graham. Recreational activities include: camping, fishing, hiking, swimming, picnicking, and boating.

There is one feature in this park that caught our attention. There is a stone-lined mineral spring that looks like an outdoor hot tub. The water temperature is ninety-seven degrees Fahrenheit and we can attest to the fact that it is the way to relax on a sunny and windy winter day in Arizona.

From the parking lot at the picnic area, we watched a large flock of red-winged blackbirds fly from one area to another. We tried for some time to get a picture of them. No success in the photography department. Maybe next time. This is a place we will return to enjoy.

Described as the "place to be" by hikers, birders and anglers, **Pena Blanca Lake** is eighteen miles northwest of Nogales. The forty-five-acre reservoir was created in 1957 by the Arizona Department of Game and Fish. Pajarito Wash and annual precipitation are the primary sources of water. The lake lies in a remote area of Southern Arizona, surrounded by rolling hills and desert vegetation. Standing by the edge of the lake, it is easy to believe that you are alone in this beautiful setting. A boat ramp, a fishing dock, restrooms and picnic areas are available.

Lake Mary is the name that describes twin reservoirs in the Coconino National Forest, south of Flagstaff.

Upper Lake Mary is the largest of Flagstaff's twin lakes and was created by the building of an earthen dam on Walnut Creek. It is a long, narrow reservoir in a heavily forested area. The scenery surrounding the lake includes large forests, green meadows and fields of flowers. Elk and deer frequent this area.

The surface area of the lake can vary greatly depending on precipitation levels. At times, the lake can be five miles long and two thousand feet wide. At other times, the lake can be significantly smaller.

The Upper Lake is considered to be a boaters' paradise. All shapes and sizes of boats, rafts, canoes, and other floating devices are welcome on this lake. We watched some young adults using paddle boards. Seems to be an enjoyable water sport. The length of the lake is conducive to water skiing as well. Other recreational activities include camping, fishing and picnicking. This area would be pleasurable for artists and photographers. The blue sky, the white clouds, the dark green forests, the light green meadows and the yellow flowers create a natural collage that is visually pleasing and relaxing.

Lower Lake Mary is the second of the twin reservoirs and lies downstream from the upper lake. During wet seasons, the lake can be three miles long; during dry periods, it can be completely dry. Elk and deer frequent it.. During our visit in May 2016, we took pictures of the small stream surrounded by miles of green grass. We also took a picture of the sign warning boaters of the water hazards. When you look at the small stream, it is hard to envision boats on the lake. The sign made us chuckle.

Patagonia Lake is located on Route 82 between Patagonia and Nogales. It is tucked between rolling hills and offers visitors the opportunity to rest or play in a beautiful environment. The two hundred and sixty-five-acre, man-made lake was created by the damming of Sonoita Creek; the lake extends for over two miles which attracts water skiers and boaters. At the marina, canoes and rowboats are available for rent. For the less adventurous, pontoon boat tours are available: they offer birding tours or interpretative tours upon request. The Lakeside Market sells supplies, fishing licenses, bait and other necessities to make your day fun and exciting.

Recreational activities include swimming, boat rentals, boating, camping, hiking, birding, picnicking and fishing. One feature of interest in this state park is the arch bridge. The bridge allows boats to pass underneath and provides a sense of excitement and adventure to all those who walk across.

John F. Kennedy Park on Mission Road in Tucson offers the public a large variety of recreational opportunities. The park complex includes: ramadas, restrooms, grills, sports fields, tennis courts, basketball courts, playgrounds, swimming pool and an urban fishing lake.

At the urban fishing lake, several picnic tables are available for public use and the size of the lake entices many to walk around and enjoy the view of the Catalina Mountains. Some shade trees are available and are enjoyed by the fishermen hoping to catch a big fish. Ducks and coots are often seen bathing and swimming. On the east side of the lake, cattails grow in abundance.

The last time we spent time near this body of water, a man was offering horseback rides around the lake. Some families with children were enjoying this activity. This is a quiet place to walk, think and just enjoy staring at water in a desert environment.

Luna Lake is located in the Apache-Sitgreaves National Forest, three miles east of Alpine. This is one of the most scenic places in Arizona. Luna Lake is a natural body of water that covers approximately seventy-five acres. The upper San Francisco River supports the water level. The body of water sits in the middle of a green, lush valley surrounded by thick forests. Recreational options include boating (small crafts only), fishing, camping, hiking and picnicking. This is a place that imprints itself in the memory. Mention the lake located in Alpine and we immediately remember the huge valley, green fields, blue sky, ranches, the deep blue water, and the reeds growing on the edge of the water, We will also remember the three year old boy running into the water with his new sneakers on. Pleasant memories.

Lake Mead in northern Arizona is the largest man-made reservoir in the United States and can contain up to nine trillion gallons of water. The reservoir was created by the construction of the Hoover Dam and the damming of the Colorado River. Lake Mead is one hundred and ten miles in length, extending from the Hoover Dam to the western edge of the Grand Canyon. Standing on the skywalk at Grand Canyon West, visitors can see the beginning of Lake Mead. With five hundred and fifty miles of shoreline and long expanses of water, the lake is popular with boaters, fishermen, photographers, swimmers, and those who wish to spend their vacation on a houseboat. There are several viewpoints in the Lake Mead Recreational area where visitors can stop and view the lake. We have always loved to see the water, but a sense of disappointment always prevails. Only small portions of this immense reservoir can be seen from any viewpoint. When we fly to Las Vegas, we always look forward to seeing the grandeur of Lake Mead from the plane. It is only then that you can truly understand the immensity of this beautiful reservoir with its blue water and bright red cliffs.

Imperial Reservoir lies eighteen miles Northeast of Yuma and was created by the building of the Imperial Dam, a diversion dam on the Colorado River. The reservoir is within the boundaries of the Imperial National Wildlife Refuge and can be seen from a viewpoint within the refuge. To access the viewpoint, visitors travel a dirt road through a colorful array of sand hills. The ride is well worth the effort. The scenery is spectacular in a very remote area of Arizona.

Lyman Lake, located in St. Johns, is a fourteen-hundred-acre lake created by an irrigation dam on the Little Colorado River. It lies within the boundaries of the Lyman Lake State Park. It is a warm-water lake that is elongated and, therefore, is frequented by water skiers. The state park contains a beach, a boat ramp, several picnic tables with ramadas, camping facilities, and hiking trails. Boating, hiking and fishing are available recreational activities. Cabins are also available for rent.

For those arriving at the site, it can be a little confusing. There is no visitor center: the Lyman Lake Market serves as the visitor center and a store for supplies, bait, and food. The striking feature of this lake is the surrounding scenery. The red sandstone cliffs, the desert areas, the rolling hills, the red sand beaches and the deep-blue water make this place a photo opportunity. What a great place to spend some time with family and friends. A true gem in a desert setting.

Lake Havasu is a nineteen-thousand-acre reservoir created by the building of the Parker Dam. The beauty of the desert environment, the dramatic rock formations and the dark blue water draws thousands of tourists to this location. Boaters, fishermen, bathers, sun lovers, paddle boarders, water skiers and photographers can come here to play, relax, exercise and dream.

Lake Havasu city, on the eastern edge of the Colorado River, is well prepared to provide all of the amenities to the incoming tourists. Within the city limits, there are two points of interest that we found enjoyable. The London Bridge is not the Tower Bridge of London, but this bridge did indeed stand over the river in that beautiful city. Jacqui, our friend from Scotland, verified its authenticity. It is definitely worth the walk to view this historical bridge.

Along the river, the London Bridge Beach offers visitors the opportunity to walk along the lake and appreciate the true beauty of Mother Nature. The park offers benches, a swimming beach and paved, flat walkways for easy walking. Along the paths, replicas of lighthouses can be found and they enhance the experience.

Throughout the year, Lake Havasu City hosts a variety of events such as a Hot Air Balloon festival and boat races. Fun place to visit in a beautiful natural environment.

Arivaca Lake is located south of the town of Arivaca and can be accessed from Ruby road. The drive to the lake is appealing to adventurers and explorers; the lake is accessed by a dirt road that winds and turns its way down to the body of water. On the way, interesting rock formations are visible. For rock lovers, there are Mexican fire agates and opals that can found in the hills along this dirt road.

Arriving at the lake, a toilet and a boat ramp are the only amenities to be seen. This is a remote and primitive area surrounded by grasslands, mountains and cattle ranches. The lake is a ninety-acre impoundment lake built by the Arizona Game and Fish Department. The lake is stocked with game fish. Water levels vary by season depending on the level of precipitation.

Recreational activities include bird watching, wildlife viewing, fishing, rock climbing, primitive camping, hiking and boating (small boats only). The remoteness of this area is very appealing. It is a great spot to escape the hustle and bustle of everyday life.

Agua Caliente Park in Northeast Tucson is one of our favorite places to visit. The park was well-known for its hot springs. It was formerly a ranch and health resort; today it is a public park for the enjoyment of everyone. Within the one-hundred-acre park, visitors will find a beautiful little pond surrounded by green grass, reeds and several of the biggest palm trees found in the Tucson area. The water level, today, relies heavily upon precipitation to maintain its water levels and can vary by season. From the shoreline, the antics of the ducks and the movement of the turtles can be easily observed.

Recreational options include picnicking, hiking, birding, wildlife viewing, sitting, meditating and escaping from other responsibilities. On one occasion, we observed a professional photographer taking family photos near the pond. What a great background that includes an excellent view of the Santa Catalina mountains. On the grounds, there is a museum and the original ranch house is available for viewing. We have returned several times to this gem in the desert and we will continue to rejuvenate our spirits amongst the huge palm trees.

The building of the Roosevelt Dam created a twenty-two mile long and two mile wide reservoir as part of the Salt River Project. The water for the reservoir is supplied by the Salt River and the Tonto creek. **Roosevelt Lake** lies within the boundaries of the Tonto National Forest and has one hundred and twenty-eight miles of shoreline. It is situated at the beginning of the Apache Trail: a scenic dirt road that connects Roosevelt Lake and Apache Junction.

This is one of our favorite lakes for numerous reasons. There are many viewpoints and pull-offs where you can spend time admiring the dark blue water that contrasts with the green background and the blue sky. Riding along on Route 188, you can see the lake for mile after mile and every turn of the road shows a different perspective. Coming down the hill from the town of Roosevelt, the lake appears before you and the scene takes your breath away.

At this lake, the recreational opportunities are limitless. There is one beach that allows camping on the edge of the water. What a great place to wake up in the morning. This is a body of water we have seen several times and each time is exciting and breathtaking.

Four miles downstream from Roosevelt Lake lies **Apache Lake**. It is the second largest reservoir of the Salt River Project and was created by the building of the Horse Mesa Dam. This reservoir has a full array of services for the traveler and visitor. There are motels, a restaurant (with good food), a campground and a store. Recreational options are numerous and wildlife viewing may occur. Apache Lake lies on the Apache Trail, in a beautiful setting, surrounded by the Superstition wilderness.

The third in the series of reservoirs along the Salt River is **Canyon Lake**. The construction of the Mormon Flat Dam created the reservoir. At nine hundred and fifty acres, it is the smallest of the reservoirs on the Apache Trail. The lake is stunning with its steep canyon walls towering over the clear, cool, dark blue waters. The Dolly Steamboat offers tours of the lake. Amenities include a marina, restaurant, boat rentals, boat rides, camping and fishing.

The fourth in the series of reservoirs is **Saguaro Lake**. We have not visited this lake.

Lake Powell, created by the building of the Glen Canyon Dam, is the second largest man-made reservoir in the United States. It is located near the city of Page. The reservoir is one-hundred-and-eighty-six-miles long with over ninety side canyons and two thousand miles of shoreline. With its deep blue water, spires, buttes, red rock cliffs and sandstone mesas, the area is impressive.

The reservoir is a boaters' paradise with several marinas and ramps. House boating is popular because of secluded coves, beaches, and numerous canyons to explore. A variety of boat tours are offered and some of the tours bring visitors to the Rainbow Bridge: a well-known natural arch. We took a boat tour through some of the canyons and the experience was memorable. Our female pilot could turn the boat on a dime in those beautiful, red and narrow canyons.

Sitting on our balcony at the Lake Powell Resort, it was

easy to fall in love with this beautiful area with its sunsets, sunrises, burgundy cliffs and dark blue water. This beautiful reservoir leaves us with the same feeling we had when we visited Lake Mead. We can only glimpse one small area at a time and it is impossible to comprehend the immensity of this beautiful body of water.

Some may ask why we included a chapter on lakes. Believe it or not, many Arizona residents will be surprised by the number and size of the lakes we have found. We will continue to stop at every body of clear, cool, blue water, continue to laugh at the frolicking waterfowl, marvel how quickly little turtles can move and continue to try picking some cattails without walking in the mud. To fellow adventurers and explorers, we wish you luck in finding your favorite water hole.

NATIVE AMERICAN SITES

*"We do not inherit the earth from our ancestors,
we borrow it from our children."*

- Native American Proverb

Traveling across the United States, we had the opportunity to experience the diversity of terrain and cultures in this great country of ours. Arriving in Arizona, we soon discovered the diversity that exists in this state. There are twenty-two Native American communities that currently reside within the borders of Arizona.

Discovering and experiencing the diversity of Native American cultures was included in our quest to explore Arizona. In this chapter, we will share with you some of the sites we have visited and some of the activities we have participated in. We will also share some rock art sites. There are three types of rock art: Petroglyphs are symbols etched into rock, pictographs are paintings on rock and intaglios (geoglyphs) are figures on the ground.

Monument Valley Tribal Park, Cochise Stronghold, Painted Rock Petroglyph Site and Park of the Canals were not included in this chapter. These sites were incorporated into other chapters. Museums exhibiting Native American Art have been included in the chapter on museums.

Welcome to another aspect of our journey as we explore the diversity of our adopted state.

Besh-Ba Gowah Archaeological Park is located in the town of Globe. This site contains the ruins of a two hundred room pueblo that was occupied by the Salado between 1250 to 1450 AD. There are exhibits that contain artifacts from the area, but the feature of the site is the trail that leads through the pueblo. There are several ruins to view and many information signs explaining the culture of the inhabitants. The Salado were farmers and hunters. The site was abandoned because of a period of climate change that affected their daily existence. This site has been placed on the National Register of Historic Places.

Garden Canyon is located on the Fort Huachuca Military Installation in Sierra Vista. A friend of ours had recommended a visit to this canyon to see the rock art. Being lovers of rock art, we arrived at the kiosk in the canyon picnic area. What a surprise! In this canyon, there are Hohokam and Apache pictographs. This was our first occasion to see Apache rock art.

The road into the canyon is a well-maintained dirt road and it rises quickly. About a mile from the picnic area, there is a sign for the pictographs. Walking up the path, there were hundreds of yellow Columbines along the stream. What a beautiful place to spend an afternoon. Up the stone steps and there they were! On the roof of the cave, there was a beautiful white dove painted on the rock by the Apaches. Harder to see, there were several red paintings left by the Hohokam (known as the Ancient Ones). What a joy to see the art left for us to enjoy.

V-Bar-V Heritage Site lies east of Sedona. It is accessed by a well-maintained dirt road. This site was originally the V-Bar-V Ranch and some of the remains of the ranch can be seen on the property.

This petroglyph site is the largest and best preserved in Verde Valley. It is estimated that there are over one thousand petroglyphs by the Sinagua Indians dated from 1150 thru 1400 AD. The US Forest Service purchased this site in 1994. It is currently a protected site that is open to the public. Interpretive tours are available.

The petroglyph site is a one-half mile walk from the visitor center, and a beautiful panel of petroglyphs greets you. The rock art is well spaced and it is easy to spot the deer, antelope, snakes, turtles, and a multitude of geometric figures. This site definitely made us smile. Well worth the trip.

Honanki Ruins are found at the base of the world-famous, red-colored cliffs in Sedona. Honanki is one of the largest cliff dwellings in Red Rock country and was inhabited from 1150 - 1350AD. The Sinagua, ancestors of the Hopi, were hunters and gatherers.

What a beautiful place to live; blue sky, green trees, red rock and salmon colored sand. That was our initial impression upon arriving at this site. The tour began and the feeling of awe continued. Several large portions of the cliff dwellings still remain and you can see them up close and personal. At one point on the tour, the guide pointed out fingerprints in the dried mud between the stones. Those are the fingerprints of the person who built this corner of the dwelling almost nine hundred years ago. We even got to put our fingers at the same place.

The amazing feature of this site is the quantity and quality of the pictographs (white and red) and petroglyphs. Some of the figures were new to us. The geometric designs can sometimes vary from one site to another, depending on the tribe. This was a site where we touched history.

Los Morteros in Marana is an archaeological site where bedrock mortars can be closely examined. Bedrock mortars are mortar holes etched into rocks in which grain or pods were ground into meal. There are many sites around the Tucson area and some may have been used as early as 500AD while some appear to be more recent. These holes tend to remain intact for many years.

At Los Morteros, a short walk from the parking area, adventurers can find a large rock with a minimum of eighteen mortar holes. Arriving at the site, it is easy to picture several women there at the same time. The function of this site could have been a combination of preparing food and social networking. Another piece of Arizona's ancient history that remains.

Walking down the path from the parking area, we spotted a huge snake. No one had to yell "stop." We temporarily suspended the exploring and waited. The snake did not move. We tossed a rock toward the snake and it still did not move. We proceeded a little closer, determined the snake was dead and continued on to find our treasure. Yes, we got a picture of the huge snake (as proof).

Window Rock is a small city that serves as the capital of the Navajo Nation. Government buildings and offices are located in Window Rock. For all adventurers and explorers, the major features are the Window Rock Navajo Tribal Park and the Council Chamber.

Just south of the Tribal Park, the Navajo Nation Council Chamber stands proudly. With its red sandstone façade and its rustic architectural style, it blends well into its surroundings. The building is stunning and it prompts the visitor to stop, pause, and look at it again. The building has been designated as an Historic Landmark; however, it continues to function as the Nation's council chamber.

Inside the Tribal Park, visitors can stroll on a paved walkway. Along the walk, the Navajo Nation Code Talkers WWII memorial is clearly visible. It is a large, beautifully designed tribute to the men who served. A sculpture of a code talker is at the center of the memorial.

The main feature at the Tribal Park, of course, is the-rock-with-hole-through-it. This is how the city got its name. The hole in the rock is the major landmark of this quaint little city and the trip to see it is well worth it.

Tucson hosted a **Festival of Indian Arts** in September 2011. Midge, Midge's grand-daughter (Elizabeth), Gypsy and

I headed for the festival in hopes of seeing some Indian dances. No disappointment on that day, only Joy! The featured dancers were the Laguna Corn Dancers and the Zuni Olla Maidens. The maidens dance with pottery on their heads. That was amazing to watch, but it made all three of us a little tense.

The festival also had a selection of vendors selling a variety of Native American Art. After viewing beautiful silver jewelry, hand-crafted musical instruments, the decision was made. We purchased two watercolor prints that depicted tribal life. The name on the prints was Michael Chiago. Being newcomers to the state of Arizona, we were unaware of his celebrity status. The prints hang proudly in our art room.

For art lovers who appreciate Chiago's art, a trip to Kitt Peak is warranted. Leaving the parking lot and walking toward the Visitors Center, there is a large piece of Chiago art that is readily visible. Great art atop a beautiful mountain.

San Carlos is located on the San Carlos Apache Indian Reservation and is the seat of government for the Apache Nation. Betty, Midge and I visited the beautiful little town of San Carlos in March 2016. Driving into town, we immediately noticed that all of the buildings were made from the same building materials. We soon learned that the town houses and government buildings were built with tufa rock, harvested on the reservation. The beautiful tan, stone structures give the town an air of elegance.

An impressive feature in the town is the San Carlos Indian Mission. The mission is built of tufa rock with a Spanish architectural style. The inside of the church is unlike other churches we have seen. The altar sits in the middle of the room, Apache symbols are displayed and a water trough is used at the baptismal font. It is a house of worship for the Native American. The Franciscan Friars help members of the community to connect to their tribal identity by blending elements of Apache ceremonies with the Catholic Mass. At the mission school, next door to the mission, the students are provided instruction in Apache culture and language.

In the book *Don't Let the Sun Step Over You* by Eva Tulene Watt, with assistance from Keith H. Basso, Eva talks about the Rice Boarding School. The boarding school is currently located in the town of San Carlos (formerly known as Rice). The town was renamed after the original town of San Carlos was flooded by the building of the Coolidge Dam.

We were hoping to see some remains of the boarding school. A lady who worked at the mission, pointed us in the right direction and there were two beautiful buildings that were once part of the historic school. Both of those buildings are also made of tufa rock. Fabulous buildings!

San Carlos is well-known for its abundance of Peridot, a green, volcanic glass stone that is found in lava fields. It is harvested in that area and we were hoping to go into a lava field and find one piece of the precious stone. That did not occur. Tours are available; however, one has to climb a huge hill to view them mining the stone. I doubt that they give free samples.

The **Pecan Festival** is an annual event in Sahuarita and the day begins with a 5K Nut Run. Activities at the festival include a tractor pull, wagon rides through the pecan groves, a pecan pie contest and entertainment. There are numerous vendors, a children's play area and a food court.

There is also a "Heritage Area" located in a white tent. This is where we got an education on basket making techniques. A Tohono O'odham basket maker patiently answered all of our questions about preparing devil's claws, what type of grass they use for baskets and where to find the materials. All the while, the other ladies continued to work on their individual baskets. What a treat it was to learn all that in one afternoon while watching the process. This was an exceptional day of learning.

The **Shoofly Village Ruins** are located in the Tonto National Forest, a short distance from the town of Payson.

There are remains of an ancient stone village with visible footprints of the original buildings. It is estimated that this area was inhabited between 1000 and 1200AD. The area covers four acres and it is estimated that the community contained eighty plus rooms with two hundred and fifty people living here. The results of the excavations have determined that the inhabitants were farmers and hunters. There is a well paved path that meanders through the site so that visitors can view the entire area.

The site is located on the edge of a mesa which undoubtedly provided protection for the community. The location also provides some spectacular scenery. Looking in one direction you can see mountains, look in another and you can see huge ponderosa pines for miles and looking from yet another angle you can see the huge cliffs of the Mogollon Rim. What a beautiful part of Arizona this is!

Montezuma Castle National Monument is near the town of Camp Verde. The National Monument was established in 1906 in order to protect this impressive cliff dwelling. It is estimated that the Sinagua Indians lived in this area between 1100-1425AD.

This five-story, twenty-room, cliff dwelling tucked into a limestone cliff is impressive. There is no doubt that the Sinagua Indian builders were skilled engineers. Strategically built into a cliff and along Beaver Creek, it afforded the inhabitants water and protection.

There is a one-third mile paved path through the grounds. One can walk amongst the sycamore trees, take pictures of the "castle" built into the cliff, explore the structures built at the base of the cliff, and stop to view Beaver Creek. At times, park rangers will conduct lectures along the path about the history of the Sinagua. The visitor center also has information about the inhabitants and their way of life.

Hundreds of years ago, the Anasazi (The Ancient Ones)

lived in **Mystery Valley**: a section of Monument Valley Tribal Park. The Anasazi lived here as early as three thousand years ago and the valley was abandoned before the Navajo arrived in this area. Today, however, there is ample evidence of their occupation in this valley.

The valley is closed to the public and can only be accessed with a Navajo guide. The area is restricted to provide privacy for the residents. In 2016, we scheduled a tour so we could explore this large and magnificent valley. Excitement was the prevalent feeling that morning and off we went in our open-air vehicle, through the sand dunes on narrow roads with deep sand. It was apparent that this would be a very interesting day.

We drove along the base of huge sandstone formations, buttes and mesas. The surrounding area was peaceful and quiet. No other tourists were seen on that day and we enjoyed having this experience all to ourselves.

The ancient ruins were worth the trip. The Square House ruin is reportedly about three thousand years old and is surrounded by pieces of broken pottery and cutting tools. The House of Many Hands treats visitors to an enormous collection of pictographs that include geometric figures, human forms, animals, and many sizes and shapes of hands. The panel of hands was a surprise and a treat to see.

At the Honeymoon Arch, another surprise awaited us. In a cave below the arch, a small, beehive-shaped rock structure was almost hidden from sight. This is the first time we had seen a beehive house. The structure was intact and a semi-intact granary was nearby.

The scenery, the rock formations, the ancient ruins, the petroglyphs, and the pictographs all enhanced the enjoyment of the day. The day, however, was not over yet. Our open-air, four-wheel drive vehicle started climbing up some rocks and stopped atop a mesa overlooking the valley. The view took our breath away. What a great way to end a tour!

Mission San Xavier del Bac is located south of Tucson and within the boundaries of the Tohono O'odham Indian Reservation. The building is large and is painted a brilliant white, thus nicknamed "The White Dove of the Desert."

The original mission was established in 1692 by Father Kino; there are no remains of the original church built on the premises. The current structure was built from 1783 through 1792 under the direction of the Franciscan Friars, and continues to serve the Tohono O'odham parishioners.

San Xavier del Bac is the oldest, intact European structure in Arizona. The interior of the church attests to a Baroque architectural style with the faux doors and curtain displays. The mission is filled with original statues, murals and paintings. The first time we entered the church it seemed overwhelming with so much to behold. This mission was unlike any other mission we had seen. Beautiful, but very different.

For some years, the mission was abandoned and was used as shelter for travelers and the poor. Restoration efforts have been ongoing for years in an attempt to restore this structure to its original beauty. The Tohono O'odham have had an active part in the restoration efforts. There is a video about the project that can be viewed in the museum. The Mission San Xavier del Bac has been listed as a National Historic Landmark.

Near the mission's parking lot, visitors will find vendors selling their crafts. One of the vendors is Joe Begay, a silversmith, who makes beautiful silver jewelry. If you visit his booth, ask to see his book of pictures. He has been in several movies and has pictures to show all those who ask. He is most proud of the time when he was given the role of an Indian.

Driving to our new home in Green Valley, we saw the brilliant white mission near the Interstate. This was the second site we visited in Arizona. All of our guests and family members are brought to this mission when they visit. This is a beautiful historic site in our own back yard.

It is estimated that **Elden Pueblo** near Flagstaff was inhabited by the Sinagua Indians between 1070-1275AD. The structures were built of stone and it is estimated that there were sixty to seventy rooms in a community of two hundred to three hundred people. During the excavations, macaw bones and shells from the California coast were found. This pueblo was apparently part of a trading system.

A burial mound was located near the site and two additional burials were found beneath the structures. During the excavation, all of the skeletons and pottery were removed and sent to the Smithsonian.

There is a gravel path that leads around the site so visitors can view the ruins. There are no information signs that share the history of the site with the general public.

The **Deer Valley Petroglyph Preserve** in Glendale is a forty-seven acre preserve that is home to fifteen hundred Hohokam, Patayan and Archaic petroglyphs. The petroglyphs are estimated to be five hundred to seven thousand years old. This is the largest concentration of rock art in the Phoenix area. The site is listed on the National Register of Historic Places.

From the visitor center, a wide, gravel path leads you along the base of a hill filled with basalt rocks. Some of the art is easily seen, but the majority are difficult to spot on the black rocks. There are some viewfinders strategically located along the path so the visitors can find some of the significant rock art.

There was a Patayan petroglyph that was close enough and we were able to take a good picture to take home. The figure is cute: a stick figure of a man with huge hands and huge feet. This was our first Patayan rock art. We were thrilled.

Tonto National Monument in Roosevelt protects two Salado pre-historic cliff dwellings believed to have been inhabited between 1150-1450 AD. There are many such dwellings in the Tonto Basin which were abandoned about five hundred years ago for unknown reasons. In this area, the Salado were farmers and gatherers. They are known for their brightly colored pottery and their woven cloth.

From the visitor center patio, the lower cliff dwelling is very visible and viewfinders are available to get a closer look. There is a steep gravel path that leads to the dwelling and, at certain times of the year, visitors are permitted to view the site up close. About three miles away, there is a pull-off to view the upper cliff dwelling. It is a long distance away from the parking area and this site is closed to the public.

Navajo National Monument near Kayenta preserves and protects, three large Anasazi cliff dwellings built of sandstone, mud mortar and wood. The inhabitants of this area are thought to have been farmers that relied on irrigation for their crops. Today, the dwellings still remain and remind us of civilizations gone by. This site has been placed on the National Register of Historic Places.

Keet Seel, built around 1250 AD, is the largest of the dwellings. Tours to the site are available for those who wish to visit the structure. It is a seventeen-mile round trip to the dwelling and a back-country permit is required.

Betatakin, a smaller dwelling, was built between 1267-1286 AD. Guided tours are available to the site. It takes approximately three to five hours to complete the five-mile round trip to the dwelling.

The Inscription House is currently closed to the public.

Irma, Dotty, Midge and I arrived at this sight and were eager to view the dwellings. After reviewing the list of tour options, only one option was viable. There is a one-mile round-trip trail that leads from the visitor center to an overlook where visitors can view Betatakin. The choice was easy and off we went. The trail was sheer rock, the sky was blue, the wind was blowing, the trail got steeper but our spirits were good.

From the overlook, the large cliff dwelling was magnificent

and we could see for miles down the Betatakin Valley. It is hard to imagine building such an enormous structure in such a remote area. We had the thrill of watching a shepherd herding his sheep. Up the trail we went, happy to have seen an historic Anasazi dwelling.

In Tuba City, about three miles from the Dinosaur Tracks, there are some well preserved and protected **Petroglyphs**. The site is accessed on a narrow dirt road which becomes sandy in spots. Arriving at the site, the *No Trespassing* sign is readily visible. A permit from the Nation is required to enter the premises. The petroglyphs, however, can be seen from outside the enclosure.

At this site, there are hundreds of well-preserved figures. Some look like corn stalks, houses, antelope, deer, turtles, but some of the geometric figures we did not recognize. A great site to view a variety of petroglyphs.

The **Tohono O'odham Nation Cultural Center and Museum** in Topawa was built in 2007 as a permanent institution to assist in the preservation of their culture. The buildings and grounds are spectacular. It is located in a pristine desert area with Baboquivari Peak in the background. It feels like you have entered a special and reverent place.

There are two main buildings, a cultural center and a museum. The cultural center is to provide tribal members with private space. The museum building is open to the public. The exhibits at the museum highlight the history of the tribe using both traditional and interactive displays. Some of the exhibits are temporary and often highlight Tohono artists.

A temporary exhibition on the creation of the Tohono O'odham people was at the museum the day we visited. What an educational treat that was! On another occasion, we danced to the rhythm of Waila music. Waila is a dance music developed by the Tohono O'odham; it is commonly referred to as "Chicken Scratch." We like the rhythm.

Homolovi State Park is located one mile north of the

town of Winslow. The State Park was opened in 1993 to preserve archaeological sites that were being devastated by looters and souvenir seekers. The park protects seven, separate pueblo ruins built by different cultures over a span of years. Of the seven ruins, only two are open to the public

Homolovi II is the largest of the sites. It is believed that the Anasazi inhabited this site between 1330-1400 AD. The pueblo contained about twelve hundred rooms, three plazas and several kivas. Visitors can walk through the site on a paved walkway. Some exposed walls are visible and the footprint of many rooms can be seen.

Homolovi I is located closer to the river and about two miles from the visitor center. A steep, uneven, gravel path allows explorers to view the remains of another pueblo site. There is one section of exposed wall; piles of rocks can be assumed to be the remnants of other buildings.

The Hopi Tribe consider this to be an ancestral site and often return for ceremonial purposes. It is a site worthy of a trip. Educational. Homolovi State Park was fun for us because we shared the experience with Irma and Dotty.

Sells is the capital of the Tohono O'odham Nation and the home to many of the tribal businesses. It is also home to the Tohono O'odham Community College.

We love to drive to Sells and enjoy lunch at the Desert Rain Café. It serves genuine native cuisine in a friendly and homey atmosphere. Guests have the option to eat indoors or on the covered patio. Be alert if you eat outdoors! You may see a herd of cows walking down the street! We did. If you choose to eat at the café, you may want to check out their Prickly Pear Smoothies. Heavenly.

Adjacent to the café, a gift shop sells a large variety of Tohono O'odham art, such as pottery, paintings, jewelry, and baskets. Another interesting feature: Basha's Grocery Store in this city uses the tribal names in their store to designate food groups. Pretty neat idea.

San Xavier Pow-Wow. The mission San Xavier del Bac, south of Tucson, hosts an annual pow-wow and the public is invited. The event last two days and features dancing, music, crafts vendors, food vendors, competitions, and award presentations. A wide variety of dances are performed and, at times, the public is invited to participate. Every tribal member participates in the festivities: young, old, men and women.

We love to attend this activity. We especially love the music, the blue sky, the beautiful costumes, the hoop dancers, the fry bread, the children, and being a part of the festivity. We love being given the opportunity to be a participant in this tribal custom.

For many years, The Arizona State Museum in Tucson hosted an annual **Southwest Indian Art Fair** on the museum grounds. It was a highly anticipated and well-attended event. Entertainment included Tohono O'odham basket dancers, Apache dancers and well-known Native American musicians. The vendors sold high quality Indian art, including blankets, pottery, jewelry, baskets and paintings.

Due to state budget cuts, the Arizona State Museum will no longer be hosting the Art Fair. The event will be missed by the multitude of people who have attended.

Da'Wa Petroglyph Site is located within the boundaries of the Hopi Indian Reservation. It is considered a sacred tribal site and access is restricted. We were privileged to be able to visit with our Hopi guide, Garrett Maho.

Driving up to the site, you see the towering, red-sandstone cliffs covered with thousands of petroglyphs, dating back to 750 BC. It is easy to spot snakes, rivers, bighorn sheep, hands, solar calendars, feet, flute players, stick figures, and a wide variety of geometric patterns.

The quality, quantity, and significance of this rock art is amazing. We always feel privileged to be at a site where ancient civilizations left messages for others, including us. No wonder that the Hopi believe it is a sacred site.

Tuzigoot National Monument in Clarkdale preserves the ruins of a Sinagua village built between 1125-1400 AD. This is the largest and best preserved Sinagua ruin in Verde Valley. Crowning a desert hilltop, the two-to-three story pueblo ruin contains one hundred and ten rooms and one bigger room at the center which was possibly used for ceremonies. Excavations have determined that the inhabitants of this site were farmers and artists. From artifacts that were discovered, they were part of an extensive trading system. This site is on the National Register of Historic Places.

Visitors can walk around the ruins on a paved path. Information signs along the walk tell the history of the Sinagua people, daily life in the pueblo, and their building methods. Walking around the ruins, it is amazing how much of this village still remains. Visitors are welcome to climb to the top level of the main house. From that position, you can see for miles in all directions, and you can see the town of Jerome.

One striking feature of this site is the lack of doors in the structure. The only door you see is in the main room. All of the other rooms were accessed through the roof. Interesting feature. This is one of our favorite Indian ruins. It is easy to imagine a vibrant community of people living here.

Pueblo Grande Ruins is an archaeological site managed by the city of Phoenix. It protects and preserves a prehistoric Hohokam Indian village that was continuously occupied from 100-1450 AD. The main feature at the site is a three acre, twenty-feet high platform mound, surrounded by brick dwellings. The site also contains a ball court.

Another historical feature is the two Hohokam irrigation canals that run along the edges of the park. What a treat that Phoenix has preserved such a significantly historical site.

Tumacacori National Historic Park in Carmen hosts an annual **Fiesta de Tumacacori**. The Fiesta is held outdoors in a field adjacent to the mission. The entertainment includes

Folklora dancers, Mariachi bands, and the White Mountain Apache dancers. There are numerous vendors selling their crafts, as well as local agencies wishing to share the services they provide. A variety of food vendors are also in attendance.

For those who wish to participate in the festivities, this is a good place to come. There are several activity areas where you can learn to make adobe bricks, identify animal pelts, identify snakes and lizards, and learn about moths, bees and other pollinators. You can even get a picture taken with a Conquistador hat on your head.

We enjoy this festival. Here, you can absorb different cultures, eat fry bread, sit at the picnic tables with strangers (who quickly become friends) and enjoy the beautiful Arizona winter.

Montezuma Well is part of the Montezuma Castle National Monument. The well is located in Rimrock, north of the Castle site. The prominent feature of this site is the huge limestone sink hole which is fifty-five feet deep and three hundred and sixty feet across. Warm springs replenish the water on a daily basis. Some of the water escapes through a breach in the rock and this made the irrigation system possible. In the late 1300s, the Sinagua Indians built a one-mile three-foot-deep trench into the bedrock to create an irrigation canal. This canal provided water to the agricultural fields. They were farmers who successfully grew corn, squash, beans and cotton. Amazingly, the irrigation canal still exists. We put our hands into the water and it was indeed warm.

This site is also special because of the diversity of people who lived here. There are remains of a pit house which was built by the Hohokam Indians about 600 AD.

In the cliffs on the edge of the well, one-room cliff houses can be seen. It is estimated that these were built around 1300 AD. These small structures were easy to build and provided the inhabitants protection and warmth.

On a small hill overlooking the well, there are remains of a twenty to thirty room pueblo constructed of limestone and sandstone. It is estimated that the pueblo was built in the late 1300s by the Sinagua Indians about the time period when the irrigation canal was built.

This site is historically significant and well worth the trip. Paved walkways guide visitors through the site. The most adventurous can even descend into the large sink-hole to put their hands in the well water.

The **Gatlin Site** in Gila Bend is an archaeological site that preserves one the few known Hohokam platform mounds. It is estimated that this area was inhabited from 800-1200 AD. There are no original structures remaining. This site has been placed on the National Register of Historic Places.

Gila Bend is developing this area into a regional Cultural Park. There is a replica of an Indian dwelling and a ramada on the site. Visitors can also view a section of the Old Phoenix Highway, the remains of an 1878 wagon road and an original Hohokam canal.

Sears Point Archaeological Site is located on Interstate 8, seventy-five miles east of Yuma. Access to the site is on a seven-mile, narrow, and very rough road. For the last mile, the road is the bed of the Gila River!

There is an information kiosk that indicates you have arrived at the parking lot. There are no maps available and the environment is daunting. A series of huge basalt flows lie next to the Gila River.

The information about the site states that some rock art can be viewed near the parking area. We did locate about twenty petroglyphs. The question remained as to where to head next. The trails are visible but not well maintained. Walking around the site, we determined that the area was too large and too difficult for us to explore any further. We did not find hundreds of petroglyphs, but we did have the opportunity to enjoy some beautiful scenery. The trip was well worth it. It is not every day we get the chance to drive in the bed of the Gila River.

The **Phoenix Indian School** was built in 1891 under the Federal Policy of Assimilation of the Native American. It is the only Bureau of Indian Affairs School in Arizona that was not located on an Indian Reservation. From 1891-1935, it served as an elementary school and served as a high school from 1935 thru 1990. It was closed in 1990 by orders of the federal government.

In 2001, the Steele Indian School Park was founded on Indian School Road in Phoenix. It is a seventy-five-acre park containing paths, picnic areas, places to rest, relax and rejuvenate. Three buildings and a large pond are the core of the Phoenix Indian School Historic District. The three original buildings are all built of brick: one is Victorian Queen Anne style, one is Mission Revival style, and the last is Spanish Colonial Style. The historic district has been placed on the National Register of Historic Places. The blue sky, the palm trees, the green grass, the pond, and the brick buildings paint a picture of serenity and beauty.

The design of the park pays homage to the site's Native American History. Many of the spaces are built in a circular fashion and quiet, private spaces are available throughout the site. On the circular path around the Historic District, information boards are posted to provide visitors with historical information about the site.

A meaningful, educational and significantly historical site, it altered the lives of many. It is a tribute to the Steele Park that it recognizes and honors Native American history.

In 2014, the Amerind Museum in Dragoon hosted an **Apache Festival**. What a great environment for a festival. The museum is located amongst the beautiful boulders in Texas Canyon. Off we went with our chairs, water and lunch.

The festival was held outdoors which allowed the public to be close to the performers. The entertainment consisted of music and dancers. Our favorite dancer, Tony Duncan, performed the Hoop Dance that day and we were no more than thirty feet away. What a great day that was.

Picture Rocks Petroglyph Site can be accessed via a short trail from the Redemptorist Renewal Center on Picture Rocks Road. The public is invited to view the petroglyphs. The center asks that visitors check in at the office prior to descending on the trail.

At this site, bighorn sheep, stick figures, geometric figures, and a large circle are visible. These petroglyphs are believed to be Hohokam and are dated from 800-1350AD. Easy site to view communication from an ancient civilization.

Casa Grande Ruins National Monument in Coolidge preserves ancient Hohokam ruins of several structures surrounded by a wall. The most impressive structure is the "Great House," the tallest and biggest Hohokam building known. It is estimated that it was built in the 1300s and the purpose of this imposing, four-story structure remains a mystery. Visitors are allowed to wander around the site. A ball court is also on site and can be accessed via a short trail.

The visitor center offers exhibits and artifacts that were found in the area. A video is available for public viewing that explains the history and daily life of the Hohokam people.

Between 1937 and 1940, the CCC built adobe houses to be used as housing and administration buildings at this National Monument.

Annually, Casa Grande has special tours during the month of March which take the public to the back-country to view additional ruins not usually open to the public.

Petroglyph Site in the Picacho Mountains is accessed by a narrow, dirt road which becomes rough in spots. To access this place, a State Trust Land Permit and a high- clearance vehicle are required. This area is very remote so accurate directions to the rock art are necessary.

Arriving at the sight, it is apparent that the drive there was warranted when you notice the dozens of hills with basalt rocks. At the first hill, hundreds of petroglyphs are visible on the rocks. The majority of the rock art in this area is Hohokam. The figures most notable are stick figures, bighorn sheep, turtles, snakes, circles, and geometric figures.

We noticed one very special figure on a rock. It was the stick figure, apparently a pregnant woman, with three wavy lines under the figure. We had seen this figure before at the Monument Valley Tribal Park in Northern Arizona and in Canyonlands National Park in Utah. Our guide in Monument Valley had explained the significance of this rock art figure. It says that this woman will be crossing the river to have her third child. How exciting it was to see this unusual art again.

This was a great site to see both a quality and quantity of rock art. Also a great place to come in the spring with the blue sky, yellow brittlebush, orange globe mallows and black lava rocks.

Walnut Canyon National Monument near Flagstaff preserves ancient Sinagua cliff dwellings. It is believed that the Sinagua people lived here from 600-1400AD. They were farmers and planted their crops on higher ground, where the visitor center and rim trail are today.

On the island trail, you can descend into the canyon and walk where the Sinagua once traveled. Visitors will be able to view up close about twenty-five rooms along the trail. A long series of steps leads to the trail. We chose to view the dwellings from the rim trail.

On the rim trail, visitors can walk along a paved trail. Two overlooks are provided and offer excellent views of the beautiful rock formations in the canyon. It is easy to spot the cliff dwellings in the canyon walls.

Canyon de Chelly National Monument (2011) is located near the town of Chinle, and is on the National Register of Historic Places.

This is a place of incredible beauty with its red sandstone cliffs, green trees, red sand and magnificent cliff dwellings with a long history of habitation. One of the main features is Spider Rock: a red sandstone spire that rises seven hundred and fifty feet from the canyon floor. Today about forty Navajo families make their homes, raise livestock and farm on their ancestral lands.

Access to the bottom of this canyon is restricted, so in 2011, Midge, Jacqui and I decided to take a guided Jeep tour with a Navajo guide. Our guide's name was Dave Wilson and he informed us that he was an Indian Chief. How cool!

The Anasazi cliff dwellings were amazing to see up close and petroglyphs abounded in the canyon. Some of the petroglyphs were different than those seen at other sites. Our guide had a herd of horses in the canyon, and when he called them, they would answer him.

It was a great day of fun, sunshine, beauty, excitement and history. It was also a lot of fun being in a Jeep at the bottom of a canyon, driving along in a dry river bed. We could see why they cancel their tours when it rains.

Canyon de Chelly (2015) We returned to Canyon de Chelly National Monument with Irma and Dotty and with a new goal in mind: seeing the canyon from the rim trail.

On the north and south rim of the canyon, viewpoints are provided so visitors can see the canyon floor from different perspectives. The Anasazi cliff dwellings can also be seen from the viewpoints. Along the rim trail, vendors sell their art in the parking areas. This is a great opportunity to meet and talk with individuals who live at the bottom of the canyon.

Spider Rock is definitely the most visible landmark in the canyon and you can view several miles of the river from the rim. The canyon looks longer, wider and more beautiful when viewed from above. Happy to have had the opportunity to view the canyon from both perspectives.

Kinisba Ruins is located on the White Mountain Apache Reservation near the town of Apache. The inhabitants of this pueblo are thought to be the ancestors of the present-day Zuni and Hopi tribes. Evidence indicates that this area was inhabited as early as 800 AD and at its peak, there were four hundred to eight hundred people living here. The remains deteriorated significantly over time so between 1935-1939, the Indian Division of the CCC provided Apache labor for the rebuilding of the south side of the pueblo. Kinishba has been designated a National Historic Landmark.

Arriving at the parking lot, there is a dirt path that leads to the ruins. Our first thought was "Wow! A beautiful large pueblo, near a water source, lush valley and majestic mountains." It is easy to see why this sight was selected to build a community. Walking along, you arrive on the north side and realize the damage that erosion and time has inflicted on this architectural wonder. The kiva area lies to the east of the ruins and some evidence can be seen. This is an excellent ruin to explore.

Near Springerville, perched atop terrains in front of basalt cliffs lies the ruins of **Casa Malpais**. The name of the ruins derives from the type of volcanic rock it sits on, and the entire complex is built of volcanic rock. It is estimated that it was inhabited from 1260 AD to 1400 AD and was as large as sixty rooms. The present-day Hopi and Zuni believe this to be sacred ground of their ancestors. At the site, the remains of the pueblo, a solar calendar, petroglyphs, and a large kiva can be seen. To access the ruins, reservations must be made for a guided tour at the Springerville visitor center.

At the visitor center, we spent time with the guide and gathered information about the ruins. Due to the rainy conditions and the volcanic staircase that is used to access the site, we did not go visit the ruins. As far as we know, these are the only ruins in Arizona built entirely of volcanic rock.

Wupatki National Monument near Flagstaff preserves many ancient settlement sites inhabited by the Anasazi, Cohonina, Kayenta and Sinagua Indians. Driving through the monument, many pueblos can be seen across the miles of prairie. The Wupatki National Monument has been placed on the National Register of Historic Places. There is easy access to five of the settlements within the boundaries of the monument.

The largest site is Wupatki which is located behind the visitor center. It is a large, impressive structure that was built with red sandstone by the Sinagua about 1100 AD. It is the largest and tallest structure built during that time period. The structure is four stories high and contains one hundred rooms, kivas and a ball court. There is a paved path that allows visitors to walk through the site and it quickly becomes apparent that the structure was built around a rock outcropping. The site was abandoned about 1225 AD. This is a very impressive ruin.

The Wukoki ruins are immediately noticeable from the parking lot. The structure is tall, red, visually pleasing, and appears to have grown out of the rock. It is said that the building displays superb architecture built by skilled artisans. It is believed to have been occupied between 1120-1220 AD. There is a sand path that leads to the ruin and visitors can enter the structure.

The Nalakilu ruins is a two-story house built about 100 AD. Rooms were added to the structure at a later date, indicating two different periods of habitation. This ruin has easy access and visitors can enter the building.

Box Canyon ruins are semi-intact structures built along the sides of a canyon. Trails lead to the remains, but the paths are sandy and rocky.

Lomaki ruins are sizable, partial buildings along the rim

of a canyon. It is believed that the Sinagua and the Anasazi inhabited this area. In one of the structures, a "T" door is visible, indicating Anasazi influence or habitation. A gravel path leads to these buildings. Along this path, we spotted a beautiful collared lizard and he graciously posed for us. His picture hangs in our living room in remembrance of our trip to Wupatki.

Wupatki National Monument is a great place to view magnificent and varied ruins. The ruins are some distance from one another, so allow adequate time to explore.

The **Hopi Indian Reservation** is located in Northern Arizona. It consists of twenty-five hundred square miles and is entirely surrounded by the Navajo Reservation. The inhabitants call their land "Hopiland." It is the center of the Hopi population and the Hopi culture. Many inhabitants keep the old traditions and customs alive. The Hopi view their land as sacred and consider Hopiland to be private property. Visitors are welcome, but restrictions apply pertaining to ceremonies and pictures.

Hopiland consists of three large islands of rock, called "mesas," on which the majority of the population still live. Some homes, however, can be seen at the base of the mesas. On Second Mesa, there is a restaurant, a museum, some gift shops and a small motel.

On Third Mesa, the village of Old Oraibi still stands after all these years. It was built before 1100 AD and it is the oldest continuously inhabited settlement in the United States. The adobe structures are beginning to disintegrate, but this village continues to be inhabited.

One day, we received an invitation from our friends, Ron and Vicki Sullivan, to spend three days on the Hopi Reservation and we eagerly accepted. Prior arrangements were made for us to spend some time with a local potter to view the pottery firing process. One day during our visit, we were invited to the

First Mesa to be spectators at the Harvest Festival. This event was closed to the public, but we were invited by Garrett and his family. We felt honored and privileged to be there

Meeting a well-known potter, Garrett Maho, watching the process of making and firing pottery, and seeing our pot for the very first time was very exciting. Needless to say, we came home with our "Rainbird" pot. Our memories of the trip include beautiful scenery, wonderful historical sites, friendly people, and magnificent art. An experience to remember for a long time.

Native American People have lived in Arizona for thousands of years. Evidence of their presence can be seen along the San Pedro River, Gila River, Colorado River, Santa Cruz River, the Snake River and in hundreds of other locations. Ancient dwellings, pot shards, fire rings, metates, cutting stones, pit houses, pueblos, petroglyphs and pictographs are all available for viewing. They stand ready to remind us of the civilizations that came before us. People just like us: building homes, raising their children, planting their crops and communicating with one another.

We have read several books on the culture and history of ancient Indian tribes and tribes currently living in Arizona. Visiting the sites and places we have listed has helped us to collect more pieces of information. The hands-on learning has been educational, enjoyable, and has changed us in many ways.

FORTS

*"The only thing that held the fragile Arizona
Territory together was a handful of army posts."*

- Roger Naylor

A few generations ago, the Territory of Arizona was on the edge of wilderness. A great migration occurred in this country and the territory experienced an influx of gold seekers, cattle ranchers, and settlers who wished to make their home here. The new arrivals settled on Native American lands and violence erupted in many areas.

In the 1800s, it is estimated that over seventy military outposts were established in Arizona. Some were temporary camps that could be moved if the need arose and others were permanent outposts. Sometimes, specific camps or forts had specific responsibilities. Yuma Quartermaster Depot, for example, had the responsibility of receiving and distributing supplies to the various forts.

In the 1770s, prior to the western migration, the Spanish constructed fortifications which were called *Presidios*. Their purpose was similar to the military outposts established in the 1880s. Protection of settlers was the primary purpose of a presidio. There are also remnants of forts that were built during the Mexican Revolution. With such a large number of various forts, it is no wonder that we decided to explore some of them in this newly adopted state of ours.

We will share with you some of the camps or forts we have visited and explored. In this chapter, you will not find

Yuma Quartermaster Depot, Camp Hyder, Fort Bowie, Camp Rucker, Camp Naco, Camp Navajo and Fort Yuma. These military outposts were mentioned in other chapters.

The forts in this chapter are not listed in any particular order, nor are they separated into different categories. They all share one common denominator; they are the treasures of the past. They remain for us to enjoy and remind us of the struggle of the people who were here before us.

Camp Beale Springs, Kingman. The springs were a resting stop on the toll road from Prescott to Hardyville. During the Hualapai Indian War (1866-1870), the springs became the location of a temporary military camp that offered protection for travelers along the Fort Mohave road and the toll road. From 1871 thru 1874, it served as a temporary reservation for the Hualapai tribe. The camp was closed in 1874 when the Hualapai were moved to La Paz, Arizona.

Arriving at the site, we found a memorial dedicated to the memory of the Hualapai ancestors who fought bravely against the attempted genocide of their tribe. The stone memorial also states: "This location was a temporary internment camp for the Hualapai people until the infamous forced march of the La Paz Trail of Tears. April 21, 1874."

A survey of the area revealed tin cans, glass remnants, cement foundations and partial cement walls. Investigation of the camp, however, was not permitted. The site is currently on Hualapai Indian land and a permit is required for entry. These grounds are considered sacred by tribal members.

Seventeen miles east of Douglas, lies an historic military site called **San Bernardino Ranch Outpost** or **Slaughter Ranch Outpost**. It was established as a US Army post in 1911 as a direct result of increased tensions along the United States and Mexican border. The unrest is sometimes referred to as The Border Conflict. The soldiers assigned to the post were the 9th Infantry African-American soldiers, referred to as the Buffalo Soldiers.

In 1916, under the direction of General Jack Pershing, a raid onto Mexican soil was initiated from this site. It was an attempt to locate Francisco "Pancho" Villa who had killed Americans in Columbus, New Mexico. The raid was not successful. The military outpost was decommissioned in 1923.

The site is located due east of the Slaughter Ranch and can be accessed by a series of stairs that climb to the top of a mesa. The literature indicates that there are few remains. Rocks along the pathways help visitors navigate through the site and several rock foundations can be seen. It is obvious that a significant military outpost had existed here. Standing on the edge of the mesa, the fence along the Mexican-United States border is readily seen. There is also an unimpeded view of the Mexican landscape.

What a privilege to be standing on this ground where, over one hundred years ago, young soldiers lived and worked. An historic site in a very desolate place.

Camp Crittenden, later known as **Fort Crittenden**, was a US Army Post built in 1867. It was located at the head of Davidson Canyon, three miles west of Sonoita. The soldiers from this camp saw much action during the Apache Wars. Their primary responsibilities were to engage the Apaches and to protect the American pioneers in the area. The fort was closed in 1873.

Today, there are reportedly some remains: crumbling adobe and mounds of earth. The remains are on private property. No directions have been found to the site. On Highway 82, heading south from the town of Sonoita, there is a roadside marker that relates the history of the camp. If you look closely in the field behind the marker, you will see a stone building in the distance. These remains are from the ghost town of Crittenden, not from the camp.

Fort Verde State Historical Park is located in Camp Verde. The fort was established in 1865 to offer protection to the Anglo settlers in the area. Conflicts between the settlers and the Tonto-Apache and Yavapai Indians were occurring. In the 1870s and 1880s, the fort served as a base for General Crook's US Army scouts and soldiers. From 1865 through 1891, the fort housed officers, doctors, families, and enlisted men.

Today, the State Park attempts to preserve parts of the Indian Wars-era fort as it looked in the 1880s. The park offers tours and living history demonstrations. The goal of their demonstrations is to offer visitors the opportunity to experience what is was like to live here. The park also has a museum with artifacts found in the area, stories of the Indian Scouts and informational exhibits. Several of the original buildings still remain and are very well maintained. Three of the buildings are on the State and National Register of Historic Places.

Arriving at this site, it is truly amazing to see all that remains of this historic place. The parade grounds, the white picket fences, the American flag waving and the buildings in a straight line along the parade ground give this place an air of elegance. Martha Summerhayes stated in her book, *Vanished Arizona*, that she liked this fort. We could understand what she meant. This site rates a "Number One" for charm. A place not to be forgotten.

Mike Burns in his autobiography, *The Only One Living to Tell*, tells his story about being the sole survivor of the Skeleton Cave massacre. He was given the name Mike Burns by the soldier who rescued and raised him. After reading his book, the passion to find his burial site was fueled. Research led us to his gravesite in the **Fort McDowell** cemetery.

Fort McDowell is located on the Fort McDowell Indian Reservation located twenty-three miles northeast of Phoenix. The fort was built in 1865 to protect trade routes in the area. It was built in Indian country, surrounded by mountains and in a very isolated area. From 1870 to 1890, the supply trail from Fort McDowell to Fort Whipple in Prescott needed protection from the neighboring Indian tribes. The Fort McDowell Indian Reservation was established in 1890 for Mohave, Apache and Pima Indians. Today, it is a Yavapai Reservation.

January 2016, our destination was the Fort McDowell Indian Reservation in search of Mike Burns' gravesite. We were not prepared for the beautiful scenery: mountain ranges, farmland, green trees, and flowers. A beautiful and peaceful area. The cemetery was easy to locate and was well kept. An American Flag was waving at the entrance. The gravesites were lined with rocks, and white crosses adorned each grave. After some searching, the grave was located. It was time to pay our respects to a man who had not only persevered, but thrived. We also found a headstone in memory of all those killed in the Skeleton Cave massacre.

Some of the original fort still exists. We located three intact buildings, one partial adobe building and two foundations. At the Yavapai Nation Museum and Cultural Center, we inquired about additional remains of the fort. We were informed that the fort had been bulldozed. It was in the same location as their new elementary school. It was a day of remembering someone who touched our lives. A day of exploration and of meeting people who helped us in our quest for knowledge.

In the 1730s, Spanish colonists began to settle in the Tubac area, the northern edge of their New World. They farmed, raised cattle, sheep and built irrigation systems. In 1751 the settlement was destroyed during the Pima Indian Revolt. In response to the unrest, **El Presidio San Ignacio de Tubac** was founded to prevent further violence and to protect the mission and the colonists.

Juan Bautista de Anza, the second commander of the Presidio, left from this site on his journey to California to protect San Francisco from Russian incursions. The garrison was moved from Tubac to Tucson in 1776. As a result, the residents closed up their homes and moved to safer areas. El

Presidio San Ignacio de Tubac is on the National Register of Historic Places.

Today, the Tubac Presidio State Historic Park preserves the ruins of the original Spanish presidio. This park, established in 1958, holds the distinction of being Arizona's first state park. Visitors can view portions of the original foundation, walls, and plaza floor.

The State Historic Park has added additional buildings to the park in the past years. Guests can enter an old schoolhouse (1885), the Otero school (1914) and the Rojas House (1890). A museum with artifacts from the site and a video explaining the role of a presidio also enhances the experience.

We participate in the various celebrations at the State Park: e.g. De Anza Day, held in October. Educational programs, tours and musical events are also offered. It is a sight worthy of exploration.

Fifty miles northeast of Tucson, **Camp Grant** was located at the confluence of the San Pedro River and Aravaipa Creek. The confluence is within walking distance of Route 77. Camp Grant was a US military outpost from 1866 thru 1871. Protection of the supply routes and Anglo settlers was the primary responsibility of the outpost. During its years near the San Pedro River, it was abandoned, destroyed or rebuilt several times. At one time, it was called Fort Breckenridge. The camp was relocated in 1872 to the base of Mount Graham near the ghost town of Bonita. There are very few remains of the original camp.

A significant event in Arizona history occurred near Camp Grant. It has become known as the "Camp Grant Massacre." In early 1871, about 500 Pinal and Aravaipa Apache Indians were living in the area. As requested by the military, they had surrendered all of their weapons. At this time, tensions between the Apaches and the Tucson residents were running high. The residents were dissatisfied that Camp Grant could not protect the supply route required for commerce. In October 1871, six Americans, forty-eight Mexicans and ninety-four Tohono O'odham Indians rode from Tucson to Camp Grant. That night, the group attacked the Apache camps and killed an estimated one hundred and twenty-four people. Ninety-five percent of those killed were women and children. Some of the surviving children were captured and taken as slaves. In October 1871, one hundred people were indicted for the murder of the Apaches. They were acquitted. In the book *Massacre at Camp Grant* by Chip Colwell-Chanthaphonh the massacre is described in detail, along with the conditions that contributed to the massacre.

The massacre site is located near Dudleyville. We have been near the site, but we have not been able to find specific directions to the exact location and according to the literature, there is no memorial. It is considered sacred land. Another piece of Arizona history that cannot be judged by the values of today.

Camp Grant was closed in 1871. It was relocated to the base of Mount Graham in 1872 and was called **Fort Grant**. The US Army installation was strategically placed in that area to protect the settlers who were constantly harassed by Apache warriors. This base played a major role during the years of the Apache Wars. The fort was abandoned in 1898.

In 1900, it was re-purposed and used as a staging point for soldiers going to the Philippines during the Philippine-American War. The land and buildings were transferred to the state in 1912 as a state school for boys, and became a state prison in 1968. The literature states that there are no remains of the fort.

In 2016, we went to explore the ghost town of Bonita. From our location, the state prison complex was visible and we decided to go to the prison in case there were remains. Speaking to one of the prison guards, we were informed that there is indeed one building remaining. The ruins are inside the prison complex and access could not be granted. Driving away from the prison, we were able to view "Angel Field," an historic airstrip. An educational trip.

Fort Lowell (1873-1891) was located on the outskirts of Tucson at the head of the Rillito River which flowed regularly at that time. The first Camp Lowell was situated closer to Tucson but was moved for sanitary reasons. It was a US Army installation which, on average, included thirteen officers and about two hundred enlisted men. The fort was never directly attacked due to its size and manpower.

The primary responsibilities of the fort were: providing protection to the town of Tucson and distributing supplies and soldiers to the outlying military installations. The fort was abandoned in 1891. The remaining buildings were vacant and were soon occupied by Mexicans who moved north to take advantage of the free housing.

When we arrived at the site, we were impressed by the number of buildings that remain. In Fort Lowell Park, visitors will find the post hospital, cottonwood lane, three officer's quarters and the quarters of the Commandant. The Commandant's house is currently the park's museum. Along Fort Lowell Road, within the boundaries of the original fort, guests can easily locate the San Pedro Chapel, the Quartermaster's Quarters and Storehouse as well as the Post Traders store. All of these buildings have been placed on the National Register of Historic Places.

The park has several information signs telling the history of the post, the usage of the buildings, the people of significance who lived and worked here and information on the Apache Wars. The museum has a significant number of artifacts from the 1800s. In one corner of the park, there is a pile of rocks that are reportedly part of the wall of the guardhouse where Geronimo was kept before he was removed from Arizona.

On the first visit, we felt that the trip was educational and we enjoyed the peaceful and serene setting. The second time we visited was during the annual "Fort Lowell Days" and the feeling was completely different. It was exciting, energizing and a lot of fun. There were horse demonstrations, soldiers in full uniform, music of the 1880s, mariachi bands, food vendors, children's activities and living history demonstrations. You felt like you were strolling through time. Another bonus on that day was that all of the buildings were open for visitors to stroll through and explore. What a great day spent in a truly impressive site.

In 1776, the Spanish-built Presidio in Tubac was abandoned and the **El Presidio San Augustin del Tucson** was built by Spanish soldiers in the current downtown district of Tucson. The presidio was the beginning of the town of Tucson. Here, Spanish settlers could live, farm, laugh and pray in safety.

The presidio remained intact until two years after the Gadsden Purchase. Once the United States purchased this section of land from Mexico, the American settlers began to migrate to the southern part of the Arizona Territory. Once the Americans arrived, the old presidio met its demise. Some of the fort walls were dismantled in 1856. The last portion was taken down in 1918. The *original presidio* was gone!

After an archaeological dig, the Northeast corner of the original fort was found. Today, a re-creation of the corner of the Presidio can be found on the corner of Washington and Court street in downtown Tucson. Visitors can now walk through and visualize what a presidio looked like. There are docent led tours that explain how life was lived in the 1700s. On the second Saturday of the month, living history demonstrations are held and guests can watch weavers, candle makers, blacksmiths, and can even sample foods eaten in the frontier days.

We went for the living history demonstrations and were

lucky enough to see the Spanish soldiers (in full uniforms) march up the street toward the fort. They even shot the cannon that day. Even though the fort is a re-creation, it gives you an idea of how it must have been to live within a fortification to ensure your personal safety. A small section of the original foundation can be seen. It is exciting to view part of a building built by Spanish soldiers three hundred and forty years ago. This site is educational and fun: a great stop for parents and children alike.

Fort Huachuca is located near the town of Sierra Vista. It was established as a temporary US Army Outpost in 1877 to counter the Apache threat and to secure the Mexican border. In 1882, it became a permanent installation. From 1913 through 1933, it became the base for the Buffalo Soldiers (African-American soldiers).

This installation has had a long history of duties and functions. The post currently exists and it is known as the US Army Intelligence Center. The literature indicates that it is currently one of the largest army installations in the United States. The post consists of seventy thousand acres; one hundred and ten of those acres are the "Old Post."

In 2011, we departed in search of the Old Post. We wanted to see where the original fort had started. To our delight, we found several intact buildings: the barracks (1882), the post chapel (adobe and stone building), Leonard Wood Hall (two-story building used as hospital), the Pershing House and the Fort Huachuca Historical Museum building. All of the above noted buildings have been placed on the National Register of Historic Places.

The "Old Post" section of the fort is well maintained. It was comforting to see that a portion of the past was well preserved for visitors to come see and enjoy. Walking in the park where the initial soldiers lived in tents, you can sense how they felt when they arrived in this truly desolate section of the Arizona

Territory. If you imagined even further, you can almost hear the sounds of the bugle bouncing off the mountain walls.

In the historical section of the installation, there are two museums worthy of mention. The Historical Museum tells the story of the US Army in the Southwest, the original fort, the Buffalo Soldiers and the Apache Wars. The museum has numerous artifacts that are interesting and educational. The US Army Intelligence Museum has some unusual artifacts, radio gear, code machines, and a section of the Berlin Wall. Both museums were worthy of our time.

This was an exciting post to view. It brought us back in time and made us visualize what it would have been like to be here in the 1800s.

Fort Whipple is a US Army post located in the town of Prescott. It was founded in 1864. The post served as the Arizona Territory's capital prior to the foundation of Prescott. It also served as a tactical base for the US Cavalry during the Indian Wars (1864-1882) and shortly transitioned into the headquarters of the Rough Riders during the Spanish American War. During WWI, it was converted into a TB sanatorium. The Army post was officially closed in 1913 and soon after became a military hospital through World War I and World War II. Today, it is a VA hospital and is listed as a major tourist attraction in the Prescott area.

Fort Whipple was on our list of places to see when we arrived in Prescott in May 2014. We were totally surprised when we got our first glimpse of this fort. It almost took our breath away. The fort is built in the shape of a rectangle with the parade grounds in the center. The warehouses, the hospital, and the residences line the outside of the area. The large residences are built on the nearby hills and are currently occupied by nurses, doctors, and their families. All of the buildings are well maintained and all are painted a brilliant white. With the blue sky, green trees, green grass, flowering bushes and impeccable landscape, the fort displays an air of true elegance.

One night, we went to the parking lot near the Yavapai Casino to get a glimpse of Prescott from above. The brilliant white buildings of Fort Whipple were easily located and it was amazing how big the fort looks. We could understand why the fort was listed as a major tourist attraction in Prescott. According to our rating system, we rank it "Number One" in historical significance, beauty, and preservation. It is the best-preserved Arizona fort we have visited.

Fort Apache Historic Park is located on the White Mountain Apache Reservation, south of Whiteriver. The historic park preserves structures from the original fort and from the era of the Bureau of Indian Affairs boarding school. The layout of the fort has not been altered and some of the structures are original: the oldest structure is the log cabin that was reportedly the residence of General Crook. The Fort Apache post office was the adjutant's building and is one of the original structures. One of the original four barracks still remains and is used to store farming equipment. The commandant's residence and the officers' residences burned and were rebuilt as exact replicas of the originals.

At the end of the Indian Wars, the fort was later converted to a Bureau of Indian Affairs boarding school for girls and boys. On the fort grounds, the boy's dormitory and the girl's dormitory sit vacant. The Theodore Roosevelt School, however, still provides education for the children in the area.

Upon arriving, the Nohwike Bagowa (House of our Footprints) Museum was our first stop. A great place to gather information on Apache culture and history. Walking around the fort was like walking through history in this beautiful and isolated place. It is exciting that a proud people have chosen to preserve their history and are willing to share it with visitors.

Searching for forts in Arizona has been exciting and very

educational. We have learned about historical events at the sites in which they occurred. This, we find, is a wonderful and meaningful method of learning. The experience has also exposed us to many areas of the state.

There is one interesting lesson we have learned from this search. Things are not always like you envision them to be. During childhood and early adulthood, we watched many western movies. We did not find any forts in Arizona that look like those portrayed in the films. The search for the Hollywood forts has ended.

RANCHES

Gene Autry, Dale Evans, Roy Rogers, Hopalong Cassidy, Tom Mix, Rex Allen, Cisco Kid, Rifleman, Bonanza, Lone Ranger, Tonto and High Chapparal. The names were very familiar in our years of development. Names you will never forget!!! Names that denote the wild west, cowboys, cattle, horses and ranches.

Every year, about eight hundred and seventy thousand cattle are raised on thirty-eight hundred Arizona ranches. Come on our journey and we will share with you some of the ranches we have enjoyed. All of them were special in their own way, and most of them have a long and interesting history. In this chapter, the Empire Ranch and Triangle T Ranch, have not been included. They have been discussed in other chapters.

As a postscript: when visiting the ranches, we rarely see cowboys. We tend to see the cowboys, aka ranchers, at Walmart, local festivals or in downtown Tucson.

McGee Ranch (also known as Sierrita Mining and Ranching Co). In 1895, three families were heading to California in search of gold. A broken wagon wheel would change their fate. During the time they were stopped to fix the wheel, the McGees, the Harris and the Livelys decided to make their home near the Sierrita Mountains.

The family eventually made their permanent settlement on the east side of the Sierritas, near the town of Tucson. Throughout the years, the families have been involved in mining, construction and cattle ranching.

We have visited their settlement and the cemetery. The

cemetery is very well maintained and the graves of the original settlers are well marked. On one visit to the ranch, Midge, Betty and I had the opportunity to speak with John Harris II who was a student in the original schoolhouse at the settlement. He shared with us his experiences in a one-room schoolhouse. He is mentioned in the book *Ranch Schoolteacher* by Eulalia Bourne. Hands-on history lessons are always valuable.

Dowdle Ranch is located southeast of Tucson at the base of the Santa Rita Mountains. It can be accessed from Madera Canyon Road. David Dowdle was born in South Carolina and ranched in Texas and California before he moved his family to Sawmill Canyon and established a cattle ranch prior to 1878. After his death in 1898, he was buried in the old cemetery on Oracle Road in Tucson.

His ranch is listed as a historical site. There are two sections of walls and two corners of the original adobe house that remain. The remaining portions measure about four feet high. Next to the adobe sections, the corral still exists. Looking around the area, it is easy to imagine why David would have chosen this location for a cattle ranch. The view of the Santa Rita mountains is stunning.

Rancho de La Osa is located in Sasabe, in the high Sonoran Desert, on the United States-Mexican border. It has a long history of ownership and usage. Part of a Spanish Land Grant, it was acquired from Mexico during the Gadsden Purchase and was part of a cattle ranching empire. In 1924, it began its career as one of Arizona's premier guest ranches.

The ranch has ten buildings on its property. One of the buildings is historically significant. In the late 17th century, Father Kino and his followers built an adobe mission outpost on the ranch property. This building still exists and has been used as a gathering place for the guests. Another historical feature that can be seen at the ranch is a cannonball. Yes! During the Mexican Revolution, Pancho Villa fired at the

Hacienda and a cannonball was imbedded in the wall of the building. Today, guests can hold one of the cannonballs in the palm of their hands.

At this unique and special ranch, a long list of world-known celebrities and dignitaries have stayed here to relax and rejuvenate. Some of the celebrities include: Margaret Mitchell, Cesar Romero, Tom Mix, President Lyndon B. Johnson, Zane Grey, Franklin and Eleanor Roosevelt, and John Wayne. It is said that William Clayton drafted the Marshall Plan in one of the haciendas in 1948.

In March 2015, the ranch property was on the market. We acquired permission to visit the ranch. Upon entering the property, the initial impression was "Wow!" It is no wonder that it was a premier ranch in its heyday. The haciendas run alongside the main square and the main house faces the parking area. The desert landscape, the sculptures, the brightly colored chairs, the pastel colored buildings, the fountains, the multiple seating areas and the eucalyptus trees gave this place an air of class and elegance. Under new ownership, the ranch was re-opened in February 2017 as a guest ranch.

Kenyon Ranch lies in the foothills of the Tumacacori Mountains, just south of Tucson. It was started in 1937 as a dude ranch and was a popular winter vacation spot for many years. Today, it is a retreat site for workshops, conferences, weddings and family gatherings. It is advertised as a peaceful environment where one can reconnect with nature. Upon arriving on the premises, their advertising is accurate. It is indeed a peaceful place with impressive scenery This is a place to come to see the stars, listen to your own thoughts and escape from the busy pace of everyday life. The stone walls and buildings, the fountains, the sculptures, the arches, the sitting areas and the alcoves create an atmosphere of serenity and familiarity. The property and grounds were very well maintained.

The **Lonely Dell Ranch Historic District** is a short walking distance from Lee's Ferry. From the 1870s -1890s, this ranch was home to the families who operated Lee's Ferry. Due to the isolation of the area, the ranch had to be self-sufficient in order to insure their survival. They grew their own food and some of the large orchards are still evident. Several original buildings remain. The National Park Service has preserved the structures. This area is harsh, barren and isolated. The scenery, however, is stunning. From here, the Colorado river is within walking distance for those who wish to soak their feet or watch the rafts depart for their trip down the Colorado River.

Sopori Ranch is about three miles west of Amado and can be accessed from Arivaca Road. This ranch is historically significant in the Santa Cruz Valley. In the 1700s, thousands of acres were given as a Spanish land grant to Juan Bautista de Anza, the second commander of the Tubac Presidio and the founder of San Francisco. A land grant was given to civilians to attract and encourage permanent settlers.

In the 1860s, the ranch was home to the Pennington family. They were one of the first permanent Anglo settlers in the area. They lived in a fortified stone house by the wash. Eventually, Apache attacks encouraged them to move to a more secure location. Two Pennington family members are buried, along with other early settlers, in a cemetery near the fortified house. At the entrance of the cemetery, there is a rock engraved with the following: "Tread softly here - These stony mounds - Shelter the bones of - Arizona's oldest pioneers." Reading these words, it was clearly understood that this is sacred ground.

The nephew of Robert E. Lee reportedly owned the ranch in the early 1900s. He was killed while horseback riding on the ranch property. There is a religious grotto to Saint Teresa on Arivaca Road overlooking Sopori Ranch. Mrs. Lee built the grotto in honor of her husband.

From 1950 through 1993, movie mogul Jack Warner

owned the property. Today, the property is owned by a family residing in Illinois. Only about five hundred acres remain in private hands. In 2004, twelve thousand acres were sold to a developer.

We have researched this property, visited the cemetery to pay our respects to some of Southern Arizona's pioneers, stopped by the roadside shrine and admired the ranch buildings from a distance. We have dreamt of having a closer look, but the ranch is posted "No Trespassing." An historical treasure in our back yard.

Eva Wilbur-Cruce, in her book, *A Beautiful, Cruel Country*, describes her childhood in the 1900s on **Wilbur Ranch** in Southern Arizona. A fascinating account of frontier life, the book is compelling and descriptive.

Researching the ranch, we discovered that ruins exist and are located within the boundaries of the Buenos Aires National Wildlife Refuge. The ranch is accessed from Arivaca Road. Parking at the Arivaca Creek National Recreation Trail, a short side trail leads from the stream to the 1870s adobe ranch house.

Arriving at the ruins, we located corrals, a collapsed barn, a semi-intact shed, two intact cattle chutes and the remnants of a beautiful adobe house. The roof of the house has collapsed, but some of the adobe walls still stand. After reading the book, you can picture this ranch in its heyday. What a great place this would have been to grow up. Luckily, some of this treasure still stands as a reminder of Arizona's pioneer days.

In the 1880's, the Dodge family built the **Acadia Ranch** in Oracle as a boarding house and a sheep farm, By the early 1900's, people began flocking to Arizona in search of a cure for "consumption." Oracle was a primary destination for individuals sick with tuberculosis. Acadia Ranch took in the sick seeking a cure. The very sick were kept in the building and others were placed in outdoor tents. In those days, it was believed that fresh, dry air was a cure for the disease. The famous sculptor, Alexander Calder, and his family stayed here for several months during his youth. A cure for TB was discovered and the patient population began to decrease.

Today, the 13-room ranch house, the icehouse and the water tank proudly stand alongside Mount Lemmon Road. A wide porch stretches the length of the building and gives the structure an air of elegance. The Oracle Historical Society has done the necessary repairs to restore this magnificent building. The ranch house is currently an historical museum which highlights the history of the ranch and the local area. In 1984, the ranch was placed on the National Register of Historic Places.

Buffalo Bill Cody is a well-known name in Oracle. He frequented this town regularly and often stayed at the Mountain View Hotel. He had interests in the Campo Bonita mines and, in 1912, he registered a claim for the High Jinks Gold Mine. Due to a lack of success and finances, the claim was abandoned in the 1920s and was sold at auction.

The **High Jinks Ranch** is on the site of the gold mine. A structure, called La Casa del High Jinks, was built by Johnny Baker and Claude Way. Johnny was a sharp-shooter and right-hand man to Cody. From 1944 to 2007, the ranch had multiple owners. Some buildings were added and renovations were made. In 2007, a couple purchased the property with the intention of restoring it to its original grandeur and making it into a bed and breakfast. The ranch is listed on the National Register of Historic Places. The property is located along the Arizona Trail.

In 2014, Midge, Betty and I headed to Oracle to see this historical and significant structure. The road to the ranch is dirt that climbs and twists through the Arizona desert. On more than one occasion, the thought occurred that Gypsy was heading in the wrong direction. All of a sudden, there appeared, a tall rock wall, a stone arch and a sign that said "High Jinks Ranch." The entrance was impressive and made one unsure whether to enter this property that appeared fortified. Heading toward us, the new owner smiled and welcomed us to his home. On that day, we received a history lesson about the gold mine, the structures, the water collection system, and Buffalo Bill Cody. Built on the side of a hill, the structure is multi-level; this feature enhances the charm and beauty of the main house. The stone arches and stairways are impressive. The location of the ranch offers a spectacular view of the San Pedro Valley. What a beautiful place to live and what a treat to stand on a piece of land once owned by Buffalo Bill Cody.

During a guided tour to the ruins of the Los Santos Angeles de Guevavi mission, the park ranger was sharing information about the **Guevavi Ranch** in Nogales. He spoke about the significance of the murals on the walls of the courtyard. Returning home, research about the ranch was our focus. Shortly after our guided tour, the owners of the ranch granted permission for us to see the highly acclaimed murals.

The Guevavi Ranch was homesteaded in 1915 and, over time, became one of the largest cattle ranches in Southern Arizona. In its heyday, it was a refuge for many Hollywood celebrities. It is well documented that John Wayne spent time at the Guevavi Ranch. The land was subdivided over the years but the ranch headquarters still remain. The Hacienda Corona de Guevavi, complete with interior courtyard, stands on thirty-six acres of land in Nogales. It is located on a hill and, therefore, offers magnificent views of the valley and mountains.

The abandoned main ranching complex was purchased by the Stovers about fifteen years ago. They lovingly restored the main house into the beautiful western retreat that exists today. Their daughter, Nisa, continues to operate the bed and breakfast.

One of the main features of the Hacienda are the murals in

the interior courtyard. Salvador Corona, the famous muralist and bullfighter, resided at the Guevavi ranch for one to two months at a time in the 1940s and 1950s. On the walls of the courtyard, visitors can view murals of indigenous Mexican peasants. There are numerous murals in excellent condition. For those interested, two large murals by Salvador Corona are on exhibit at the Pimeria Alta Historical Society Museum in Nogales.

There are rooms in the main house for guests and two casitas are also available. With large porches, several sitting areas, individual patios for each room, this is a place where one can come to rejuvenate, relax and dream. In January 2016, at a birthday party, Midge's daughter Marie stated, "I am looking at the same scenery John Wayne saw!"

Ward Ranch in Sonoita no longer exists. We debated whether to include this ranch in our book. The answer was yes because of it's historical significance. Here, in 1861, an event occurred that altered the fate of many settlers and slowed the development of Southern Arizona. There is sign on Route 82, heading south from the town of Sonoita: "Arizona pioneer Johnny Ward established a ranch here in 1858. In 1861, Indians kidnapped his Mexican stepson, Felix Ward. Army officers assumed that local Eastern Chiricahua Apaches were responsible, leading to the infamous conflict between Lieutenant Bascom and Cochise. In fact, the Pinal band of the Western Apaches took Felix..."

The event that occurred at this ranch and the ensuing conflict led to the twenty-five-year-long Apache wars that affected the lives of all settlers and military in Southern Arizona.

Rancho Santa Cruz lies along the Santa Cruz River, south of Tubac. Doris Oestig purchased one hundred acres from Tol Pendleton in the 1940s and established the famous Rancho Santa Cruz. Reportedly, this is the area where the Spanish Army camped during their exploration of the New World.

In its heyday, the ranch attracted many wealthy patrons and celebrities, including Stewart Granger and John Wayne. Throughout its existence, it has had many lives: a famous guest ranch, a children's camp, a church retreat center, and a business and conference center.

The ranch was on the market until recently (2016). The new owners wish to restore it to its original grandeur and re-open it as a guest ranch. On the grounds, there are several large cottonwood and mesquite trees which give the property an air of wealth. On the one hundred acres, there are several intact structures; ten guest rooms, three guest suites, one honeymoon cabin, a swimming pool and a fifty-person restaurant.

Another interesting historical feature about the ranch is the fireplace. One of the fireplaces was built from stones that came from the hotel that stood at the original Calabasas townsite. The townsite was located next to the Rio Rico Golf Course on Pendleton Drive.

The day we went to see the historical site, the new owners arrived and took us on a personal tour of the property. What a treat to view this property up close and personal. We will maintain a relationship with our new friends.

Canoa Ranch is south of Green Valley and can be accessed from East Frontage road. In 1912, Levi Manning established what is known as the current Canoa Ranch. In the following years, Canoa became the largest cattle ranch in Southern Arizona. The ranch land was estimated at five hundred thousand acres.

Levi's son, Howell, turned this ranch into the jewel of the Santa Cruz Valley. Howell raised Arabian horses, two of which were famous. In the 1940s, the ranch employed about fifty ranch hands located in several locations on the property and had ten to twelve families living at the ranch.

The ranch headquarters was similar to a small town: a blacksmith shop, a bunkhouse for the single men, adobe houses for the families, a school, corrals, barns and a five-acre pond stocked with fish. In 1939, the movie *The Westerner* with Gary Cooper was filmed on the property.

After the death of Howell, Levi Manning started selling off parcels of land in 1953. In 2001, Pima County purchased about four thousand acres. The goals - preservation of this historical site and education of the public. Some of the buildings have been restored and some are in progress.

Tours of the historic ranch are available. When we went to visit, we were amazed at the number of buildings that remain. Walking through the site, it feels like you are at a working cattle ranch. This is a significantly important site and is well worth the visit. The Canoa Ranch Headquarters Historic District is listed on the National Register of Historic Places.

San Bernardino Ranch, also known as Slaughter Ranch, is located seventeen miles east of Douglas. It is accessed by a well maintained gravel road through the Arizona desert. The ranch is located on the United States-Mexican border.

In 1884, John H. Slaughter purchased sixty-five thousand acres and established his ranch. The Slaughter family lived on this property until 1936. The property changed hands several times after John's death. The property is well-known due to John's contribution to the state of Arizona. He was the famous sheriff of Cochise County who reportedly helped tame the Wild West, and was held in high regard.

The grounds of the property are visually pleasing. Huge trees, water retention ponds, green grass and well-maintained buildings. There are six structures on the ranch: a barn, main ranch house, wash house, ice house, granary, and commissary. All of the buildings are open to the public and guests can view artifacts of the era, read articles about the Slaughter family, and view some of the farm animals roaming free.

John Slaughter made a valuable contribution to this state and we were pleased to have spent time at the historical site.

Then, we discovered another piece of information. In 1983, the ranch was purchased by the Johnson Historical Museum of the Southwest and the US Fish and Wildlife Service. In the water retention ponds there are Yaqui Topminnow and Yaqui Chub. These are two endangered species that are only found in this particular valley. John loved people, children and animals. We think it would be OK with him to share the spotlight with the topminnow and chub.

In 1938, Rex Hamaker established the **Rex Ranch Resort.** It is located south of Arivaca, off the East Frontage road. The fifty-acre resort contained thirty-two guest rooms and casitas, a restaurant, meeting rooms, a day spa and the first swimming pool built in the Santa Cruz Valley. In its heyday, it was a prime vacation destination for winter guests, birders, artists and Hollywood celebrities. It was the place to come for relaxation, socialization and rejuvenation.

One of the buildings on the property was built in the 1880s by a cavalry soldier who was granted the piece of land when he retired from the US Military. The other buildings were built after 1936.

The resort closed in 2012 and was put on the market. Proud new owners took possession of the property in 2014 and changed the name to La Bella Rex Ranch. Unsure about their intentions, the decision was made to find and explore the ranch as soon as possible. Permission was granted for us to enter the property. It is hard to describe the feeling when we drove up to the main building. A huge, salmon-colored Spanish-style building was shining in the direct sunlight. The arch above the doorway contained a bell and two stone lions lay alongside the walkway. What a magnificent sight. It is no wonder that the rich and famous came here to vacation!

All of the buildings at this resort are salmon colored and are strategically placed amongst the trees to offer shade and privacy for the guests. The setting was peaceful and would please any nature lover. This was a premier ex-guest ranch that we visited. We wish the new owners the best in their endeavors.

Rancho San Cayentano on Santa Gertrudis Lane in Tumacacori was one of the Showcase ranches that were established in Southern Arizona. In the 1930's, owning such ranches was viewed as a symbol of wealth. Tol Pendleton established the Rancho San Cayentano during this period of time. He imported cattle from Texas and raised horses. For many years, Santa Gertrudis Lane was known as "Booze Alley" due to all of the parties taking place; one night at one house, another night at another house and so forth. Georges Simenon wrote a book called *Bottom of the Bottle*. His book was fiction but was indicative of the party atmosphere at the Showcase ranches in the area.

Today, the ranch is still there and is currently used to board horses. Driving to the ranch is an adventure; down a narrow dirt road and through the Santa Cruz River which flows in this section. Once you get to the ranch's gate, the beauty begins. A beautiful lane, lined with huge trees, lies ahead and beckons you to the ranch house. The house is white stucco with red tile roof, arches, and large porch. The house is ideally located on the property.

Everywhere you look, there are green pastures, green trees, handsome horses and phenomenal views of the Santa Rita Mountains. Even today, it is indeed a "Showcase" ranch.

Guest ranches and dude ranches still exist in Arizona. They cater to a population who wish to get a Wild-West experience combined with luxury. Most of the existing ranches provide a wide variety of entertainment options for their guests and provide the Western or Spanish environment with modern amenities. The Wild West still remains appealing!

We have seen many more ranches and we have enjoyed every one of them. Each ranch is unique and we have learned another piece of Arizona history at each site. By the way, on some of these ranches we did see cowboys. We are always on the lookout for them!

MUSEUMS

Museums, for us, have been a refuge from the summer heat and have been an excellent source of historical information. In this section, we will share with you some of the museums we have visited in many areas of the state. The list is long, therefore, we will share with you the features we found most interesting or educational. Some museums will not be included in this chapter; they were mentioned in other sections.

Browsing through museums has significantly increased our knowledge of the history of Arizona. It is interesting that, over time, the areas of interest have shifted. Enjoy this journey through selected Arizona Museums.

Arizona Sonora Desert Museum is located in Tucson. This is the first place we bring guests in order to expose them to the desert, flora and fauna. If our guests are lucky, they will have a hummingbird greet them or have a hawk fly over their heads at the Raptor Exhibit. This is a great museum for new residents and guests. You can walk at your leisure, eat lunch in an outdoor garden, listen to a docent explain the lifestyle of a Gila Monster and see a Kestrel up close.

During the summer, the museum has "Cool Summer Nights" from five to ten pm. Some of the topics include Full Moon, Bat Nights, Creatures of the Night, Arts and Music. It is fun to participate in their activities. Looking for scorpions is an activity we stay away from, however, children seem to find this activity the most enjoyable.

Superstition Mountain Museum in Apache Junction is located at the base of the Superstition Mountains. Pulling into the parking lot, the scenery is spectacular. The museum contains a collection of mining equipment and Anasazi Indian pottery shards. As part of its collection, it has several maps that indicate where the Lost Dutchman's mine is located. When we looked at them, the location of the mine was different on the various maps. To this day, prospectors and visitors are still searching for the location of this mine.

The museum contains a lot of interesting information about the surrounding area. One example; Ettore "Ted" DeGrazia, a famous Tucson artist, came to these mountains and destroyed some of his art in protest to the inheritance tax laws. It is estimated that the art was worth one million five-hundred thousand dollars. There is also information about the Apacheland Movie Ranch that was established in the area. *Have Gun Will Travel* with Richard Boone as Paladin was filmed at that location. Several movie stars frequented the area during filming and their pictures are on the premises for guests to see. The gallows used in some of the movies are on the property.

This was a fun and interesting museum to visit. It contained some information not found in other locations. For the Elvis lovers, there is an Elvis Memorial Chapel on the grounds. Guests can visit the chapel.

Tucson Rodeo Parade Museum in Tucson has an amazing collection of horse drawn wagons of all shapes, sizes and uses. Such as: Circus wagons, dairy wagons, covered wagons, stagecoaches, chuck wagons, mud wagons and a Tohono O'odham Indian cart. The surrey "with the fringe on top" that was used in the movie *Oklahoma*, starring Gordon MacRae and Shirley Jones, is also on exhibit. Great collection. Fun museum.

Museum of the Horse Soldier is located in Trail Dust Town in Tucson. The US Military's mounted services are highlighted and honored at this museum. The exhibits include saddles, swords, uniforms, insignia, rifles and testimonials of military personnel. The artifacts are professionally exhibited.

In another room, there is an exhibit that attests to one man's perseverance and devotion. One man's dream was to find remains at the state's many abandoned forts. Today, guests can view bullets, insignia, buttons, belt buckles, horseshoes, forks, spoons, bones, and padlocks that were located at different forts. The size of the exhibit and the number of artifacts is astonishing. What a wonderful experience!

The building and grounds of the **International Wildlife Museum** in Tucson are well appointed and make the visitor feel welcome. Inside, the museum is a testimony to the art of taxidermy. We are not fans of such museums, but the exhibits in this particular museum were tasteful and pleasing to the eye. The number and variety of animals was amazing. They even had a Woolly Mammoth!

There was also an exhibit of butterflies. This was absolutely fascinating. For all the species, they had both sides of the wings displayed. The colors, patterns, and the variety made this exhibit special. Butterfly lovers should consider visiting this museum.

The **Courthouse Museum** in Florence contains exhibits about the history of the Florence area. It also has a comprehensive exhibit on the Florence Prisoner of War Camp during WWII. In 1943 and 1944, German prisoners of war from the African Corps were imprisoned in Florence. The exhibit contains a map showing the exact location of the camp, pictures of some prisoners and information about their activities and work duties. Comprehensive information about some interesting history.

University of Arizona Mineral Museum in Tucson prides itself in educating the public through its rotating exhibits. We have viewed two of their exhibits: Chinese minerals and Trilobites. The information is consistently thorough and well presented.

Downstairs, there is a permanent exhibit that focuses primarily on Arizona minerals. How exciting to see all of the minerals that have been found in this state. Guests can also view fossils that have been discovered in Arizona. When we go there, we always slow down at the gold exhibit. How come we can't find a nugget like that in a ghost town or a tailing pile? It sure does prompt us to continue exploring and dreaming! This is a great place to visit if you love rocks.

Pinal County Historical Society and Museum is located in Florence, and has many historical artifacts on display. Florence is known for its number of prisons, so it was not a surprise to find an exhibit devoted to executions. There were hangman nooses, pictures of the men who were executed and an electric chair.

Another exhibit of interest was information on Winnie Ruth Judd, known in Arizona as the Trunk Murderess. There is a book of the same name about this incident in history. To date, this is the only museum where we have found an exhibit on Winnie Judd.

Arizona History Museum is located on 2nd St in Tucson. The museum has a large variety of interesting and historical artifacts for guests to view. There is also a mining exhibit which is interesting and informative.

There are some special features in this museum. Its entrance is a remnant of the historical *convento* which was located at the base of Sentinel Mountain. Beautiful memento of the past preserved for us to enjoy.

The Geronimo exhibit at this museum is the most comprehensive collection we have encountered. What a treat to see the number of photos and information presented. It was surprising and thrilling to see his signature, death certificate and photos we had never seen. Great exhibit.

Another exhibit that caught our attention was about the Silverbell artifacts. The silver crosses that were discovered were reportedly from a Roman colony that existed in the Tucson area from eight hundred to nine hundred A.D. We will leave it to the readers to determine if it is a Miracle, Mystery or Hoax.

Huhugam Ki Museum is in the Pima-Maricopa Community. In 1986, the community built a Youth Home constructed of Saguaro ribs and mud. The decision was made to place the museum in the former Home. The architecture of the building is impressive.

Pottery, baskets and tribal information are on exhibit. One etching by the famous artist, Frederic Remington, tells of the contribution of the Pima Indians in the development of this country. The Pima provided safe passage through hostile territory to settlers and gold seekers. Remington's etching is entitled "Pima Indians Convoying a Silver Train in Mexico." It is prominently displayed in the museum. Great historical find.

In Page, the **Powell Museum** pays tribute to John Wesley Powell. In 1869, he was the first man to boat down the Green and Colorado Rivers for eleven hundred miles. The museum exhibits include information about Powell's life, maps and information about the river trip. A replica of the boat that was used on the historical trip is also included. There are also pottery, shards, petroglyphs and dinosaur tracks to view. The book and gift shop attached to the museum offers a great collection of Arizona books. Brought home some books from there.

Researching our trip to Prescott, the **Smoki Museum** sounded interesting so we put it on our list of things to see. Driving up to the museum, turned into a moment of awe. The structure is built with river stones and stands out. What a great arrival! We were eager to see their Indian art collection.

The collection of Indian exhibits lived up to its reputation and included pottery, baskets, moccasins, art and sculptures. It was educational and pleasing to be at this museum. In the back room, however, we encountered an exhibit about a topic unknown to us. There was information and photos about the Smoki. The Frontier Days Rodeo used to be a money maker for the town of Prescott, but attendance dwindled.

The businessmen brainstormed and came up with a solution: Dress up like Indians, take some aspects of the Indian dances and make them into dramatic performances for the paying audiences. The idea was financially viable and the Smoki continued for seventy years and performed more than three hundred different dances, including the Snake Dance. The Smoki no longer exist.

It happens all of a sudden. We are faced with a piece of history we have trouble understanding. This is when we remember the statement: You cannot judge the actions of the past with the values of today.

The **Desert Art Museum** in Tucson advertises that it contains a large collection of Southwestern art. The museum lives up to its claim. The museum contains many square feet of extraordinary exhibits which include clothing, blankets, wall hangings, jewelry, sculptures, photographs and paintings. More than once, we stopped and exclaimed "Wow!"

The museum was also exhibiting some photographs by Scott Baxter. For the centennial anniversary of Arizona Statehood, Scott took photos of one hundred Arizona ranchers. A book entitled *100 Years 100 Ranchers* by Scott Baxter is available.

The blanket exhibit was stunning and some of the photography on exhibit was some of the best we have seen in a museum. We will return to this museum and we would recommend it as a place to explore beautiful art.

Amongst the wonderful rock formations of Texas Canyon, there lies a Spanish Colonial Revival-style building that houses the **Amerind Museum.** The Amerind Foundation began in 1937 with a focus on archaeological research. In 1985, the museum opened to the public and exhibits a large number of artifacts of Indian tribes ranging from Alaska to South America. The artifacts and information are well displayed. It is worth the trip to the museum.

The museum hosts many special educational and cultural

events throughout the year. Guests also soon discover that being in Texas Canyon can be a refreshing and enchanting change from the desert environment.

Atop a hill in Flagstaff, a tan stone building with a white porch stands proudly amongst the tall trees. The **Pioneer Museum** was the Coconino County Hospital for the Indigent from 1908 thru 1938. The remarkable feature is that the structure was built of Pumiceous Dacite (pumice stone) from the Mount Elden eruption that occurred five hundred thousand years ago. The building has been renovated and looks stunning.

Museum exhibits include artifacts from the pioneer days, history and equipment from the hospital era and Route 66 memorabilia and information. On the grounds, two railroad cars can be readily viewed and photographed.

Green Valley has the distinction of having the only United States silo with an anti-ballistic missile. Of course, the warhead has been removed. Visiting the **Titan II Missile Museum,** guided tours are available. Visitors can descend into the silo, enter the command room, and view the missile up-close and personal. Tour guides disseminate valuable information about the site, the Cold War Era and duties of the crew. Special tours are also available: e.g. longer tours to see more of the facility and tours with personnel that served at this military establishment. Interesting historical site.

Airplane lovers beware! The **Pima Air and Space Museum** in Tucson will astonish you with its collection of aircraft. Aircraft of all types can be seen in numerous buildings and on the grounds. There is also a tour available to the "Boneyard" to view retired military aircraft. This museum is an all-day adventure as you go from one magnificent plane to another. All of the aircraft can be seen up-close. Great place for kids of all ages. Postscript: look up as you stroll along because there are many treasures hanging from the ceiling.

Tucked away in a residential neighborhood in Tucson, you will find the **Franklin Auto Museum**. Housed in three buildings, the owner displays his collection of antique Franklin automobiles. All of the vehicles are restored, shiny and absolutely beautiful. For antique car lovers, this is a good place to explore.

The **Zelma Basha Salmeri Gallery of Western American and American Indian Art** (referred to as Basha's Gallery) is located in Glendale at the company's offices. There are over three thousand pieces of art displayed in several rooms and include Native American baskets, pottery, Kachinas, sculptures, oil paintings, acrylic paintings and etchings. Visitors will find several pieces from the same artist. The art was usually purchased directly from the artists. They believed in supporting living artists and became long lasting friends with some. At times, some of the art in this gallery is loaned to other galleries or museums.

We spent a whole afternoon at the gallery. It was not enough time; we could have spent the whole day and still not have seen all of the art. Over the years, they have amassed an incredible collection of beautiful pieces. A wonderful place to spend some time. Guests are surprised when they arrive; there is no admission. The gallery is free to the public. It is their pleasure to share it with all of us.

In the quaint western town of Wickenburg, visitors will find a well-known museum known as the **Desert Caballeros Western Museum**. The museum has a large display of pioneer and western artifacts. Guests can see a Concord Stagecoach, a chuck wagon, and a surrey. A variety of local cattle brands are available for viewing. Rotating exhibits are routinely featured. On one occasion, we went to see the "Cowgirl Up" art exhibit which featured Arizona female artists. Fun museum to explore.

In front of their lower museum, there is a sculpture worth noting. It is a large sculpture of a horse and a kneeling cowboy by the artist Joe Beeler. It is entitled "Thanks for the Rain." Wonderful piece.

Across the street, we found a very interesting site. An information sign states the following: From 1863 to 1890, outlaws were chained to this tree. They also claim that escapes were unknown. Today, the tree remains and a mannequin is chained to the tree. Great history presented in a humorous way.

We were asked several times if we had seen the **MIM** (Musical Instrument Museum) located in Phoenix. It finally made it on the list of places to see on our trip to the big city. Arriving in the parking lot, it was immediately apparent why others kept telling us to plan on spending an entire day here. The building was not only beautiful, but huge.

The first obstacle we encountered (besides the enormity of the lobby and the size of the museum map they gave us) was the headsets they gave us. We are not headset people. The goal was not to use them. After a few exhibits, the headsets were on and we danced throughout the museum for the entire time we were there. One can listen to great music at each exhibit. Fun, fun, fun.

At this museum, guests can find any musical instrument from any country in the world. The exhibits are well displayed and space is available to sit, relax and listen to music. We will return to this museum someday and we are sure we will enjoy it as much as we did the first time.

Snaketown was an archaeological site near the city of Phoenix. Many Hohokam Indian artifacts were excavated at this site. Some of the artifacts can be viewed at the **Huhugam Heritage Center** on the Gila River Indian Reservation. It is located off of Interstate 10 near the Wild Horse Casino.

This heritage center is one of our favorite places to visit. In front of the center, there is a huge mound of earth. To enter, you must pass through the earth and through a huge red-framed door. The architecture is stunning and symbolic.

There is an amphitheater representing a ball court in the center of the courtyard. Two of their exhibits are permanent and the museum has rotating exhibits as well.

One of their exhibits contains information and photos of tribal members who have served in the US military. Guests can read information about Ira Hayes: one of the soldiers that raised the flag at Iwo Jima. Ira was born in a small town not far from the Cultural Center.

The other permanent exhibit is located in the main building and displays artifacts from the Snaketown excavation and information about the Gila River Indian community. The pottery and baskets are priceless artifacts from a prior civilization. Fantastic place to visit.

The **Jewish History Museum** focuses on the contribution of the Jewish community in the development of Tucson. Next door, there is a Holocaust Museum honoring relatives of Tucson residents and survivors of the Holocaust. Oral testimonies and photos are part of the exhibit.

Located in the Old City Hall building in Nogales, visitors will find the **Pimeria Alta Museum.** The exhibits include an antique fire wagon, printing press, information on the local ranches and several other historic artifacts from the Nogales area.

We found two interesting items at this museum. There is a painting of the Virgin of Guadalupe from the early 1700s that was brought to this area by a well-known early resident, Pete Kitchen. The painting was damaged in an Apache raid, but was restored and given to the museum for all of us to view and enjoy.

There are large murals hanging in the biggest room. Two of those murals were painted by Salvador Corona, the famous muralist and bullfighter.

The **Mohave Museum of History and Arts**, located in Kingman, is a recommended stop for anyone in the area. The museum has a collection of old mining equipment, cattle brands and other Western artifacts. The murals, however, are one of the key features in this museum. Large murals depict Arizona history in brilliant color. There is also information about the tattooing traditions and styles of the Mohave Indians.

In one room, there is an exhibit on Andy Devine, a local boy. Good information and great photos. This was an educational and interesting place.

If you love tiny, well-crafted things of all kinds, colors and shapes, you will love the **Mini Time Museum of Miniatures** in Tucson. There are miniatures that will excite anyone. There are houses, furniture, clowns, stuffed animals and angels. The houses come in all sizes (tiny, of course) colors and shapes. There is also a collection of German-made doll houses made in the 1600s and 1700s. One special feature for us was the fairy tree. A neat experience. Beware! This museum is likely to bring out the child in you. Midge's daughter, Teresa, was impressed with the collection of miniatures.

While researching museums in the Tucson area, we found the **Postal History Foundation**. Arriving at the site, we soon realized that it is not a museum, but after taking a tour with a volunteer, we were grateful we had found this place. The foundation gathers old postage stamps and collections and volunteers sort the stamps into specific categories. Stamp collectors can purchase the stamps. The interesting aspect of this foundation is the educational component. They have designed teaching plans that incorporate postal stamps in the educational plan. Teachers can request these teaching tools with the accompanying stamps at no cost to the teacher or school.

The **Gila Bend Museum** is located on the main street. The exhibits include historical artifacts, information about the Indian sites in the area, pottery and other Indian artifacts. One exhibit caught our attention: detailed information about the Oatman Massacre site. We were going to see that site the following day. It is where the Oatman family was massacred and the raiding Indians captured two, female children. Small museum but interesting.

The **Heard Museum** in Phoenix is a must-see destination for anyone who loves Indian art of all kinds. The building is stunning, the collection of art is phenomenal. The pottery, the baskets, the Kachinas, the rugs, the life sticks, the sculptures, the jewelry and so much more kept us occupied and enthralled for hours.

On that day, they had an exhibit of Georgia O'Keeffe paintings. Wow! We saw some of her art for the very first time. What a treat. After that exhibit, we were glowing with the excitement of it all.

Then, we moved onto the next exhibit. The name of the exhibit: Indian Boarding Schools. Information about the purpose of the schools, the policy of taking children out of homes, the jailing of parents who refused to send their children, the placing of children in schools two thousand miles away from home, burying children who died in the school cemetery and informing their parents two months later. The more we read, the more depressed we became. It is a part of American history, but on that particular day, the statement that you cannot judge the past by the values of today did not work very well. Spending some time outdoors amongst the beautiful sculptures rejuvenated the spirit.

There was a newspaper article about the opening of a new museum in Tucson, **The Old Pascua Museum and Cultural Center.** Upon arriving at the site, we found a small adobe house in a residential neighborhood. The museum consisted of information about the Yaqui tribe and some beautiful Yaqui ceremonial masks. The museum was small but the experience was large due to our interactions with the docent. He gave us information about the persecution of the Yaquis in Mexico and their journey to the Tucson area. Our knowledge base significantly increased on that day.

The **Museum of Northern Arizona** in Flagstaff is so much more than a building that contains artifacts and information about the Colorado Plateau. True, their collection of Indian artifacts is extensive and their information is educational, but their mission also extends to providing the community an opportunity to interact with artists, educators and nature. A variety of learning opportunities is offered at this museum.

Scottsdale's **Museum of the West** is a recent addition to the exceptional museums in Arizona. Upon arriving at the museum, it was amazing to see the quality of art in this new museum. The building is large and constructed in a way that the place is bright and airy. The pottery, the paintings, and the sculptures are from renowned artists and are exquisitely exhibited. One of the exhibits contained pieces of art from Basha's Gallery in Glendale.

Some of the items exhibited here were unique: rifles, arrows, lassos, holsters, sheriff badges, leg irons and handcuffs. Large collections of each were exhibited. On the way out, we stopped at the Heritage Gallery: a wall of pictures honoring numerous individuals who contributed to the development of the West. This museum was a great experience.

University of Arizona Art Museum in Tucson is an interesting adventure. The museum has two permanent collections; all other exhibits are temporary and have included such artists as Andy Warhol and Salvador Dali. The museum gives the community the opportunity to view art from a large variety of mediums and artists.

On the first floor, there is an permanent Jacques and Yulla Lipchitz exhibit containing some of the artist's sculptures, clay models and some of his tools. Guests should not miss the permanent exhibit on the second floor. It contains fully restored and magnificent Medieval/Renaissance art.

In an historical part of Tucson and on a very small plot of land, a building was erected to house the **Tucson Museum**

of Art. The inside of the building contains wide ramps which guide you from one exhibit to another and one floor to another. Their permanent collection is the Art of Latin America. This museum features several rotating exhibits per year. They feature current artists as well as renowned artists. Admission to this museum is free every second Sunday of the month. Every visit to this museum has been educational and enjoyable.

Prescott is host to one of the well-known museums of Arizona: **Sharlot Hall Museum**. The museum is on a sizable piece of property and contains a collection of historic buildings. The goal is to preserve these treasures of the past. One such treasure is Fort Misery; the oldest log cabin in Arizona. Another significant building on the museum property is the log cabin that served as the first Capitol of Arizona. A minimum of eight buildings have been protected and preserved through the efforts of Sharlot Hall. The buildings on the property are open to guests and contain information about their usage as well as historic artifacts. Information about Sharlot Hall and her contribution to the history of this state is also available in the main building.

We have shared with you some of the museums we have visited in our adopted state. You mean there are more? Oh, yes! We did not include the museums that we visit at specific sites, e.g. Fort Lowell. Besides reading and researching, we have used museums as a reliable source of collecting dots. Dots are little pieces of Arizona history that someday will become a collage.

GHOST TOWNS

*"Only in seeking is there mystery,
without which there is nothing."*

- Marion De Grazia

We were born and raised in New England and are accustomed to the terms; blizzard, thunderstorm, ice storm, sleet, freezing rain, snow, humidity, rain and floods. The term "Ghost Town," however, is not frequently spoken in New England. As a matter of fact, we do not recall ever seeing one in that part of the country.

Arriving in Arizona, we went to the Chamber of Commerce to gather information and came home with every magazine they had. Wow! A picture of a ghost town. Daily, Midge read the paper and, every week, they featured a mining camp or town. I would browse through tour information on the computer, and find information on ghost town tours.

How many ghost towns can there be in this state? After some research, we came up with this information: it is estimated that Arizona has two hundred and seventy-five ghost towns. There are many other smaller historical sites with very few remains. That answer sounded like a challenge to us. Two hundred and seventy-five towns to see, so better get going! From the very beginning, the goal has been to see as many towns as possible.

One of the things we had not yet discovered is that some ghost towns still have people living there. A ghost town has no post office, but may have ranchers and other residents within its boundaries. The majority of the towns or camps were mining towns, railroad towns or temporary camps. Some of the sites look like everyone moved out yesterday and left all their belongings behind. A few of the places have one tin can and a piece of lumber left behind to show proof of occupation. Sometimes, on the ghost town websites, they claim there are no remains. To date, we have always found some proof that someone once lived there.

Our friends will gladly climb aboard Gypsy to go explore a new town; they always add to the enjoyment of exploring a new site. They also add to the humor of bouncing on the rough dirt roads and driving through rivers. We will share with you some of the towns and camps we have explored. We hope the journey will be as enjoyable for you as it was for us.

Helvetia was our introduction to ghost towns. Helvetia was founded to provide lodging for the men who worked in the surrounding copper mines. In its heyday, there were three hundred inhabitants, mainly Mexicans. The town also had a hotel to accommodate visitors. It is located in the foothills of the Santa Rita mountains in Pima county.

The directions led us to the cemetery. Reportedly, the remainder of the town had been bulldozed and buried. On that day, we did find the cemetery, took pictures and proudly returned home.

About two years later, the adobe ruins of the Helvetia hotel were standing straight and proud in front of us. Two adobe corners, about five feet high, still remain. Fence posts, roof covering, lumber and rusty tin cans are scattered in the area of the hotel. After months of research, we had finally found proof that Helvetia had existed.

A couple arrived in their ATV and pointed out an abandoned mine about a mile down the road. At the site, there was a tailing pile with an abundance of obsidian rocks. There was also a shaft with no lock on its door. It was tempting to open the door and look inside. We chose not to look.

Pearce is located in Sulphur Springs Valley, south of Wilcox. When you arrive in the small town you are greeted by a welcome sign: "Historic Pearce Townsite. Gold discovered in 1895. 1920 population 1,500. 2000 population 15." This ghost town has current residents. Some families chose to stay in the area when the post office was discontinued and the mines closed.

Our first visit was in December 2010. This was when we thought we had become rich beyond all our dreams. Think millions!!! Let me explain how this happened. Abiding by the *"No Trespassing"* sign and taking our pictures by the gate, a little rock appeared before us. It was sparkling in the sunshine and it obviously contained a flake of gold. It was immediately picked up and adored. It returned to Green Valley on that day and remains in a prominent place in our "Box of Rocks." Even today, the monetary value of that beautiful "nugget" remains unknown. Could we possibly be incredibly rich?

Pearce includes several historic buildings, the old and new jail and the cemetery. The cemetery is well-kept and well-marked. We found grave markers of Union soldiers, Confederate soldiers, General Sherman's adjutant, and one very special grave marker of Sgt. George H. Platt (1832-1906). He died in Pearce AZ in August 1906. He was a member of the Union Light Guard of Ohio. This division was formed for the sole purpose of acting as body guards for President Abraham Lincoln. What an interesting find.

Currently, the gold mining has resumed. New mining technology now enables companies to extract gold from tailings and old mines. The tailings are gone and they are currently mining one of the hills. We will continue to monitor the progress of the mining operations.

Cerro Colorado is an uninhabited ghost town located on Arivaca Road between Amado and Arivaca. It was established by Charles Poston, the owner of the Sonora Exploring and Mining company. In 1861, Charles's brother, John, was in charge of the operations. The mine is remembered in Southern Arizona for the murder of mine employees by Mexican *banditos*.

Cerro Colorado was a silver mining operation and all the mines were pit mines, Today, some of the mines are fenced off and caution signs have been posted. There are, reportedly about fifteen open pits; we found only five during our explorations. Several foundations, mining ruins, tailing piles and a field of sludge remain.

One of the exciting activities in a ghost town is digging through the tailing piles in search of fame and fortune. A beautiful rock was found in this town. Unsure of the type of rock, we requested assistance from our geology professor. It was hematite and he was excited to see such a beautiful specimen. It currently sits on our patio with many other beautiful examples of perfection.

On one occasion, Jacqui, our friend from Scotland wanted to see a ghost town. Cerro Colorado seemed to be the perfect choice. She got out of the car and went to see one of the open pit mines. When she got into the car, she told us a story about seeing some strange critter looking up at her from the shaft. We had no idea what to tell her. When we looked at the picture, however, we all discovered that an owl was looking at her. Lesson to be learned. You never know what you will find in a mine shaft.

The main reason to bring family and friends to this site is to show them the sarcophagus. Yes, a sarcophagus! Alongside the dirt road, you will find the burial site of John Lee Poston (1830-1861). The grave marker says that Mexican banditos murdered him. It is questionable who is buried at this site. Some even say that no one is buried there. Let the historians debate the issue. We still enjoy bringing others to see the site. It is not every day that you see a sarcophagus on the side of a dirt road in an Arizona ghost town.

Apache is a small dot on the Arizona map on Route 80 south. It is located about thirty miles north of Douglas. Sue Smith, Midge and I headed to Apache. No town is evident. We saw two buildings: one that looked like a store and a little building by the railroad tracks. An old railroad car stood alone, apparently abandoned, by the tracks. The only movement in the area was the tumbleweed rolling down the street.

Our destination was the historical monument, not the ghost town. Alongside the road, a twenty-foot stone monument was erected to commemorate the surrender of Geronimo in 1886. The actual surrender site is about five miles from the existing monument, but it was placed by the road so it would be accessible to the public. It was built by the Civil Works Administration (CWA) in 1934. There is a plaque on the monument that explains in detail the actual surrender. The stone monument is impressive and the insertion of metates (grinding stones) into the stonework increases its beauty. What a nice touch. Impressive historic site. Exciting day.

Gleeson is a former copper mining town that is currently listed as a ghost town. There are some current residents and ranchers in the area. In its heyday, there were an estimated one thousand residents. This is a great place to explore. There are several existing structures: remains of an adobe hospital, a saloon, a school, and several residences. During exploration, parts of other structures, foundations and walls are easily found. This is a great ghost town if you want to easily see and photograph a mine. Another interesting feature of Gleeson is the restored jail. You can visit the jail by appointment only.

Another item on the list of places to see was called Rattlesnake Crafts and More The road to the crafts site was a one lane dirt road through the desert. It would be very easy to imagine that one was lost and heading in the opposite direction. Arriving at the two trailers, the amount of merchandise displayed was astonishing. One trailer contained a large variety of crafts made from rattlesnakes e.g. vertebrae necklaces and rattler key chains. In between the trailers, there was an incredible variety of items that are sometimes difficult to find: red wagons, flat irons, branding irons, wooden pitchforks, and multiple artifacts. One particular item came home with us and is currently hanging in our living room. He is a Spanish Conquistador made of foam. A great wall hanging. He did not rescue us, we rescued him.

American Flag is currently listed as an abandoned ghost town. It was founded in 1871 as a small mining town of no more than forty people. By 1890, the town was unoccupied. The founder later built the American Flag Ranch and concentrated his efforts on raising cattle, rather than mining. In 1880, seeing the upcoming demise of the town, the post office was moved to the American Flag Ranch. Today, the post office stands proudly next to an old barn and corral. It is the oldest surviving territorial post office building in the state of Arizona. It is listed on the National Register of Historic Places. The historical building appears majestic, with the flag waving, it's brilliant white walls surrounded by natural beauty. To ensure it's preservation, the post office can be viewed only from the outside. A fence prevents anyone getting too close.

The post office is located next to the Arizona Trail and we took the opportunity to walk the trail. Great day. Love to see some of the treasures that have been preserved in this state.

On our three-day trip to Portal in December 2015, **Camp Rucker** was on the agenda of places to see. Early one morning, Midge, Sue Smith and I took off in search of this camp. Heading down Route 80 and then on twenty-one miles of dirt road. The old fort is located in a remote area of the Chiracahua Mountains in the southeast corner of the state. Camp Rucker was a military outpost from 1878 - 1880. After reading the directions for the tenth time, we finally found the pull-off and exited the vehicle. The scenery was spectacular. What a beautiful site for a military outpost. However, you could also call it isolated!

There were several intact and semi-intact adobe structures from the original fort. It was the first time we had ever seen so many adobe structures in one location. There were some signs on the buildings indicating their usage. On the same site, there are also the remains of a 1930s ranch house, barn and corral.

What an exciting site to see. We were indeed proud of ourselves for finding it! Oh, another exciting thing happened here. On the way out of the site, a Montezuma Quail was spotted and it even posed for us. Another great Arizona photo opportunity.

Brigham City was a Mormon establishment founded by families from Salt Lake City. The town was formerly known as Ballenger's Camp. It was founded in 1876 and was abandoned in 1881. The lack of water for agriculture was the primary reason the establishment was left unoccupied. Brigham City is located about one mile north of current day Winslow.

The homes were built inside a protective wall. Today, a large section of the stone wall still remains and gives the settlement an air of mystery, intrigue and elegance when you walk toward the entrance. There are some semi-intact adobe remains, some foundations, portions of smaller walls and one intact stone building.

It was an interesting site to visit. It was a deviation from the mining camp and the railroad town. It is currently listed as an abandoned ghost town and has been placed on the National Register of Historic Places.

In April 2015, we arrived at the ghost town of **Camp Hyder**. The history of this camp is very interesting. As the story goes, General George Patton selected a desert area in Arizona and California in which to train his troops in preparation for deployment to the North African desert. About one thousand troops were trained in this area. The camp was active from

1942 through 1944. When we arrived, the first thing we noticed was the isolation of the camp.

It was definitely a great place to explore. Several wooden structures still remain. Looking at the buildings, our guess was that they were the living quarters for the high-ranking officers in the area. The exploration, however, was limited to the exterior of the buildings because of the abundance of "No Trespassing" signs. It was exciting to visit this ghost town. Can you imagine that we walked where General Patton once walked? Great piece of history. The only unfortunate part is that there is no information on-site that tells the public about the historical value of this site.

Greaterville. Every time we hear about this ghost town, we think of the phrase, "There is gold in them thar hills". One day, we took off through Box Canyon in search of this town. There are current residents in this area and it is on private property. The road to the town has a gate with a "No Trespassing sign." Pictures of one of the remaining buildings can be taken from the gate.

The thrill, however, was not in visiting the ghost town. The excitement was being in the area. Currently, gold hunters still come to the area with metal detectors searching for surface gold. Reportedly, gold nuggets are still being found. We drove slowly through the area hoping to spot a huge gold nugget on the side of the hills. Zero nuggets came home.

The name **Sasco** stands for Southern Arizona Smelting Company. This town processed the copper ore from the Silverbell Mine. In its heyday, about six hundred people lived in this town. The smelting operations were closed due to a lack of profit. The town is currently unoccupied.

In April 2014, we drove to Red Rock and headed down a paved road, which later turned to a dirt road, which later turned to a poorly maintained dirt road. At one point, the dirt road crossed the Santa Cruz river; the river always flows in this section because it is downriver from the water treatment plant. At the river, the cows were standing in the water and the water level appeared to be above our comfort level. Then, a rancher came from the opposite direction and crossed the river. He told us to stay on the left-hand side. The cows watched us cross!

What a great find this town was. There were several remains: a semi-intact stone hotel, a dynamite shack, foundations, storage areas, and remnants of a large smelter. The area was worthy of exploration on both sides of the road. Near the smelter remains, there is a wall with the letters SASCO on it.

In the springtime, the surrounding area is a great place to come see the wild flowers. We have seen an incredible bloom of orange globe mallows in this area.

Pantano Station is currently listed as an unoccupied ghost town. In its heyday, it was a vibrant railroad community. In the late 1950s, the railroad service terminated and in 1960, the railroad took down all of the existing structures. In April 2014, we ventured out into that area and went to explore this town. The literature indicated that the only remaining features were a water tank near the railroad tracks and a cemetery. We found the water tank, several foundations, cement stairs, part of a fence, rusted tin cans, glass and pieces of dinner plates. The cemetery was not located. There is an information kiosk at this site that highlights the history of the town.

Salero is a ghost town we read about in the book *Landscapes of Fraud* by Thomas E. Sheridan. It is located in the Santa Rita Mountains, east of Tubac. The Salero mine has a very interesting history and a list of re-incarnations. In the 18th century the Jesuits mined it for silver. In 1857, the mining area was moved and mined by the Salero Mining Company, with its headquarters in Tubac. The mine was relocated in 1870 and is currently located a few miles east of its original location. The current site is located on Salero Ranch land and is closed to the public in an attempt to preserve the structures.

It took some effort to find the directions to the site, but, in 2015, Mary, Irma, Midge, Gypsy and I headed to find this historical site. With plenty of drinking water, lunch, and plenty of gas, a successful trip was inevitable. Forging a river, Gypsy headed west in search of our goal. Arriving at our destination, there was a problem. There was a gate on the road up to the town and there was a huge "No Trespassing" sign. On that day, the pictures of the remaining structures were taken from the top of a boulder near the gate.

Salero is reportedly one of the best-preserved ghost towns in Arizona, so for months we searched for contact information. Finally, permission was granted for us to walk around the gate and visit the town. In February 2016, Irma, Betty, Midge, Gypsy and I returned to the same gate. What a joy to be able to walk through this site. The only living creatures spotted on that particular day were cattle who were definitely curious as to why we were there.

There are remains of adobe structures, intact buildings (with replaced roofs), stone buildings and remnants of other buildings seen in the area. Core samples from the mine can be seen strewn around the area. When walking up toward the town, the mine is clearly visible. We did not explore the mine area or the cemetery. Ghost town websites report that Horace C. Grosvenor is buried in the Salero cemetery. Reports also state that two other owners of the mine were killed in Salero by Apache raiders.

It was a great site filled with history. The trip to the mine is filled with beautiful scenery and the ride through the river is exhilarating. This site remains closed to the public and permission to visit is required prior to entering on private land. The caretaker at the mine site takes his job very seriously.

One of the fond memories of Salero was the noise level in the back seat when we crossed Sonoita Creek in 2016. Betty was clapping and announced to the world that she felt like a pioneer woman. Irma could not stop laughing. Our friends definitely enhance the enjoyment of exploring our new state.

Kentucky Camp is currently listed as an unoccupied ghost town. It was a mining town using hydraulic mining in search for gold. The camp is located in the Coronado National Forest on the east side of the Santa Rita Mountains. The nearest town is Sonoita and it can be accessed from Highway 83.

The drive to the town is on a dirt road through hills and fields covered with golden grass. Driving slowly on this road increased our ability to appreciate the scenery. Upon arriving, a short, steep road leads to a cluster of houses. There are five adobe buildings, the remains of a barn and one other building on the site. The camp is a cluster of structures that used to serve as offices and residences for the mining employees. The mining operations occurred on the other side of the hill. There is a path to the mining site. The mining site and the piping that provided water are still visible.

A special celebration was happening: one of the hydraulic guns had been returned to the site. Tours of the site were being offered on that day and rangers were available to answer any questions the guests might have. What a wonderful history lesson we received on that day.

This town site is currently being preserved. The Friends of Kentucky Camp are working with the Coronado National Forest to preserve and protect this state treasure. The camp has been placed on the National Register of Historic Places.

Ruby is one of the best-preserved ghost towns in the state. It was founded in 1907 as a mining town. It was originally called Montana Camp. The mine produced gold, silver, lead, zinc and copper. In its heyday, the population of the town was twelve hundred.

With our directions and adventurous spirit, Gypsy, Midge and I turned left on Ruby Road and headed south. The paved road is bumpy and not well maintained and with little notice, the road turns into a dirt road. The scenery along this stretch of the road is phenomenal. The road gets bumpier and crosses a stream about three times. At one point, a group of white cows was staring at us. It takes some time to get accustomed to the concept of open range. Onward toward Ruby!

Arriving at the townsite, we paid our admission fee to the caretaker and the day of exploration began. The literature says that most of the original buildings still remain. We saw several intact buildings, some partial wooden buildings, some partial adobe structures, and a lot of structures in a state of disrepair. This was our first experience in a large ghost town. It did not take us long to understand that "best preserved" meant that the buildings were still there. It did not mean painted and restored.

Better informed, the exploring and adventuring continued. To the south of the mine shaft, there is a tailing field. The tailings are grey and appear to be sand. When walking on the tailings, it is not hard to imagine being at a beach There is also a pond. Fishing and camping are allowed at the site.

The central feature of the site is the mine shaft. It is tall and quite obvious. They have closed off the road to the top, but it is visible from the ground level. The caretaker told us that, at dusk, about forty thousand bats come flying out of the shaft. What a sight that would be to see!

After walking around and exploring all of the remaining buildings, we wondered where everyone lived. There were not enough houses for twelve hundred people. Another lesson learned. The houses were for the mining company executives, the assayer, the doctor, the school teacher, and mining supervisors. One building was a schoolhouse and one was a mercantile. The employees who worked in the mine lived in tents in the surrounding area. On that particular day, a lot of knowledge about ghost towns was acquired.

It is always a joy to share this site with our friends and family. It is easy to imagine having lived here. On one occasion, we brought Midge's daughter, Cathy, to see Ruby. Our first stop was to show Cathy the mine shaft at the ghost town of Oro Blanco. The road abruptly ended; it had been washed away. The next stop was to show her California Gulch. The stream that crosses the road was running fast and the water level was above our comfort level. Never mind. Let's head for Ruby. That town was still there! Trip accomplished!

According to a newspaper article, the Ruby schoolhouse is in the process of being converted into a museum. What a wonderful addition this would be to an already interesting site.

Fairbanks is one of the easiest ghost towns to find and is also handicapped accessible. It is located ten miles west of Tombstone on State Route 82. Fairbanks was founded in 1881 as a railroad supply point and stage terminal, and was the nearest stagecoach stop to Tombstone. It later become a depot for shipment of cattle and silver ore from Tombstone.

Visitors can take a self-guided tour of this once booming and thriving Wild West town. Today, there are six structures remaining: the schoolhouse, a large commercial building, two residences, foundation of the hotel, stables, and outhouses. There is also a cemetery in the area. The buildings are well preserved. The day we arrived, another visitor shared with us the picture she took of the resident rattlesnake. She even pointed to where she had found the snake. Needless to say, the pictures of that building were taken from far away.

During another visit, it was surprising to find that the museum in the schoolhouse was open. We had the occasion to speak to the ranger and gathered information about the surrounding hiking trails.

The town site of Fairbanks is along the San Pedro River. As we cross the bridge over the river, we always look for water. We have always seen water flowing in this section of the river.

We found an article about the **Patagonia Back Road Ghost Towns.** The article described the route as a journey back in time. Midge, Gypsy, Mary, Bernadette and I decided to make it a full day of ghost town hunting. Our supplies included a tank full of gas, a cooler full of cold drinking water and lunch.

Leaving Patagonia, the dirt road was wide and very well maintained. The further from town, the narrower and less maintained the road became. It did not matter, our adventurous spirit and enthusiasm continued to move us south. The first stop on the journey was to watch the wild horses run in the field; the second stop was to view a wildflower up close; the third stop was to admire an intriguing rock formation. This could indeed become a very long day!

We finally arrived at the **Harshaw** town site. At one time, Harshaw was the largest producer of silver in the state of Arizona. There are current residents in the town and some of the remains are on private property. There are three, semi-intact buildings remaining: two adobe structures and one wooden structure. There is also a cemetery built on a hill; some of the gravesites are badly eroded. It was eerie to see the shovel leaning on the fence in the cemetery. Wonder why it was there!

Mowry was a mining community producing silver, lead and zinc. According to the directions, the town should have been visible. The town was not located on that day.

The next on the list of ghost towns was **Washington Camp**. It was used as a supply community for the mining town of Duquesne. In its heyday, the community had a population of up to one thousand residents. The town contained a general store, a school, and bunkhouses for the miners. The adventurous group was eager for more exploration. Success propelled us southward toward the next experience.

The next town was **Duquesne.** A right turn onto a rough dirt road led us to the town. There are several buildings remaining, some of which are old homes and the mining headquarters. There are numerous "No Trespassing" signs but all of the remains are close to the road and can be easily photographed. We saw no evidence of current residents.

At this point in our journey, the scenery began to change. There are fields of golden grasses and ranches with horses in the pastures. Something else is changing too. It is becoming obvious that we have been in the wilderness for too long. Mother Nature is calling! A border patrol car arrives and we asked him for directions to the nearest ladies room. He looked embarrassed by the question and looked distressed in having to tell us that the closest was in Patagonia. OK. That is how it goes sometimes when you travel the back roads and wilderness of Arizona.

The group became quieter, but proceeded south. Maybe the border patrol agent was wrong. A few miles down the road, a beautiful monument appeared. The monument is in honor of Fray Marcos de Niza, a Franciscan friar, who entered Arizona in 1539. He was the first European to enter the United States, west of the Rockies. We photographed the monument and looked at the beautiful scenery. Then, in a moment of need, Midge, Mary and I used the back of the monument to relieve the pressure in our bladders. Bernadette is the only one who declined.

The happy group entered the vehicle and went in search of the community of **Lochiel**. At one time, the community had a population of four hundred residents. Several buildings can be seen from the main road, but access to the town is blocked. The town is on private property. The one building that you can approach and explore is the schoolhouse. It was evident that attempts are being made to restore and preserve the beautiful little school. Lunch was eaten on the school grounds and photos were taken of the buildings visible from the road.

The border patrol agent had recommended that we do the return trip through the San Rafael Valley. Usually, taking recommendations from people who know about the area adds to the enjoyment of the journey. What a surprise was in store for us! Golden grass as far as you could see. The grass was glistening in the sun. Passing by the San Rafael Ranch, the group quickly exited the vehicle. The primary focus was to take pictures of the ranch and the miles and miles of golden grass. Such beauty is hard to ignore. By the way, John Wayne reportedly slept at this ranch.

Heading north through the valley, golden grass, gorgeous mountain ranges, cattle grazing and several calves were seen. Every so often, Bernadette would ask how far it was to Patagonia. We drove on. Eventually, Patagonia was in sight and Bernadette's first stop was to use the facility.

This was a day trip that will be remembered for a very long time by all the participants. We will remember the scenery, the sense of adventure, the laughter, the gold grass, the bond that was formed amongst friends and, lastly the monument to Fray Marcos that was used as a relief in time of great need.

A funny postscript to this trip. About two years later, Irma went on a tour to the San Rafael Ranch. On the way there, the van stopped at the monument to Fray Marcos. Immediately, she thought "Oh! This is the monument they were talking about!" Thank you, Irma, for not telling everyone on the tour about the monument story.

The ghost town of **Pearce Ferry** is located at the bottom of the Grand Canyon. From Route 93, it is accessed by Pearce Ferry Road. The last five miles of the journey are a steep and bumpy dirt road.

This was the place where John Wesley Powell reportedly pulled his boats out of the Colorado at the end of his Grand Canyon expedition. In the 1930s and 1940s, it was a popular destination for Hoover Dam tourists. There were plans to build a resort on that spot. The resort plans did not materialize and, today, very little remains.

In the area, there are signs posted by the National Park

service that explain the history of the tourist stop and the involvement of the CCC in the area. A public restroom and a picnic area is available for canyon guests.

The remains of a CCC building, a concrete slab and the remnants of a wooden structure are visible. The mile-high canyon walls were a spectacular backdrop to this unique and intriguing ghost town. We were thrilled to have found this historical place. For some, however, the road may appear daunting. A four-wheel drive is not necessary to access this ghost town.

We have visited dozens of Arizona ghost towns. We have shared some of the sites with you in an attempt to demonstrate that there is a wide variety of unoccupied, abandoned, preserved, restored and occupied ghost towns in this state. We have enjoyed every one of them. To us, they are the settlements of days gone by. In these places, people lived, laughed, prayed, married, gave birth, and died. It feels like an honor to walk amongst them.

Sometimes people ask us where we find all of these towns. We use websites as our main resource. There are several sites to choose from. If you find a website that has banjo music in the background, you have found the site that we use. In selecting which of the towns you will visit, read the information carefully. Some of the dirt roads to these towns can be narrow and poorly maintained. Sometimes, narrow roads can cause what they call "Desert Striping" (scratches on the car, produced by trees branches near the edge of the road). If you choose to explore, you may see us in the wilderness, searching for one more site where someone once lived.

ROUTE 66 IN ARIZONA

The name "Route 66" always instills a sense of adventure and excitement. It is almost a challenge to come see and experience. On our twenty-one-month adventure across the United States, we saw many sections of Route 66 in several states. We loved seeing the blue whale, Paul Bunyan (with his axe), teepees, narrow trestle bridges and red bricked roads.

When we became residents of Arizona, we were thrilled to discover that our adopted state has four hundred miles of Route 66 for us to discover and enjoy. The Arizona route extends from the New Mexico border to Needles, California. We have discovered a large portion of the route, one section at a time. We will share with you some of our adventures on The Mother Road and we will be traveling from east to west.

In October 2015, Midge, Dotty, Irma and I left for a road trip to Chaco Canyon in New Mexico. On the return leg of the trip, we entered the **Painted Desert** and the **Petrified Forest National Park** from the western entrance.

When we entered the Painted Desert, we immediately noticed that the array of colors was stunning. It is as if you do not know where to look, where to point the camera or where to stand to get the best view. The scenery was colored red, grey, brown, yellow, green, tan and black. Some of the colors are in layers, some are mixed and some stand alone. What a magnificent sight to behold. Mother Nature definitely puts on a spectacular show in this park.

We drove through the park (slowly, so we didn't miss anything) and after a while we started seeing some of the petrified wood. Erosion has done its work - we can now see remnants of a time long ago. We also stopped to see the Indian ruins and the petroglyphs. The petroglyphs at Newspaper Rock can be seen from a distance through a view finder. It is well worth a stop at this attraction.

Then, we arrived at this surprising stop. The signage reads as follows: *"Highway of Dreams - Petrified Forest is the only National Park in the country with a portion of Historic Route 66 within its boundaries. You are currently standing where the Mother Road used to be, with the line of telephone poles paralleling its alignment through the park. This stretch of Route 66 was open from 1926 until 1958 and was the primary way millions of travelers initially experienced Petrified Forest and Painted Desert. Imagine driving to this spot in the 1932 Studebaker before you, when this road was in its heyday!"*

We could see the telephones poles stretching for miles across the land and heading west. Got a great photo of the Mother Road on that day. Also got to explore and experience two beautiful parks.

We visited **Holbrook** on two separate occasions. There are some endearing Route 66 attractions in the downtown area and many good eating places. There are two places, however, that we fondly remember. The Rainbow Rock Shop is a great place to find any type of rock you wish, as well as pieces of petrified wood. The other location that was intriguing and memorable was the Wigwam Village Motel. When we stopped to see the attraction, some of the wigwams were occupied. We have discussed on many occasions that we would like to stay in one of the wigwams someday. Maybe on our next trip.

Winslow is thirty-two miles west of Holbrook. We had the opportunity to stand on the corner in Winslow Arizona. We did not sing the song: we did not want to offend the residents. We did, however, get our picture taken with the statue of the man with his guitar and we even hugged him. An additional sculpture was added to the famous corner in 2016. This should add to the enjoyment.

At the intersection, there is a large Historic Route 66 sign painted on the road. Similar signs are visible throughout the downtown area. The area is worthy of exploration. We walked east from the corner of Second and Kinsley and we found a bathtub on top of a building - it even had a mannequin in it! We also found an historical marker indicating that a historical wagon road ran right through Winslow starting in 1858.

The La Posada Hotel was designed in the 1920s by architect Mary Jane Colter. It is described as her Southwestern masterpiece. In it's heyday, during the 1930's, the list of celebrities and dignitaries who stayed at the La Posada is staggering. The list includes: Mary Jane Colter, Charles Lindbergh, Carole Lombard, Bob Hope, Gene Autry, Barry Goldwater, Howard Hughes, President Franklin Roosevelt, President Harry Truman, Isabella Greenway, Amelia Earhart, Will Rogers, Shirley Temple, Clark Gable and Albert Einstein. Yes, even John Wayne slept here. The hotel was closed for forty years but has been fully and lovingly restored. It was reopened in 1998. After singing on the corner and staring at the man in the bathtub, this is a treat we highly recommend. It is an elegant, extravagant hotel which has the ability to bring you back in time. If you choose to eat in their dining room, their chocolate soufflé is a decadent extravagance, if they have it on the menu. Midge, Irma, Dotty and I consumed the soufflé in about seventeen seconds.

Meteor City is fourteen miles west of Winslow. From Interstate 40, it is easy to spot the abandoned Route 66 attraction. The feature that is most prominent on the site is the domed gift shop. The teepees and large dream catcher add to the ambience. It is apparent that its been closed for some time. The debris and broken signs speak of it's painful demise.

Amongst the beautiful murals and the graffiti, there is

a silhouette that is haunting to look at. It is the stenciled silhouette of a man, dressed in black, holding a face in his hand. The face of whom is unknown and the significance remains a mystery. Very interesting!

At this site, we walked around taking pictures of the murals, structures, signs, debris, and the dream catcher. Here, we even had the opportunity to take a picture of the original Route 66. Walking around, Irma stubbed her toe on a rock and discovered that it was a beautiful piece of petrified wood. We all left with rocks, as souvenirs, from the remains of a Route 66 attraction.

The sign says "*Welcome to **Two Guns**.*" It is the remains of a Route 66 theme park. Several structures remain at this site: a gas station, a campground, a gift shop, a diner, a pool, and several stone structures that appear to have been a hotel and a zoo. One of the buildings has Mountain Lions stenciled on the front, so that must have been part of the zoo.

It is a large site and we walked around looking at all the stone structures. One of the structures looked like a Hogan, another looked like a tower, and along Canyon Diablo, the structures appeared to have been hotel rooms. If you stop here, make sure to check out the murals on the water towers.

It is easy to imagine that this would have been an inviting stop for travelers on Route 66. Today, it is listed as a ghost town. It was definitely a great site to explore.

Twin Arrows is alongside Interstate 40. Do not fear. You will not miss the site. The prominent feature is two, very large arrows sticking in the ground. The arrows are truly impressive and unique. They would definitely have enticed travelers to stop at this site. It sure prompted us to stop. They currently have jersey barriers near the road so you cannot drive into the parking lot, but visitors climb over the barriers to explore this interesting place.

The site contains a cafe, a trading post, and several other

smaller structures. It is in a state of disarray and has apparently been closed for some time. The buildings are littered with graffiti and five stenciled silhouettes of a man, dressed in black, holding a face in his hands. Wait a minute! This is the same silhouette we saw at Meteor City. We left this site hoping that, someday, we will meet the artist so we can understand the significance of this haunting silhouette.

Heading into Flagstaff, we did not forget to stop in **Winona, AZ.** There is an original trestle bridge with an original section of Route 66 at this stop. We stopped at the bridge and walked on the original road. There is signage that indicates that the bridge has been placed on the National Register of Historical Places. It was a great opportunity to photograph an original section of the route. We then traveled west on Winona Road, the original Route 66, toward Flagstaff.

Flagstaff is an enjoyable and energetic city. A former lumber and railroad town, it continues to prosper due, in part to the influx of students (Northern Arizona University), ski enthusiasts, outdoor lovers and tourists. The San Francisco Peaks offer the city some spectacular scenery.

Route 66 snakes it way across the city. The route is currently marked Business 40. When we drove the route across town, we saw many remnants of days gone by. The existing original Route 66 motels and restaurants are mixed in with the new businesses. Some of the neon signs are impressive and surely must have enticed travelers to stop, rest, and eat.

Flagstaff was less affected by the demise of Route 66 than other cities and towns. Currently, the city takes great pride in the fact that it was on the Mother Road. One place to check out is the Museum Club. It is a renovated structure; it is currently a club and a museum. A cool place to take a photo. We have been to Flagstaff several times and we always enjoy the time we spend in the area.

Williams is the westernmost city to be affected by the

Route 40 bypass. Today, it is the gateway to the Grand Canyon. When you arrive, it is apparent that Williams, like Flagstaff, takes full advantage of their Route 66 heritage. The town has old-fashioned streetlights, several gift shops with Route 66 memorabilia, antique cars, beautiful murals, neon lights, a soda fountain, a gas station museum with vintage gas pumps, and diners with statues of Betty Boop.

We found it both relaxing and exciting to walk around this beautiful downtown. They also offer horse and buggy rides for those who choose not to walk. We have recently heard that there is new attraction in town: a zip line in the downtown area. Enjoyable town to visit.

Ash Fork is easily accessible from Interstate 40. The town is known as the Flagstone Capital of the United States. It was a former railroad town and later became a stop on Route 66. Currently, the town has approximately five hundred residents.

There are two main streets through the town and many original Route 66 signs and structures can be seen in the downtown area. Zettlers Route 66 store is one of the original buildings. They are currently open and they sell a wide variety of Route 66 memorabilia. The owners were pleased and eager to share information about the area. Ash Fork is seeing an increase of Route 66 visitors from the United States and abroad.

On the north side of town, there is a memorial to the railroad which contributed to the development of Ash Fork. At the memorial, a plaque explains the growth of the town and its significance in the development of the West. This town was a great find and it is a fun place to explore.

Leaving Ash Fork, we headed west and, at the next exit, we took **Crookton Road**. This is a section of the Historical Route 66 that leads to Seligman. We always find it fun and exciting to travel on part of the original road. At Zettlers store in Ash Fork, they had shared with us that we were in for a treat. Look! Prairie dog mounds. My goodness, they were everywhere. Look! A prairie dog looking at us! How thrilling to see them.

What are those signs up ahead? They can't be Burma Shave signs! Yes, they are! We saw three sets of Burma Shave signs. One example: "The one who drives when - he's been drinking - depends on you - to do his thinking - Burma Shave." Of course, we had to stop and take pictures of the historic signs. While we were taking the pictures, a prairie dog was staring at us, so we took his picture.

What an incredibly relaxing road to travel. It was easy to imagine the excitement of the travelers in the 1930s and 1940s. Golden grasses, rolling hills, prairie dogs, trains heading west, trains heading east, blue sky and puffy white clouds. Beautiful terrain. Nostalgic signs.

Seligman is one of our favorite stops on Route 66. We believe it is one of the best places to feel the spirit of the old route. The town retains its character and offers visitors great photo opportunities and plenty of time to dream of how it used to be when visitors arrived here in the 1950s and 1960s. This town makes us smile and was the inspiration for the town of Radiator Springs in the movie *Cars*.

Several historic structures are still evident in this town: the Cottage Hotel, the Rusty Bolt, the Copper Cart and the famous Snow Cap Drive-In. There is an abundance of Route 66 memorabilia and dozens of antique cars and trucks. There is also a sign-a-truck where you have the opportunity to sign your name on the vehicle. Photo opportunities appear on every block. You can even take a picture of the back of a plane sticking out of a building.

What a great place to walk around and feel the excitement of the visitors. Every time we have been to Seligman, tour buses have arrived and a whole new group of visitors appear surprised and awed by what they are seeing. I can only imagine how many visitors and children have relived the wonder of the Old Route 66.

In 2016, we returned to Seligman to spend an overnight at the Stagecoach 66 Motel. We wanted to experience an overnight in one of our favorite Route 66 stops. This gave us the opportunity to explore the town when all of the daily visitors were gone.

We checked into the motel and off we went to explore our themed rooms. Dotty headed for her Harley Davidson room and we headed to our Elvis room. What a surprise when we opened the door. Bright red bedspread, a life-size cut out of Elvis, pictures of Elvis everywhere and ELVIS in the tile leading to the bathroom. There was no doubt that we had entered the Elvis room. We got plenty of pictures and then we headed next door to see Dotty's Harley room. Both rooms were really cool. What a great way to attract customers. We will never forget our overnight stay in Seligman.

Grand Canyon Caverns is a twenty-mile drive west of Seligman. You will find a large green sign indicating that you have arrived. The complex is located on the Old Route 66 loop and it is quite noticeable. There is a forty-eight-unit motel with store, swimming pool, laundromat, diner, and an old gas station. For those interested in caves, the caverns offers tours, cave exploring and even has a cave suite you can rent for a good night's sleep.

We walked around the grounds to take pictures of the large dinosaurs, the antique cars and trucks and to absorb the ambiance of a Route 66 attraction. The gas station at the caverns is called Radiator Springs; the same name as the town in the movie *Cars* (released by Pixar Animation Studios starring Lightning McQueen and Mater). There are plenty of antique cars and trucks to admire. There is also one very special truck: the Radiator Springs Gas Sign-a-Truck. There are markers near the old truck and all who come are invited to sign the truck. Some cute drawings and sayings on the vehicle!

We had checked the grounds and headed indoors to check the gift shop and diner. Before we left, we made sure to get a picture of Michael Flynn with Betty Boop: our souvenir of a great stop.

Peach Springs is located on the Hualapai Indian Reservation. The Hualapai Lodge and the tribal community center is located in the town. At the Hualapai Lodge, they provide services such as food and lodging. Permits to drive down to the bottom of the Grand Cavern can be purchased at the lodge. At their gift shop, you can view or purchase the world-famous dolls made by the Hualapai members. The town is currently listed as a ghost town.

In **Valentine**, we found an historical site that is worthy of mention. In 1901, a two-story schoolhouse was built to serve as a day school for the Hualapai children and a boarding school for the Apache, Havasupai, Hopi, Mohave, Navajo and Papago children. The Truxton Indian school was closed in 1937. When we drove by the site, Midge asked that we stop and explore the remains of the school. She had just finished reading the book *People of the Blue Water* by Flora Gregg Iliff. Flora Gregg journeyed to Arizona in 1900 to teach elementary school at the Hualapai and Havasupai reservations. Midge was thrilled to see the actual school described in the book. The two-story school building remains, as well as two other structures. One of the structures has beautiful murals on the side. The town is currently listed as a ghost town.

An interesting note about Valentine. In its heyday, the Valentine post office would receive hundreds of cards from individuals who wanted their cards postmarked "Valentine, AZ" for their sweethearts.

Truxton was a town that existed only because of Route 66. It has no history prior to The Mother Road. It was built to accommodate travelers by providing food and lodging. The only remnants are a motel and a café. The town is currently listed as a ghost town.

Hackberry is an old silver mining town. The main attraction is the Hackberry General Store. This is the real-life counterpart of Lizzie's Curio Shop in the movie *Cars*. The movie idea originated after a discussion about the small towns that were affected by the re-routing of Route 66. Several towns and locations have been used as the inspiration for the movie.

As you enter the town, you cannot miss the sign: "*You Are Here - Hackberry General Store.*" There are plenty of antique cars and trucks, vintage gas pumps and Route 66 memorabilia to take pictures of. The store is a combination store and gift shop. All types of Route 66 souvenirs are available for those who are interested. The town is currently listed as a ghost town.

Before we left this fun attraction, we took a picture of Carolyn Flynn with Elvis: a cardboard Elvis, of course. Another unique stop.

Kingman has long been a main stopping place on Route 66. It is the main place to stop for lodging if you are traveling from Las Vegas to Phoenix on Route 93. It has predominantly been a railroad town. We had traveled through Kingman on two occasions but we had just driven through.

In 2014, we read that Kingman would be hosting the International Route 66 Festival on August 14-17. That meant we had to go. We made plans with Mike and Carolyn Flynn and the four of us went to participate in the event.

What we found was exciting. Route 66 signs everywhere, hundreds of antique cars and trucks, vendors, performers, and lots of Route 66 fans. We had the opportunity to explore the town, visit the Powerhouse and Route 66 Museum, attend some of the performances and we ate at Mr. D's Route 66 Diner. We also visited the courthouse and the Mohave County Jail. The jail was built in 1910 and has been placed on the National Register of Historic Places.

We sang, took plenty of photos, dreamed of owning some of the beautiful cars and we laughed. We had a fun time and have lots of fond memories of Kingman.

From Kingman to Oatman, the old Route 66 passes through desert and mountainous areas. The road is narrow and curves are plentiful. This is mining country, with depleted and current mines. We assumed that the next town would be Oatman. All of a sudden, we spotted a little complex called **Cool Springs**.

In its heyday, this establishment offered lodging, hot meals, water and gas on this lonely stretch of Route 66. Today, it is a small store, a museum and a gift shop. There is also an outhouse for those in need. Old cars and Route 66 memorabilia are abundant around the structure.

This remnant of a larger establishment stills offers some respite for those of us who travel. It also offers beautiful scenery and warm hospitality. One other feature we spotted offered us a photo opportunity. There is a Route 66 flag across the street and Midge got her picture taken there.

Traveling west to Oatman, we stopped at one of the pull-offs on the side of the road to admire the scenery. We could see some old mining remains in the distance and then we heard a burro. We looked and looked but we could not locate it. How cool was that!

Oatman is the westernmost town on the Arizona Route 66. The town is named in honor of Olive Oatman, who was captured by Indians, and later released. The town has a long history of mining, boom and bust. On the side of one building, the history of the town is written for all to see.

The town looks like a movie set, with its narrow streets, slumping buildings and the feel of the Old West. It feels like it has always been. We have been to Oatman on two occasions, but we would willingly go again. We have often thought about staying overnight at the Oatman Hotel. It is said that Clark Gable and Carol Lombard stayed there the first night after they were married in Kingman. If you wish to stay overnight, you go to the bar, put down your thirty dollars and they give you a room key. The policy is first come, first serve. Not having reservations has dissuaded us from staying there. Kingman is twenty-eight miles away if no rooms are available.

Anyway, Oatman will always hold a special place in our hearts. The first time we went, we were eating lunch in a gravel lot by the side of the road. A little burro walked back and forth, staring at us. Oh, I forgot to tell you about the burros! They were left to fend for themselves when the miners left and they have populated quite well. It is estimated that there are about two hundred living in the area. About twenty of those have claimed the town and the tourists as their own. People used to buy carrots to feed them. Currently, the store sells hay cubes to feed the cute burros. As long as you carry your bag with the hay cubes, you will always have friends in this town. The last time we visited the town, we saw several baby burros. How cute. This will always be one of our favorite towns on the Old Route 66. A lot of fun, western atmosphere, friendly people and many photo opportunities.

Everyone should have the opportunity to experience the beginning of auto travel. Take the time and get out there to "Get your kicks" on Route 66.

OTHER INTERESTING SITES

When we were developing the outline for the book, we thought that establishing categories for the sites was a great idea. Soon, we began to realize that many places do not fit in any of the categories. No problem. We just included another chapter. Welcome to the chapter that includes many places worthy of exploration and places that helped us piece together the history and fabric of Arizona.

Papago Park is a fourteen-hundred-acre municipal park that lies within the cities of Phoenix and Tempe. This hilly desert park contains picnic areas, hiking trails, bike paths and other recreational facilities. The park also contains several small lakes which are surrounded by tall palm trees. The water, the tall trees, the red dirt, the red sandstone formations, the green grass along the water's edge and the reeds in the lakes create an environment of spectacular natural beauty. There are benches strategically placed along the edges of the water for visitors to sit, relax, enjoy and be thankful for such a beautiful place in a city environment.

A striking feature in the park is the Red Sandstone formations that stand proud and tall. The Hole in the Rock is readily visible in one of the sandstone formations. It is listed as an Archaeological Site and it is believed that the hole was used as a calendar device by the Hohokam tribe. Today, it is a destination for hikers and photographers.

On the top of a desert hill, we spotted a pyramid style structure. Upon investigation, we discovered that it was the tomb of George Hunt, Arizona's first governor. Near the tomb, there is a marker indicating all of the family members buried there. The tomb is quite large and can be easily accessed from the parking lot. The tomb has been placed on the National Register of Historic Places. There are also benches at the site where visitors can sit and enjoy a great view of the city of Phoenix.

We enjoyed the natural beauty and serenity of this park. However, we must admit that we came to this site because of its history. Between 1942-1944, this area was a POW camp that was initially designed to house Italian prisoners. In 1944, the decision was made to house only German prisoners at this camp. In this desert environment, there stood a camp surrounded by barbed wire fences and guard towers.

There were other POW camps in Arizona during WWII, but this camp is famous for the "Great Papago Escape." In 1944, twenty-five German prisoners exited the camp via a one hundred and seventy-eight-foot tunnel. All were captured. The event, however, is well documented in several Arizona books. There is a detailed description of the escape in the book *Arizona: A Cavalcade of History* by Marshall Trimble.

This park is a beautiful and historic site. It has been designated as a Phoenix Point of Pride.

Picacho Peak State Park lies along Interstate 10 near the community of Picacho. The beautiful rock formation in the park appears to be a volcanic neck, but it is currently believed that it is a tilted rock that was covered by a lava flow. There are two, well-preserved spatter cones in the area that remain as proof of past volcanic activity. The unusual rock formation served as a guide to early settlers and still serves as a guide to travelers. We use this rock as a guide regarding distance from home.

The park has camping facilities, picnic areas and hiking trails. The beautiful desert landscape includes a wide variety of desert flora and saguaro cactus. This state park is well known for its spring wildflowers after a good winter rain. One spring, we visited the park during the spring poppy bloom and it was beautiful. We have not, however, seen the entire mountain side covered by brilliant yellow poppies. The locals say it happens every seven to ten years, so we will be lucky someday.

The park is also known for its annual re-enactment of the Battle of Picacho Pass. This was the second westernmost battle of the Civil War in which three soldiers were killed. In early March, you can see several white tents and men in grey and blue uniforms. A unique event. There is a memorial to the battle near the entrance of the park.

There is also a memorial to the Mormon Battalion trail. In 1846, the Mormon Battalion camped in this area on their way to California. There are many memorials to the Battalion located around Arizona.

Picacho Peak became a star when it was featured in the novel *The Host* by Stephanie Meyer. This park allows visitors the opportunity to enjoy time in a beautiful desert landscape and the chance to absorb the historical significance of this place.

Biosphere 2 is a forty-acre site located near the town of Oracle. It was originally built to be an artificial living environment to see if the closed system could sustain human life. Its mission is research, outreach, teaching and learning about earth. There have been a variety of missions and different owners throughout the years. Since 2011, the University of Arizona has owned the facility.

Arriving at the site, the architecture of the building was surprising. We had never seen a complex like this. With its glass, spires and domes, the structure is beautiful, stunning and oddly unfamiliar. It is clear that we had arrived at a site that is interesting, different and important.

Guided tours are available and the public is able to view many areas of the complex such as a rainforest, an ocean with a reef, mangrove wetlands, savannah grasslands and a desert area. The tours also bring visitors to the building that contains the "lung" which provided oxygen to the complex. During the tour, current research projects are described.

This is an historical site and a one-of-a-kind. The information provided was valuable and we left better informed than when we arrived. For those who wish to spend more time at the facility, food is available. A beautiful complex in a gorgeous natural setting. A great site to visit and to bring family and friends.

The sign at the rest area says: "This landscape is a hotbed of Volcanic activity. With more than 400 volcanoes within fifty miles, the **Springerville Volcanic Field** is the third largest in the continental U.S." The volcanic field lies between Show Low and Springerville and can be seen driving along Route 60.

Some of the rocks in this area have been estimated to be two million years old. The newest rocks in the area are estimated to be three hundred thousand years old. Driving along on Route 60, it is easy to tell the newer flows from the earlier activity. The older areas have more vegetation and the newer parts are covered with grass and little vegetation.

We love driving in this area. The beauty of the rolling hills, the green grass, the blue sky and the occasional black rock give the area a sense of peace and surreal beauty. On occasion, we saw some of the remains of lava flows. Sometimes, it is hard to remember that every rolling hill is a distinct cinder cone and that what we are seeing is the visible remnants of an explosive past. For those adventurers who wish to explore the volcanic field in great detail, the Springerville Visitors Center has a guide book for sale. It contains a driving tour with descriptions and colored photos.

From 1937 through 1959, **Taliesen West** in Scottsdale was Frank Lloyd Wright's winter home and school. Today, it is the main campus for the Wright School of Architecture. The site is open to the public and tours of the facility are available. The tours allow visitors to view the grounds, selected areas of the residence, the movie theatre, the orchards and the gardens. Other structures such as dormitories can be seen on the premises and the studio can be seen from outdoors. The tour highlights some the architectural features that were used in the construction of the structures.

The architectural style of the main building is visually pleasing. The curved walkways, the triangular pool, the green grass, and the mountains in the background add to the beauty of the building. Interesting adventure to share with Bill and Lisa (Midge's son and daughter-in-law).

The **David Wright House** in Phoenix is a Frank Lloyd Wright residence built in 1952 for his son, David and his wife. The two-level house was originally built in an orange grove and was built off the ground so the house would be above the orange trees. The ground level contains some outdoor living space and a pool; the second story contains the living quarters with a deck on the upper level. The house is built in a spiral design and the residence is accessed via a wide, curved entry ramp. The house was occupied until 2008 when Mrs. Wright passed away. The David and Gladys Wright House Foundation currently owns the property.

In 2016, we visited the site and were surprised. We had seen pictures of the residence, but it seemed so much prettier in its environment. The spiral design, the view of Camelback Mountain in the background, the curved paths, the green grass, the ornamental rocks, the agave gardens and the impeccable landscaping made the building look like a masterpiece. It was very easy to picture what this house looked like when the orange grove was surrounding it.

Public tours are available and allow visitors access to the interior of the residence. Our first thought was: "Wow!" What a cool place to live. The house has multiple windows, round fireplaces, round bedroom, round living room. We do not remember seeing one straight line in this residence. It was different, intriguing, and definitely beautiful.

Something exciting happened to us that day. Waiting for our tour, we were waiting in the guest house for the rest of the tour group to arrive. The great granddaughter of Frank Lloyd Wright entered the room and we had the occasion to have a chat with her. How cool was that!

Currently, the residence is being renovated and one of the plans is the replanting of the orange grooves to return the building to its original setting. The public tours are currently suspended pending completion of the renovations.

Paolo Soleri, an Italian-born architect, settled in Scottsdale in 1956. Paolo was always concerned about the effects of urban design on the ecology of an area and on human society. He spent one and one-half years studying at Taliesen West under the tutelage of Frank Lloyd Wright. Over the years, he has become well-known for his ceramic and bronze wind bells. We have had the privilege and honor of visiting three of the landmarks that Soleri left behind in the State of Arizona. These three sites are a testimony to his love of art and his love of unique urban designs.

Cosanti, in Scottsdale, was his studio and gallery. It was also the permanent residence for him and his wife until his death in 2013. This site is an experiment in urban design with its terraced landscape, earth-formed concrete structures and the many structures that are below ground level to provide insulation against the cold and heat.

Visitors are welcome to visit the site and can explore the grounds. The architecture is indeed unique and different yet it is charming and memorable. On the grounds, there is a tubular building that was previously used as a dormitory, the residence of the Soleri family, a swimming pool, an outdoor studio, a half-shell for outdoor performances, a huge oven, an area for finishing the bells, and an area where dozens of wind bells are hung on display. The gift shop was one of our favorite buildings. The structure is earth-formed and the columns used for support are huge tree limbs. Very unique building. Very interesting place to visit. We bought our bronze wind bell at Cosanti and every time it rings, we think of that great place.

Another Soleri present to Arizona is the **Soleri Bridge and Plaza** in Scottsdale. The pedestrian bridge is anchored by two, sixty-four-foot pylons and spans the Arizona canal. It is the central feature of the plaza. At one end of the plaza, embossed panels created by Soleri are worthy of close examination. The pylons are strategically placed: the shadows they cast indicate times of the solstice or equinox. Basically, Soleri built a bridge that is also a solar calendar. The design of this bridge is artistically creative, elegant, and stunning. When we walked over the bridge, we felt special and honored to walk on this piece of art left for all of us to enjoy. There are benches in the plaza for those who wish to linger. For the adventurers, look for the one Soleri wind bell that hangs behind the pylons.

Arcosanti is a community environment built by Soleri to test his urban design theories: a sustainable urban environment with urban agriculture and community living. It is an experimental town built, over the years, by architectural students. The community is located in a desert environment near the community of Cordes Junction. It cannot be seen from the highway and it blends into its beautiful natural environment.

At the time of our visit, eighty-seven individuals were living at Acrosanti. Yearly, about fifty thousand visitors visit the community and the cafeteria is open to the public on a daily basis. Guest rooms are also available for those who wish to stay overnight. Weekly stays are an option for those who wish to experience communal living.

The cafeteria and gift shop are accessible to the general

public. Tours of the facility are offered for those who wish to see the complex. We chose to eat at the cafeteria and to purchase a charming ceramic bell in the gift shop.

In 1923, George Legler built a storyland in Tucson that was meant to foster the imagination of children of all ages. With two hundred tons of stones and eight hundred sacks of cement, he created **Valley of the Moon**, an environment where fairies would live and where children could come to be entertained. He provided tours of the park, told stories to the children and amused them with performances. His wish was to make children happy.

The park contains stone grottos, stone structures of various sizes, underground "caves," ponds, waterfalls, walls with niches, and a grassy area. It was meant to be a unique park where visitors can wander freely and have picnics. The Valley of the Moon is listed on Arizona's Register of Historic Places and, in 2011, it was placed on the National Register of Historic Places.

On our first visit, this site fascinated us. It is indeed a very unique place with numerous stone structures, unique forms, fairy houses and a variety of fairies located throughout the park. Our joy, however, came from watching the children who ran from path to path, building to building, in and out of the caves, and searched for every fairy they could find. There are parts of the park that are difficult for adults to access, but we kept reminding ourselves that it was built for children. It was apparent that the children were having a great time.

In the grassy area, families had gathered. Some families had blankets and others had chairs. All of them, however, had brought food for picnics. In the same area, a young man (dressed like a tree) was singing children's songs to the children gathered around him. This is what this place was about. The park is open the first Saturday of the month and on special occasions.

As we were leaving one night, we met a young lady at the entrance gate. She appeared to be about twenty-five years old and was very excited to be returning to the park. She had spent some time here when she was a child and she remembered it fondly. She and her boyfriend would be enjoying it again.

We love taking guests to show them one of Tucson's oddities: the **Diamondback Rattlesnake Bridge**. The pedestrian bridge spans Broadway Boulevard and resembles a rattlesnake. At the beginning of the bridge, the snake's jaws are open and its fangs are visible. There is a place to stand to get a great photo before entering the body of the snake. The bridge is covered and the texture resembles the diamond-like skin of a rattlesnake. The body is lit at night for safety and aesthetic purposes. Continuing through the body, the tail comes into view. The tail stands upright and is quite imposing. We do not tell our guests that there is a motion sensor as you approach the tail that produces a very loud rattle. It is a great place to bring guests and hopefully scare them. After all, it is listed as one of Tucson's Public Art.

The **Poston War Relocation Center** is located on Route 1, north of Ehrenberg. This was the largest of the ten American Concentration Camps during World War II. It was built on the Colorado River Indian Reservation and consisted of three camps: Poston I, II and III. The peak population of the three camps combined was over seventeen thousand in August 1942. All of the detainees were Japanese and Japanese-American; the detainees were mostly from southern California. At its peak population, this internment camp was the second largest "city" in Arizona.

Because of the remoteness of the area, a single fence surrounded the three separate camps and no guard towers were erected. Today, there are a few original buildings that remain and they are used by residents in the area. The atrocities and conditions of the camp are well documented in Arizona history.

We went to visit the area to see the Poston Memorial Monument that was built by the survivors of the camp. It was built in 1992 in honor of all those who were here and all those who survived. The memorial, which resembles a pagoda with a spire on top, is a beautiful testimony to survival and honor. The round concrete plaza, the stunning memorial, the curved walkway, the tall palm trees, the blue sky, the white clouds and the desert scenery lend an air of elegance to this small area that honors those who were here before us. We left honored to have seen the memorial, glad to have paid our respects to those who suffered and a bit sad.

Ajo is the gateway to the Organ Pipe Cactus National Monument and the community that visitors pass through on their way to Rocky Point Mexico and the salt-water beaches. This town currently has about thirty-seven hundred residents and is redefining itself after the mines closed. Ajo has the proud distinction of having the first known copper mine in the state of Arizona and the mining continued until 1985. Today, it is home to many retired individuals, Border Patrol agents and young families.

To us, Ajo is so much more that a gateway community and a prior mining town. This town to us has a large number of wonderful places to explore and admire. One such feature is the Curley School. From the town square, visitors can see the building. It is worth the walk to the building to admire this architectural masterpiece. It resembles some of the great buildings found in affluent cities. The historic school has been renovated and offers live-work space for artists.

For those who love to venture away from the center of town, a ride up Indian Village Road is worth the trip. On the way up the road, the Greenway mansion is visible. This is the residence that John Greenway had built for his wife, Isabella. The mansion is on private property, however, we got close enough to take some good photos.

At the lookout, there is a parking area so visitors can stop and see an open-pit copper mine. The data says that it is two miles across and one-mile deep. Standing there, looking at the hole, it does not look that big. However, at the time, it was one of the biggest holes we had ever seen.

At the end of Indian Village Road, you will arrive at St. Catherine's Indian Mission. This Spanish-style mission administered to the spiritual needs of the Papago Indians. The Catholic Church abandoned the mission in 1968. In 1975, the Ajo Historical Society took possession of the building. Today, the mission building contains a museum with artifacts and memorabilia of Ajo's past. Wonderful historic site.

Arriving in Ajo for the first time, we were unprepared for the beauty that exists in this small town. We passed the mine tailings, modest houses, a variety of businesses and then we arrived at the plaza. To say that we were surprised is an understatement! The historic Spanish-style plaza surrounds a large green area and creates a town center that is refreshing. The plaza runs along two sides of the green area, the historic Railroad Depot is on one side, and two mission-style churches finish the town square.

We love spending time here walking around the plaza, browsing in the stores, eating at the restaurant and visiting the Chamber of Commerce. It is said that John and Isabella Greenway believed that if they built an environment that pleased the miners' wives, the miners would stay in Ajo. We like the elegance of the town square and we bet that the miners' wives liked it too. This is such a beautiful and exciting place to spend a day.

We read the The *Hummingbird's Daughter* and *Queen of America* by Luis Alberto Urrea. In his books, he introduces Teresita Urrea (also known as the Saint of Cabora) to his readers. When we were preparing our trip to **Clifton** and Morenci, seeing the burial site of Teresita was high on our list of priorities. We went to the cemetery to pay our respects and then set out to explore the town of Clifton.

Clifton is a small town that was strategically built between two mountains with a railroad track and a river running through the valley. As of 2010, the population of Clifton was listed at thirty-three hundred residents. The large majority of the residences are built on the sides of the mountains. It is an old mining and railroad town whose main economy was based on processing the ore from the Morenci copper mines. Today, the remains of the smelter remain visible, but closed.

There are some historical features in this town and we started our adventure at the Greenlee Historical Society. The museum has several artifacts of Clifton's past and the docent was very knowledgeable about the town's history. For those who wish to learn more about the history, the book *The Great Arizona Orphan Abduction* by Linda Gordon details the life and history of this small town.

Other features to explore are the San Francisco River which provides green spaces for the residents, the historic railroad houses that still stand proudly along the railroad tracks, the historic downtown with renovated facades, and the 1913 Historic Train Depot. Another interesting stop is the Clifton Cliff Jail that was built in 1881. The jail was built into a cliff and still stands for the public to see. This is a town worthy of exploration as well at the town of Morenci that lies north of Clifton.

John (Jay) Gammons had a dream of owning his own Old West Town. As a youth, he spent some time around film crews in the making of western movies. One day, John purchased ten acres of land and, along with his wife, set out in pursuit of his dreams. The town of **Gammons Gulch** was born. The site in Benson is located in a remote desert environment and it is the perfect setting for the 1880s-1930s western town.

Upon arriving, the size and authenticity of the western

town impressed us. It felt like we had arrived at a well-preserved ghost town. It was easy to feel like we were transported back in time. The number of artifacts they have accumulated over the years is amazing. They even included a gold mine shaft on their property. This was indeed an impressive western town, movie set and museum.

Calling ahead is mandatory since their availability for tours varies depending on filming sessions or private events. Arriving for a tour, you will be greeted by John and given a personal tour.

Meteor Crater (also known as Barringer's Crater) is located on Interstate 40, eighteen miles west of Winslow. The central focus of the site is the meteorite impact crater that was caused as a result of an asteroid colliding with Earth approximately fifty thousand years ago. The evidence of the impact is one mile across and five hundred and fifty feet deep. There are several meteor craters throughout the world, but the Barringer Crater is the best- preserved site.

About two hundred thousand visitors explore this site annually. Outdoor observation trails, docents, a theatre and a discovery center are available to provide information and make the visit more educational and enjoyable. There is a Subway shop on the premises for those who wish to linger. In the Discovery Center, we found displays and exhibits that caught our attention. There were global maps with red dots indicating all of the meteor craters that have been discovered. Never knew there were that many impact sites! Our time spent in this area proved to be very educational. There is one picture that is a photo opportunity. If you take a picture of someone standing in front of this display, it seems that they are standing at the bottom of the crater. Needless to say, we took pictures and posted those on our Facebook page (with no explanations, of course). This was a fun and educational stop.

In 1904, two brothers who were lumber barons married

sisters and built a home that would house both families. The **Riordan Mansion**, in Flagstaff, is a two-story duplex with forty rooms and thirteen-thousand-square-feet of living space. Each family had their living quarters, with a common room joining the two living quarters. This mansion, tucked away amongst the ponderosa pines, is an impressive building with its Arts & Crafts-style architecture. The exterior has log-slab siding and huge lava rock arches. Stained glass windows were used in some of the windows on both sides of the house.

Visitors can take self-guided tours of the grounds and the exterior of the building. Maps highlighting the features are available at the visitor center: the map will help guide the visitor in finding the gargoyle on the side of the building. Guided tours are required to view one-half of the building and last about one hour. Our docent was very knowledgeable about the history of the building and its occupants. In the other half of the building, visitors can roam freely to view the displays.

This site is listed on both the Arizona and National Register of Historic Places. It is a site worth seeing and gives the visitor a view of the lifestyle of a prominent family in the early 1900s.

Isabella Greenway, the widow of John Greenway, is best known as the first US Congresswoman in Arizona history and the founder of the **Arizona Inn**. Isabella was a lifelong friend of Eleanor Roosevelt and was a bridesmaid at the wedding of Eleanor and Franklin D. Roosevelt.

Isabella was involved with a furniture-making enterprise that helped disabled World War I veterans find permanent employment. With the depression in the 1930s, the enterprise was failing. The decision was made to build the Arizona Inn for two reasons: to build an inn that would provide individualized service, privacy, quiet, and sunshine for her guests, and to increase the demand for furniture that would keep the enterprise viable.

Thus, the Inn was built in 1930 and, today, it is listed on the National Register of Historic Places. Set in a residential setting, this upscale boutique hotel is readily visible to all who drive down the street. This Spanish Colonial style complex with its salmon colored buildings and blue awnings catches the attention of all newcomers.

For generations, the Inn has been owned and operated by family members and has been lovingly restored and renovated. It is a world-renowned resort known for its quiet, beauty, elegance, privacy, and sunshine.

We love spending time at the Arizona Inn, walking around the grounds and eating at the elegant café. The grounds are a treat because of the various gardens, the number of different flowers and impeccable landscaping. Eating in the cafe always feels special due to the excellent service provided in a beautiful and elegant environment. Spending time at the Inn makes us feel special.

A lot of other people also enjoyed spending time at the Inn. The list of celebrities that have stayed there includes: Clark Gable, Spencer Tracy, Katherine Hepburn, Gary Cooper, Jimmy Stewart, Cary Grant, Bing Crosby, Bob Hope, John F. Kennedy, John D. Rockefeller Jr., Frank Lloyd Wright, Salvador Dali, Howard Hughes, Ansel Adams and, of course, Eleanor Roosevelt. This is a list of selected individuals: there are many others who have enjoyed the hospitality of this special place in the desert.

Isabella Greenway would be proud to know of the legacy she has left for Arizona, Tucson and for us to enjoy.

Arizona is full of "Other" interesting places that challenge, educate, excite, thrill, surprise, sadden and amuse us. Such a great variety in such a diverse state.

OUR FAVORITE PLACES

We have visited many locations in this great state of Arizona and there are several places we could call "Our Favorites." At first, we thought it would be difficult to pick the favorites, but it proved to be very easy. The places mentioned here have made an impact on us. We not only explored the sites, but they became part of us. We felt the goose bumps, felt transported back in time, and sometimes felt sad. These places changed us in some way because we were there. All of them are fondly remembered. Enjoy!

One of our favorite places is **Cochise Stronghold**. The site is located in the Dragoon Mountains and is accessible through the beautiful Sulphur Springs Valley. The entrance to the Stronghold is on a narrow dirt road. We could feel the intrigue and excitement of being there.

Along the road, there is signage about the early Anglo settlers in Cochise Stronghold and the remains of the Shilling House. The narrow dirt road stops at a picnic area which provides plenty of shade for the warm summer months and multiple tables for several visitors. When we got out of the car and looked at the beautiful cliffs and the seclusion of the area, it was easily understood why this area was chosen as a natural fortress and hideout. The area provided the inhabitants with water and shade, as well as protection.

We went to the Stronghold in 2012. The feelings that the site produced do not require a return trip to the area to remember their impact. Walking around the site on the designated paths, we passed manzanita trees with their red trunks, yucca, gold grass, and interesting rock formations. The natural beauty of the area was truly impressive. Cochise and his warriors had probably walked along the same paths and we were looking at the beautiful scenery that Cochise himself saw! That was enough to give us goose bumps!

Walking around, it was not difficult to remember the people who lived there, raised their children, those who died and were buried there. It was easy to think that a family could have lived in this small area. It was also easy to think that a family could have been hungry, sad or scared in the same area. Sometimes, history in Arizona gets inside of you and changes you a little.

It was here, in the Stronghold, that we first learned about Tom Jeffords. He was a white man who became Cochise's blood brother. The depth of their friendship lasted until the death of Cochise. Cochise died in the Stronghold and was entombed there. Tom Jeffords is the only white man who knew where Cochise was buried. Several books have been written about their friendship. Our favorite book is *Blood Brother* by Elliott Arnold. For history seekers, Tom Jeffords is buried in Evergreen Memorial Park in Tucson.

Cochise Stronghold will always remain on "Our Favorites" list, because it is just one example of the Arizona sites where history comes alive. When we visited we not only looked at the site, but felt and experienced the area. What a wonderful experience to have been there.

Tuba City lies within the Painted Desert at the western end of the Navajo Reservation. The town has a population of about eight thousand residents. Entering the town from Route 89, the Hopi Reservation is on the right side of the main road, the Navajo Reservation is on the left side. The Explore Navajo Interactive Museum and the Code Talker Museum are must see attractions if you visit Tuba City.

The main attraction for us, however, lies five miles west of the town. Some call this place "The Land Where the Dinosaurs Danced." It is an area of dinosaur tracks that mother nature has preserved for us to see and wonder about. This attraction has been rated as a Top Place to go in Arizona and people from all over the world have stopped here to dream about a world gone by.

When you stop at the attraction, a native guide will show you around the area. They will highlight the tracks for you, point out dinosaur dung, dinosaur eggs, and dinosaur bones. Hundreds of dinosaur tracks are visible. The tour is worth the time, effort and donation.

There is some debate about what type of dinosaur prints are there, but they have been verified. You are seeing Dinosaur prints! National Geographic lists the site on their Navajo and Hopi tour. Let the experts debate what type and size of the dinosaurs who walked there. We will just continue to be amazed when we look at the prints and imagine a baby walking alongside its mother. We have been there several times and still get as excited as we were the first time.

The years must have erased some of the information we gathered in school, because we did not recall that dinosaurs lived on this continent millions of years ago. Now, we can see the evidence whenever we choose. We use every occasion to go to the site and have brought friends, family, and stop whenever we are in the area.

Another treat, in the same area, is the occasion to pick up some jasper alongside the road. In this area, the conditions were perfect for the formation of the stones and they can be found on the surface. Erosion has made the dinosaur tracks and the jasper visible. We have found red, red/black and grey. One thing we love about jasper is the feel of the rock itself. It feels like it has been covered with wax. They say that jasper is a protection stone. We have one stone hanging from our rear-view mirror and it has protected us this far.

If you come to Arizona and have time to explore, go to Tuba City and let the child inside be amazed and enjoy the wonderment of it all.

Monument Valley Navajo Tribal Park is located in Northern Arizona on the Navajo Tribal lands. It is one of the grandest and most photographed parks in the United States.

In August 2009, during our twenty-one-month adventure across the United States, we arrived at Monument Valley. It was one of the top ten places on our bucket list and on that day, the ride to the park seemed long and endless.

Throughout the years, we had seen numerous pictures and TV specials about the area. However, when we arrived, it was much more than what is captured in pictures. It is hard to describe its rich red sand, the rock formations made by years and years of erosion, the famous "Mittens," the big blue sky, the expanse of the valley and so much more.

We had read that the road through the Tribal Park was rough and tour books recommended taking a guided tour. We chose to take a private jeep tour with Vida, our Navajo guide. Vida was born and raised in the valley and said she would show us her childhood playground.

That wonderful day we saw the red, rippled sand dunes, wild horses, petroglyphs, Ear of the Wind, Moccasin Arch, and the Sun's Eye. Midge even had the experience of laying on a rock with Vida to view the sky through a hole in a rock. We saw several of the beautiful rock formations, and had time to spend asking the multiple questions we had about marriage ceremonies, burial ceremonies, and sovereignty of nations. What a glorious day spent in a beautiful park.

In November 2010, we relocated to Arizona and became permanent residents. Being new to this state, we set upon the task of becoming educated about the culture of the Indian tribes that live in our adopted state. We took courses, went to lectures, visited tribal lands and read many books about current residents and their ancestors. From 2010 - 2014, we visited Monument Valley at least seven or eight times, stopping there whenever we are in the area.

We took our second tour of Monument Valley in July 2014. Again, it was a private tour - Midge, Midge's daughter (Marie), Don Mose (our Navajo guide) and I. This second tour was magical. We saw the formations, the petroglyphs, the arches, and the red sand dunes. This time, however, we realized that Monument Valley had become more than just beautiful spires and red sand. The conversation with Don Mose included discussions about the migration of the Navajo people, preservation of their language on Rosetta Stone, the effects of Uranium Mining on the Tribal lands and government boarding schools. We talked about events in history that affected the *people* of the Valley.

Human beings have lived in this valley for thousands of years and evidence of their existence still remains. Some individuals continue to live in the valley according to the customs, beliefs and traditions of their ancestors. We left Monument Valley on that day, in July 2014, with the knowledge that this valley will always feel different. It will no longer just be a beautiful place, it is so much more. We will continue to return again and again.

We often attend activities at the Community Performing Arts Center in Green Valley. One of our favorite activities is attending lectures by Jack Lasseter. Jack is a retired lawyer and currently an historian. Jack loves to share his knowledge and love of Arizona. One evening, toward the end of his lecture, he was sharing with the audience that he was leading a tour through the Western National Parks Association to Cochise Stronghold and **Dragoon Springs Station** in the coming weeks.

Can you just imagine the conversation between Midge and I on the way home? What? A stage station in Dragoon?

How come we did not know that? Wonder where it is? Should we go on Jack's tour? No! We will find the directions and go on our own.

We did find specific directions and off we went the following week to see the historical site. Our first challenge was to find Old Farm Road that leads out of the town of Dragoon. It is a dirt road and it is not easily located. Someone had to help us find it.

Once we started down the road, the scenery was striking. Red dirt road, Dragoon Mountains on the west, a mountain range on the right, cattle grazing, and beautiful golden grass everywhere. What a beautiful little valley. The road, however, was not so beautiful. Ruts and holes were commonplace, but we persevered in our task and we reached it.

When we arrived in the "parking area," we saw a red, wooden information sign that says: "Dragoon Springs Station. Established 1858 in the heart of Apache country. Westernmost stone fortified station on Butterfield overland mail route. Stage stop used until 1862."

After a brief walk along a well-maintained trail, we arrived at the remains of the station. The remains were about five feet tall. It was surprising to find so much of the structure still standing. It was a pleasant surprise. Near the remains of the stage station, there are four graves, three of the graves belong to Confederate soldiers killed by the Apaches. Signage at the site gives information about the soldiers. This historical site is another example of the ability to touch and experience history.

In March 2014, off we went with a packed cooler and clothes for four days. We were headed to Wickenburg to explore the area. Some points of interest included the Vulture Mine (a ghost town), the Desert Caballeros Western Museum, Lake Pleasant Regional Park, the historical section of Wickenburg and the **Hassayampa River Preserve.**

On the list of Places to Explore, the Hassayampa River

Preserve was definitely on the top of the list. The Hassayampa River flows for one hundred and thirteen miles - it runs south from Prescott through Wickenburg toward Hassayampa; there it flows into the Gila River. The Hassayampa flows mainly underground, but a flow may be seen at the River Preserve most of the year.

When we got to the Preserve, we explored the museum and marveled at the large palm trees in the area. We walked the paths around the pond. The area was a beautiful place to relax, meditate, enjoy birds and nature. But, wait a minute, where is the river? We wanted to see the river flowing.

We then spotted a path that led down to the water and off we went. Voila! There was a small stream of water flowing south. The river was about eighteen to twenty-four inches wide; the water was clear and glistened in the sunlight. The main reason we wanted to see the river was because of all of the legends regarding drinking the water in the Hassayampa. Legends vary according to the teller of the tale, but they have one common denominator - whoever drinks water from this river will never tell the truth again. We stood there and looked at the clear, flowing water and chose not to have a drink.

Fort Bowie was a United States Army Outpost that was established in 1862 to deal with the ongoing conflicts with the Chiricahua Apache Indians in the area.

We had read that there were ruins left of the fort, so we decided to go check it out. In December 2011, we ran through our checklist - water, hats, camera, directions and walking sticks. Let's go see this beautiful historical site. Little did we know what was ahead of us on that day.

We got to the parking lot and got ready to follow the sign that said, "Fort Bowie Trail - 1.5 miles." Off we went, past the mesquites, the yucca, gold grass and absolutely beautiful scenery. One of the things we had not anticipated was the extent of the history lesson we would be getting on that day.

Signage is plentiful along the trail and highlights the history and significance of the Bascom Affair, Apache culture, and the Butterfield Overland Mail. We also saw ruins of a miner's cabin, a surveyor's cabin, and remains of the Apache Pass Stage Station. Also on the walk, you can view Apache Springs which provided water for the first fort. You can also see the remains of the first Fort Bowie.

One of the surprises of the day was arriving at the post cemetery. It is a well-kept cemetery with several tombstones. One tombstone, however, caught our immediate attention. "Little Robe" was the two-year-old son of Geronimo and is buried in this cemetery. Wow!

We took a breath and headed to the remains of the second Fort Bowie. As we approached, it was incredible to see how much remains of the fort. It was abandoned in 1894 and, yet, several structures can be seen. We went into the visitor center to pay our dues and explore their small museum. To our surprise, they informed us that they do not charge to explore the fort. They figure that you already paid your dues by walking in. The park ranger suggested that we take the ridge trail back to the parking lot rather than repeating the same trail.

Off we went to explore the ruins, take pictures and tried to imagine what life was like in the 1800's in Apache Pass. We reflected on the fact that Geronimo and Naiche were held here for a few days after their surrender to General Miles in 1886. We were ready for more adventure so we headed up the ridge trail and guess what? We ended up on top of a small mountain, looking down at the fort below. What a great place for Apaches to watch the fort!

At the end of the day, we had walked a total of about four to five miles and we were exhausted, educated and challenged - both physically and mentally. Fort Bowie will always remain one of our favorite places. One can still sense the history of this place. Cochise walked here. Geronimo walked in this valley. Apaches hunted here. We walked where they walked. We hope you get to experience Fort Bowie and its history.

Midge, Mary, Gypsy and I took off in April 2015 for a three-day adventure to explore one part of Southeastern Arizona we had not seen. We had anticipated this journey for a while and could not wait to see all the places on the list. The **Gadsden Hotel** was a high priority on this adventure.

Our first stop was Bisbee. We had been to Bisbee before, but this time, we wanted to see more of it. We decided to stay at the Copper Queen Hotel (haunted, of course) and we survived the night with no trauma. We also took a Lavender Jeep Tour of the city and suburbs. It was a great way to see the entire area and was well worth the time. The tour driver also pointed out a lot of places mentioned in J.A. Jance's books.

On the trip, we also went to Naco to see one historical point of interest. We went to Camp Naco, which is the only remaining fort that was constructed during the Mexican Revolution. There are several structures remaining and preservation projects are reportedly underway. The fort is called Camp Naco, Fort Naco, or Fort Newell. Interesting place to visit.

Another stop was Miracle Valley: the site of a former religious community. It was abandoned and is currently being restored by a young couple. The main building was impressive and we hope that it will be restored to its former beauty.

The most impressive place, however, was the Gadsden Hotel in Douglas. We walked around the downtown, took pictures of the beautiful murals, located the historical train depot and admired the Gadsden Hotel from the outside. It is an impressive building sitting on a corner in the downtown district. And then, we went inside! It was impossible to go inside the lobby and not have your chin drop. What a truly magnificent site: White Italian marble staircase, four marble columns, Tiffany windows that run the length of the lobby. It is a spacious, beautiful main lobby. This hotel is one of the last of the Grand Hotels.

On the seventh step of the white Italian marble staircase, there is a chip. It is said that Pancho Villa rode his horse up the stairs and damaged the step. Be it lore or legend, it was interesting to find that the chip does exist.

The Gadsden Hotel was built in 1907, burned down and was rebuilt in 1929. It is listed on the National Register of Historical Places. In 2016, the owner died and a local couple purchased the property. It is so great to see that someone wishes to preserve such a magnificent and historical building. By the way, this hotel is reportedly haunted if you seek such places.

Driving south on scenic Route 83 toward Sonoita, you will arrive at the entrance of the **Empire Ranch**. We first went to the Ranch in 2011 and fell in love with the area. Upon entering, you see beautiful mountains in the background, a large expanse of golden grass blowing in the wind, grazing cattle, pronghorn antelope, and hawks.

The Empire Ranch has been a working cattle ranch for over one hundred and thirty-five years. It was one of the larger ranches in southern Arizona. Currently, the ranch is public land administered by the Bureau of Land Management. The Empire Ranch Foundation remains involved in the preservation of the ranch buildings. Today, cattle can still be seen grazing in the golden fields.

The Empire Ranch was listed on the National Register of Historical Places in 1976. Throughout the years, over twenty movies were filmed on the property. There are several ranch buildings remaining. You can visit the interior of most of the buildings and they have included signage in the buildings to explain their usage. Every time we visit the ranch, it is easy to picture the activity that occurred in this ranching complex. It is understandable why they chose this location to live: the scenery is spectacular and the air is fresh.

In November, there is a Roundup at the Ranch. Here was our chance to be surrounded by horses, cowboys, cowboy music, cowboy hats, cowboy food and Buffalo soldiers. What a great time and we got to use our cowboy hats for a day. We will participate in this activity again.

Enough about the beauty surrounding the ranch complex. We also go there to see a very different beauty. Off we go, down the red dirt roads, bumpy and rough, in search of the prairie dogs. Years ago, we read in the newspaper about the prairie dog colonies at the Empire Ranch and we have made it a mission to visit the little guys every chance we get.

One time, we went looking for a newly established colony of prairie dogs. We went up and down dirt roads, looking everywhere and wondered where they could possibly have put them. All of a sudden, a large pink snake, about five feet long, went flying across the road and disappeared down a hole on the other side of the road. Wow! That made up for not finding the relocated critters. Later, we were told that the snake was a coach whip. Sorry, we did not get any pictures of the pink thing.

Movie lovers may spot scenes of the ranch in several films. Some of the movies filmed in the area are: *Red River* with John Wayne, *Oklahoma* with Gordon MacRae and Shirley Jones, *Hombre* with Paul Newman, *The Outlaw Josie Wales* with Clint Eastwood, *Desperado* with Antonio Banderas and *Broken Lance* with Spencer Tracy. The surrey used in the movie *Oklahoma* is on exhibit at the Tucson Rodeo Parade Museum. During one visit, Dot and Cathy (Midge's daughters) sang "Oklahoma" in the back seat of the car.

We feel comfortable and at home at the ranch. It feels like the Old West. What a great place to renew your energy and soothe your spirit.

We love to go to **Old Tucson Studios** when we want to be enveloped in the Old Wild West. With the Can-Can shows, the stagecoach rides, the shoot-outs, the stunt shows and the sheriff greeting you, it is not hard to believe you are in the

Wild West. On occasion, you can even see a five-year old dressed like Wyatt Earp.

At Old Tucson Studios, over two hundred movies and commercials have been filmed. A list of the movies and the actors can be found in the museum. Some of the old buildings still remain and you can recognize them. It is a fun and interesting place to visit.

One day, we heard about **Mescal Studios** in Benson. It is another movie set owned by Old Tucson Studios and many films were made at this location. One Saturday morning, Midge, Ed, Olga and I took off for Mescal Studios to check out the site. It is an isolated site at the end of a dirt road. Golden grasses and surrounding mountains offer a beautiful backdrop. There are no stunt shows or Can-Can dances here. All you feel is the sun, all you hear is the wind and your imagination.

We were met in the parking lot by a movie historian who lived at the site. Of course, he was dressed like a real cowboy. Well, that started our tour off right!! When we turned the corner, it was like being back in time. We were looking at the town in the movie *Tombstone* starring Kurt Russell, Bill Paxton and Sam Elliott. The movie was filmed at Mescal, with three scenes filmed at Old Tucson Studios. How cool is that.

There was another feature that attracted our immediate attention. It was a huge saloon that stood on the corner in front of a dirt plaza. An impressive building. It was the saloon featured in *The Quick and The Dead* with Sharon Stone, Gene Hackman, Russell Crowe and Leonardo DiCaprio. During our tour, we also saw the hanging tree and the cemetery from the feature film.

We found that tour very exciting. We saw the mansion used in *Buffalo Soldier*s starring Lamont Bentley, Tom Bower and Timothy Busfield; the schoolhouse from *Little House on the Prairie;* and many other structures used in several Hollywood films. The tour was worth the time, the effort and the donation.

When we got home, we ordered the movies and scheduled a movie night. The four of us had a great time seeing the details we had seen on the movie set. Great times in the Old West.

The Hohokam Indians settled in this area about two thousand years ago. When you go to the **Casa Grande Ruins National Monument** in Coolidge, you can view maps of the area in which they settled and the expansive canal system they built. They were farmers and used the canals for irrigation. The canals are considered to be an engineering marvel. It is mind boggling to think about building a large canal system without current equipment.

Some of the canals currently utilized by the Central Arizona Project are the same canals, just renovated to meet current needs. We were absolutely fascinated by the information and knew that someday we would get to see one of the canals.

About two years later, we were in a used bookstore browsing through a book entitled *Arizona: Journey Guide* by Jon Kramer and Julie Martinez. The book included a site called **Park of the Canals** in Mesa. Upon returning home, we researched the park and found the directions. Sure enough, there was an original Hohokam canal in the park.

Midge, Sue Smith and I were going on an adventure to the Apache Trail. That was a great opportunity to take a side trip to see the canal. At the park, visitors have the opportunity to walk through the Brinton Desert Botanical Garden which contains desert flora.

In back of the Botanical Garden, there is one original Hohokam canal. It looks like a huge wash. It is hard to imagine that human beings dug this canal by hand. It is easy to admire the Hohokam for their ingenuity, perseverance and technical abilities. We had wanted to see one of the original Hohokam canals and now we were actually standing in one!

In October 2012, we took off for Willcox - Destination: Rex Allen Days and Parade. We got there early and were eagerly awaiting the parade because we hopefully were going to see Rex Allen, Jr. A couple came and sat near us and we had no idea the history lesson we were about to get on that beautiful morning.

This couple had lived in the area for many years and were thrilled to share some information with us about Willcox, Dos Cabezas, the Chiracahua Mountains, Dragoon and, most interestingly, the **Triangle T Ranch**. They asked if we knew that Japanese prisoners were held at the Triangle T Ranch during World War II. What great information we gathered from them.

Those of you who know us, you can already guess that the Triangle T Ranch was placed on the bucket list of places to see. Not long after, we headed off to the ranch to explore. The ranch is located in Texas Canyon, off of Route 10 between Benson and Willcox. The ranch is situated amongst gigantic boulders and beautiful rock formations. What a quiet, peaceful location to rejuvenate the spirit.

We headed to the office to request permission to look around the property. We spent a lot of time looking at the pictures on their wall - what a list of dignitaries: John F. Kennedy, General Pershing, and several more. The list of movie stars was much, much longer than the list of dignitaries. Interesting! By the way, John Wayne also slept at this location.

They told us about the building on the premises that was in the movie *3:10 to Yuma* (1957) with Glenn Ford and Van Heflin. It is still standing and we got a great picture of it. They also shared with us the history of the high-ranking Japanese POWs. The Japanese ambassador to Hawaii, his entourage and their children were held at the ranch; they were eventually released as part of a prisoner swap.

We finished the day by having lunch at the Rock Saloon and Grill. The atmosphere is western, the food is great, and the people were welcoming. Oh, one interesting item about the saloon - it is built around a huge rock. Great day on the ranch. Great information gathered. Needless to say, we have introduced the Triangle T Ranch to friends and family. Their annual Garlic Festival is a fun event.

Ettore "Ted" DeGrazia is an artist who became well-known because of the UNICEF Christmas cards. We enjoy seeing his art displayed in many areas of Arizona and we have fallen in love with his little Indian children.

One morning, we went to explore the **Gallery in the Sun.** On ten acres of land, Ted DeGrazia built several structures which include: a guest house, his residence, an artist studio, a chapel and a gallery which includes a courtyard. The buildings blend in with the desert surroundings. Ted and his wife are buried between the chapel and the gallery. It is a peaceful and reverent place.

The chapel caught our attention. It is built in the Spanish style with an open roof and numerous murals on the walls. It always makes us feel like we are in a far-away country. Exiting the chapel, a sign reads: "This mission is dedicated to Father Kino in honor of Our Lady of Guadalupe for the Indians." It is signed by DeGrazia and dated. A touching and meaningful dedication.

The gallery contains DeGrazia art; many art forms can be found and the exhibits change from time to time. The Gallery is listed in the National Register of Historical Places. The book *DeGrazia: The Man and the Myths* by James W. Johnson with Marilyn D. Johnson offers an insight into the man's life and art. An excellent read.

Talking about enjoyment, in December, there is the "La Fiesta de Guadalupe." It a time of enjoyment: Latin music featuring Domingo DeGrazia, Indian dancers, folklora dancers, piñatas, procession and native foods. It is a memorable event. We love to return to the Gallery in the Sun whenever we can. It is always relaxing, educational, interesting and we always manage a trip to the chapel.

During the centennial anniversary of Arizona, the book *Arizona, 100 Years Grand* by Lisa Schnebly Heidinger was released. In that book, we found an interesting site we wanted to explore: **The Garden of Gethsemane**.

Felix Lucero was injured and dying in a field during WWI. He promised that if he lived, he would dedicate his life to making religious art. Felix fulfilled his promise. While he was in Tucson, he lived under the Congress Street bridge and he produced religious statues made of sand from the wash and cement.

The sculptures in the Garden of Gethsemane were preserved in his memory by the City of Tucson in collaboration with the Knights of Columbus. The setting displays his art in a serene and beautiful environment. His sculptures include Christ on the cross, Christ in his tomb, the Holy Family and the Last Supper.

We have been to the Garden on several occasions. We have talked to the artist who renovated the sculptures, spoke with a person in the neighborhood who knew Felix when he lived in a cardboard box under the bridge, and met his niece when she came to visit the Garden. His niece was pleased to know that people visit the site in memory of her uncle.

When we went on an adventure to Prescott, we stopped at the Shrine of St. Joseph in Yarnell to see more sculptures by Felix Lucero. We go visit the Gethsemane Garden whenever we can and we have introduced friends and family to the site.

To us, this place is special because when the artist was restoring the sculptures, he enlisted neighborhood residents, made molds of their hands and used those hands on the sculptures. That act makes this place special to that neighborhood and to Tucson. One more gem!

When we first decided to become permanent residents, people used to ask us if we had been to Yuma. After several questions, we decided that it was time for us to go on a road trip to see **Yuma** and the surrounding area. We left in March 2012 for five days of exploring.

When we got to Route 8 heading west, we were astonished to see Mother Nature's present. The road was lined with brittlebush on both sides of the road. The plants were in full bloom and it felt like we were driving down the yellow brick road. What a treat to behold as we smiled all the way to Yuma.

As part of the road trip we stopped to see some petroglyphs at the Painted Rock Petroglyph Site, thirty-five miles west of Gila Bend. It is a great site to see petroglyphs. Many are at the base of the butte, and for the adventurous, the top of the butte is easily accessible. This was a great addition to our trip.

Off we continued on the yellow brick road and we began to sense that Yuma was not far away. People had told us that Yuma was known for its lettuce fields, but that did not prepare us for the miles and miles of green produce. My goodness, all of the people in Arizona could not eat all of this produce in one year's time!

We stayed in Yuma for the duration of the trip because we could easily access all the sites we wanted to visit from that location. The first place we visited was **Yuma Territorial Prison State Historical Park**. The museum was full of great information about territorial days, the prisoners and the prison. The prison, however, was a surprise. We did not expect the open cells with Arizona temperatures, the overcrowding, and the solitary cells. It is hard to describe the site. This place needs to be visited to be understood. This is another occasion when history changes you a little. We had to remind ourselves again that you cannot judge the past by today's values.

From a patio at the Territorial Prison, we watched teenagers swimming in the Colorado River. The river appeared to be about fifteen to twenty feet wide. Didn't we just read that steamboats used to go up the river to Ehrenberg? A boat could not do that today!

Our next stop was **Yuma Quartermaster Depot State Historic Park**. The park has many original structures, great signage and great artifacts. Walking around, we sensed that something important had happened here. Supplies were brought by steamboat to the Quartermaster Depot and from here, they were shipped overland to the several forts in the Arizona territory. It is a tribute that this site, as well as the Yuma Crossing site, was preserved for the public to view and enjoy.

If there is a fort in the area, it automatically becomes a must-see site. Off we go to visit **Fort Yuma**. It is on the top of a hill and there are several original structures left. It was originally built to quell Indian unrest, but it is currently part of the Fort Yuma Indian Reservation. The tribe uses many of the existing buildings as administrative offices and health clinics. It was surprising to see how much of the fort still exists.

Having finished all of the Yuma sites, it was time to branch out and explore some of the surrounding areas. Off we went through the Yuma Proving Grounds to the **Imperial National Wildlife Refuge.** The refuge is located twenty-five miles north of Yuma. We checked out the visitor center, got our directions and took off on a narrow dirt road looking for a lookout to see the Colorado River. The road had many, many dips, hills and curves, but the scenery was spectacular. It almost reminded us of the colors found in Badlands National Park in South Dakota: with its red, tan, gray and gold sand. We did get to see the river and it just added to the already existing beauty.

On our final day in the Yuma area, we headed to a ghost town called **Castle Dome**. It is approximately thirty miles north of Yuma. The town was known for its silver mine, but in later years, it was known as a major lead producer. There are many structures still standing and the buildings are well maintained. Some of the buildings were relocated from other mining sites in order to preserve them.

The list is done. Time to head home via the yellow brick road. Only one difference heading east - the car weighed more! We had purchased a very heavy rock at Castle Dome; a rock containing lead as a reminder of our great road trip.

We arrived in **Quartzsite** looking for a very special gravesite - a pyramid with the silhouette of a camel on top. It honors a man who came from Syria to the Arizona Territory and participated in the experiment of using camels as pack animals to move supplies. His grave marker lists his occupations as camel driver, scout and packer. For over thirty years, he was a faithful aid to the US Government.

We found the grave and we were pleased to find signage explaining the Camel Corps. There is also another sign that shares the following information: Legend says that the remains of Topsy, Hi Jolly's favorite camel and companion, are also placed in the bronze time capsule. What a fitting tribute to a man who participated in an historical experiment in the development of the Arizona Territory. His gravesite is on the National Register of Historical Places. We had the honor of introducing Sue Smith and Jacqui to this site.

Every year, Quartzsite has a Hi Jolly Daze Parade in honor of the Camel Corps Experiment in that area. Sometimes, there is even a live camel in the parade. This is an event we have on our bucket list.

This place is special because it makes us smile and transports us back into a time we can only imagine. Some days, as we travel across Arizona, we wonder if there could possibly be a camel left, roaming somewhere in the desert.

The term "Favorite places" means so many different things to us. Some of our favorite places we return to many times, sometimes it means only one visit. The **Arizona State Museum**, located on the University of Arizona campus, is definitely one of our favorites that we visit often. This museum educates us, challenges us, and inspires us to learn more, do more, be more. It introduces us to ideas and information we did not know. It pushes us to develop a new way of thinking, and sometimes a new way of feeling.

It is the largest anthropology museum in the Southwest. It has a large collection of Southwestern Indian pottery and has an ongoing exhibit entitled Paths of Life: American Indians of the Southwest and Mexico. Both of the ongoing exhibits are extraordinary and well displayed,

Some of the guest exhibits have been very educational and enlightening, Those exhibits have included Southwestern baskets, photographs by Edward Curtis, drawings by Indian youth, photographs by Adriel Heisey and *retablos* on loan from Gloria Giffords. From the photographs of Heisel, we learned about intaglios (also known as Geoglyphs) that exist along the Colorado river. This newly acquired knowledge will take us on more adventures. This is a great place to visit.

In January 2016, the Arizona Daily Star published a story that immediately caught our attention. The article informed the public about an archaeological discovery on **Sunset Road** just west of Interstate 10. In a prehistoric agricultural field, the oldest human footprints in the Southwest were discovered right here in Tucson. The newspaper article also invited the public to come view the footprints before the site was covered and the road construction continued.

We were thrilled that we would be able to view human footprints more than twenty-five hundred years old. We checked the dates of the tours, and off we went to Sunset Road. When we arrived, we were surprised to see the number of people who were there waiting for the next tour.

Our guide brought us to the edge of the archaeological site and explained what they had discovered. He pointed out the dirt berm that surrounded the field, pointed out some of the footprints, and explained how they gardened in mounds of earth to preserve water. After the explanation, we were allowed to go into the site to see the footprints up close.

Standing in the field, we placed our feet next to one of the prints, looked for the children's prints, examined the prints up close and noticed that the toes were readily visible. We took pictures of the prints going across the field; it was as if we could see them crossing the muddy field years ago.

What a great opportunity to participate in a significant event in Tucson. Every time we pass by Sunset Road on Interstate 10, we look over and see the construction of the road in progress. We remember what is underneath the road and we will always remember the day we stood in that field.

There were more than one hundred and twenty CCC camps in the state of Arizona. A well-preserved camp is located on a bluff overlooking the Gila River, near the city of Safford. The **Sanchez CCC Camp Historic Site** contains the historic remains of camp eleven which was occupied from 1935 to 1936 by two hundred men from Texas and Arizona. Their main goal was soil conservation to counteract the erosion that was occurring in the area.

Directions to the historic site are available and it is easy to locate. At the intersection with the dirt road, we were unsure if this was the correct turn, so we asked a gentleman in a pick-up who was exiting the road. He verified that this was the road to the camp, then proceeded to inspect our vehicle. His opinion was that our vehicle was suitable for the three and one-half mile trip on the dirt road. A little while later, it became clear why he checked out our car. The road has many bumps and erosion spots, and two areas that require a high-clearance vehicle. After a while, the camp came into sight. What a pleasant surprise to see the number of structures that remain. The semi-intact rock buildings are a proud reminder of the work that was done here. The buildings were accessible, signage was provided with information regarding the usage of the buildings and walking paths were well kept for those who wished to spend some time in an historical setting.

At an elevation of fifty-nine-hundred feet, **Crown King** is nestled in a pine forest in the Bradshaw Mountains. The population of the small community is about one hundred and thirty residents. The historical significance of this area makes up for its lack of size. Some of the historical structures include the saloon, the 1907 one-room, red schoolhouse, the general store, and the 1904 railroad bunkhouse. Historic water tanks, outhouses and a ticket office remain from the time that Crown King was a railroad town. The main industry for the community was mining; currently, the main industry is tourism.

In preparation for our trip to this mountain community, we decided to take the easiest route to our destination. We took the twenty-eight-mile dirt road through Bumble Bee and Cleator, along some of the old stagecoach routes. The road to the ghost town of Cleator was windy and sometimes bumpy. The road changed once we left the ghost town. The road became narrower, steeper and then, we started up the side of the mountain. On the last section, the road was an old railroad bed that was built for Murphy's Impossible Railroad. In some areas, the road was one-car wide, with one-lane bridges. The switchbacks going up the mountain side provided us with some spectacular scenery of the Bradshaw Mountains. Suddenly, you cross a one-lane bridge and you are magically in a small community nestled in a ponderosa pine forest.

We spent two nights in this community and explored all of the historical sites in the area. We had the opportunity to spend time with some of the residents. We gathered information about the history of the settlement and the residents were willing to offer information. Upon leaving, the ride down the mountain-side was as exciting as the ascent. This was a trip filled with laughter, good conversation, beautiful scenery and tons of memories. We will always remember some of the residents we left behind when we returned home.

The town of **Bouse**, a mining camp established in 1908, is located about twenty miles east of Parker. The current population is approximately one thousand residents. The current economy of the town is agriculture, retirees and tourism.

Midge, Jacqui, Sue Smith, Gypsy and I headed to this small community with one goal in mind. We were searching for the tank. Our first stop, however, was the general store. We needed to know how to correctly pronounce the name "Bouse." The store clerk informed us that it was pronounced like mouse, house or louse. Now, we knew. Off we went in search of our goal.

During WWII, there was a highly secret training camp that was established on the outskirts of Bouse to train tankers for combat in North Africa. The camp was never placed on the list of General Patton's training camps due to its highly secretive training. Today, an historic park exists in this small town in honor of the men who trained here. When we got to the park, there was the tank we wanted to see. Really, there were two tanks, a truck, historical markers, murals, and one wall with the message: Kilroy was here! This was an exciting way to gather historical information.

Intaglios. This was a word unknown to us until we attended an exhibit by Adriel Heisey at the Arizona State Museum. His photograph of an intaglio took us on a rewarding, educational and exciting adventure.

Intaglios are figures on the ground that are created by scraping away the top layers of rock or desert soil to expose lighter colored materials. These figures were first discovered in the 1930s. Six hundred figures have been recorded in the Southwest and more than two hundred of those have been found from Nevada to the Gulf of California.

These giant ground paintings are geometric designs, animals, and human forms. Most of the human forms are located along the Colorado River. It is believed they were made by the ancestors of today's tribes who live along the river as a communication with their ancestors or gods. All of the intaglios are believed to be prehistoric. Exact dating, however, is difficult due to the nature of the art.

The wonderful and intriguing pieces of art are best seen from the air, but they can be hard to spot if the exact location is unknown. The same is true for the adventurers on the ground. They are not easy to spot, so very good driving directions are necessary for a successful adventure.

At Fort Mohave, we were fortunate to find the intaglios of the "Twins." The larger figure reportedly represents Good and the smaller of the two represents Evil. They are in a fenced area and visitors can view them up close. The size of the figures is surprising and they can be seen clearly. Looking at them, it is easy to picture human beings scraping away the top layers of rock to create this picture on the ground.

On another occasion, we drove to Blythe California to view the intaglios that were found fifteen miles north of the city. The site is clearly marked and easy to locate. This is the most well-known site to see the figures. There are six distinct figures in three separate locations: there is a human figure in each of the sites as well as geometric designs and animals. The largest figure in this area is a human form that measures one hundred and seventy one feet.

All of the sites are fenced in order to protect the intaglios, but all of the sites are easily accessed from the dirt road. All of the figures are clearly visible and easy to photograph. What an honor to stand there and view these magnificent pieces of art.

About nine hundred years ago, a volcanic eruption, that changed the surrounding area, occurred north of Flagstaff. Evidence of this geologic event can be seen at **Sunset Crater Volcano National Monument**. The beautiful cinder cone is surrounded by lava flows and many other dormant volcanoes.

Photographers are treated to the beauty of the lava flows, the colors of the surrounding cinder cones and the beauty caused as a result of the eruption such as twisted trees and lava tubes.

We love to stop at the National Monument and to walk amongst the surreal landscape and to wonder how this landscape used to be before it was changed forever. There is a sense of peace and tranquility at this site. Visitors walk around quietly, stop to admire the few flowers that grow in the cinder fields and look up in the trees in search of an Albert squirrel. The Albert squirrel is a sight to behold with their big tufted ears, white bellies, long fluffy white tails and a red patch on their dark grey backs. Sometimes, it almost feels like a reverent place.

For flower lovers, the meadow in front of the volcano is an excellent place to spot spring, summer and fall wildflowers. It is also an excellent location for taking a photo of the Sunset Crater and the San Francisco Peaks.

Like many other travelers on Interstate 8, we had driven by **Gila Bend** without stopping. One day, however, that changed. We had purchased the book *Chasing Arizona* by Ken Lamberton and after reading his chapter on Gila Bend, we were in total agreement. Gila Bend was put on the top of our places to visit and, soon thereafter, we headed west to explore.

Gila Bend is a small town of about two thousand residents. At an elevation of seven hundred feet, the arid desert community holds the claim for some of the hottest summer temperatures in the state. We believe that is also holds the prize for the most humorous welcome sign. Upon entering the town, we encountered a sign that says: "Gila Bend Welcomes You. Home of seventeen hundred people (an outdated number) and five old crabs." At the bottom of the sign, there is a list of the five old crabs. The sign earned a hearty laugh from us.

Being the curious explorers that we are, we made it a mission to learn more about the crabs. We asked everyone we met about the tradition of designating and publicizing their "crabs." Reportedly, it is an honor to have your name on the welcome sign. Everyone said they personally knew them, but we did not have the occasion to meet one. Maybe if we return we will have that honor.

When we arrived in town, it seemed unimpressive and ordinary. The longer we stayed, the more we learned to love this wonderful little town with warm, welcoming and friendly people. For three nights, we stayed in the middle of town in the Best Western Space Age Lodge and we ate our meals at the Space Age Restaurant. For those who choose to stay at this Lodge, it is easy to find - there is a space-ship over the lobby. Interesting theme. It was great to interact with some of the people who live in Gila Bend. One of the young men who worked at the restaurant became an instant friend. We earned his respect because we were staying there for three nights. In amazement, his comment was, "Nobody stays in Gila Bend."

This community is mainly a pass-thru community so we became well-known as the people who stayed. The second day, our waitress was very happy to hear that we would be spending some time in the area. She gave us directions to find some exceptional petroglyphs along a dirt road near the Gillespsie Dam. The style of these petroglyphs was new to us: unique forms and figures.

Having friends in town was very comforting, but we still wanted to venture out and explore the surrounding area. Gila Bend's nickname is "Crossroads of the Southwest" because of all the stage and freight routes that converged in this area. We were lucky to find an old Butterfield Overland stage route and an old road from Phoenix. We also enjoyed exploring the Gillespie Dam and the Gillespie Dam Trestle Bridge.

Surrounding the town, there are agricultural fields and fields of solar panels. We were told that the solar industry is growing rapidly in the area. In town, we visited the Visitors

Center and the Museum. The museum is small, but the information is plentiful about the native tribes who lived in the area, the development of the town of Gila Bend, and the Oatman Massacre site.

We will always have fond memories of this town and the people who live there. Gila Bend will also be remembered as the only community (we know about) that advertises the names of its "crabs."

The **Naco Paleo Site** lies about twelve miles east of Payson on Highway 260. We heard about the site from one of Bernadette's friends and thought it would be exciting to play the role of fossil hunters. In a short period of time, we decided on an itinerary and off we went in search of fossils. The site contains specimens that date back to three hundred million years old when Arizona lay beneath shallow seas that were forty to fifty feet deep.

Heading out with our hiking poles, gloves, box and geology hammer, we were ready to gather up some beautiful (and maybe priceless) fossils. Upon arriving at the site, it was obvious that we would not be climbing up this steep hill in pursuit of riches or fame. Reading the sign, the fossils at the site were identified with beautiful colored photos and names. Huh! No dinosaur bones were on the list! A large variety of sea shells, however, and off we went in hot pursuit of some of the beautiful old fossils.

At the bottom of the slope we found an area rich in loose and well-preserved specimens. We found a variety of sea shells, brachiopods and a crinoid stem. We were happy fossil hunters and came home with samples for friends. One of the fossils is at rest in our coffee table as a reminder of the great day we had pretending to be "Great Fossil Hunters."

In 1989, **Prescott** was designated "Arizona's Christmas City," and in 2012 it was named "The Number One True Western Town of the Year." Throughout the years, it has received other honorary titles as well as being the first permanent capital of the Arizona Territory.

This beautiful city of thirty-nine thousand residents has numerous events throughout the year including the Oldest Rodeo in Arizona, Frontier Days and Christmas Lights. Prescott also has a large variety of tourist attractions and we explored a few of them including: the Sharlot Hall Museum, the Smoki Museum, Goldwater Lake, Watson Lake, the Dells and Fort Whipple.

One of the attractions we particularly enjoyed was the sculpture garden at Yavapai College. The quality of the sculptures, displayed in the garden amongst the flowers and trees, made for a pleasurable afternoon. Such a peaceful and serene place.

One of our favorites parts of the city was the Courthouse and the Central Courthouse Plaza. The plaza is known as a gathering and meeting place. Several performances and concerts are performed here in the summer months. This block is a wonderful place to stroll, greet other visitors, stop to rest and admire the clean and beautiful downtown. A fascinating feature is located to the north of the Courthouse. A World History Timeline is embossed and painted into the concrete sidewalk. We read the timeline on the day we were there, along with many other tourists. Very well done. Another interesting point about the courthouse: Barry Goldwater launched his presidential campaign from the steps of this building.

Across the street from the central plaza and courthouse, visitors can enjoy the historic buildings of Whiskey Row. The notorious red-light district and row of bars has been converted to restaurants, bars, and boutiques. After reading the history about this block, it is easy to picture it as it was.

Prescott is also home to the Arizona Pioneers' Home and the home for disabled miners. It was designed to provide a care facility for pioneer families and individuals and has grown throughout the years to include other individuals. A point of interest: "Big Nose Kate" Elder, a Hungarian-born prostitute and longtime companion of Doc Holliday, is buried in the Pioneers' Home cemetery.

The Hassayampa Hotel is a restored 1927 hotel on East Gurley Street. Upon entering the lobby, we were unprepared for the elegance of the lobby with its hand-painted ceiling, its dramatic murals, the stone arches for windows and doors, the wooden beams across the ceilings, the historic fireplaces and the chandeliers. This modernized boutique hotel has preserved the past and blended it with today's amenities. Celebrities such as Will Rogers, Greta Garbo and Clark Gable have rested here.

What a great city for the adventurer and explorer. We enjoyed every moment we spent in this town and will always remember the feeling of being there.

J.A. Jance, in her book, *Queen of the Night*, tells the legend of a beautiful night-blooming cereus. After reading the book, we were on a mission to find this beautiful cactus flower. We researched where to find the cactus, how to see the flowers in bloom and one option met our needs. Tohono Chul Park hosts an annual "Bloom Night" when the public is invited to come enjoy the night-blooming cereus.

There is no set date for the "Bloom Night," and in order to be notified on time, joining the e-mail list is mandatory. The park sends out alerts to keep the public informed. Notifications are sent out often alerting everyone to the upcoming bloom, then the notice arrives. Tonight is Bloom Night! This is the night when a large number of blooms will be visible. Sometimes, as many as one hundred and seventy-four blooms can be seen.

As many as eighteen hundred people have attended this much-anticipated event that last from dusk to midnight. The event includes guided tours, drawings, refreshments, and the telling of the legend. Everyone arrives with cameras and plenty of excitement and anticipation. The evening begins with a live telling of the Tohono O'odham tribal legend about the origin of the Queen of the Night. During the live telling, sometimes snakes are seen and one was seen the night we participated.

After hearing the legend, the guided tours begin. Off we go down dirt paths, through the desert flora, in search of the beautiful, white, fragrant flower. Before you reach the first destination, a sweet and pleasant scent is detected. This is the only cactus flower with a scent and it smells delicious. The flower is a brilliant white and is in bloom for only one night.

You would never find the plant of the night-blooming cereus. Its thin branches grow four to eight feet tall and blends in with the desert flora. Upon examination, the branches look like dead sticks with no leaves. What a wonder that it produces one the most sought-after flowers. What an experience to be in a desert environment, on a dark night, smelling a wonder of nature.

Writing this section was a trip down memory lane. Whenever someone mentions these places, or we read about them in a book, the feeling of being there returns. We wish that all adventurers and explorers in Arizona find those places that make the skin tingle and change you forever.

CONCLUSION

Arizona, with one hundred and fourteen thousand square miles, is the sixth largest state. It is known as one of the four-corner states where visitors can stand at a designated spot and have their feet in Arizona, Colorado, Utah and New Mexico all at the same time. This state has a history that traces back twelve thousand years and evidence of that habitation still exists and can be seen by explorers and adventurers.

This state is the land of breathtaking sunsets, magnificent sunrises, stunning mountain ranges, unique red rock formations, spectacular canyons, expansive lava fields with spatter and cinder cones, torrential monsoon rains, dry river beds, wide-open unpopulated spaces, herds of wild horses and burros, expansive blue skies and fields of green and gold grasses.

Arizona contains the third largest volcanic field in the United States, two hundred and seventy-five ghost towns, bombing ranges, General Patton trainings camps, two of the largest WWII Japanese Internment camps, WWII prisoner of war camps, the largest contiguous ponderosa pine forest in the United States, spiritual vortexes, twenty-two national parks, twenty-two American Indian tribes, the Grand Canyon: one of the Seven Natural Wonders of the world, Monument Valley: the most photographed place in the Southwest and thirty-one State Parks that preserve natural, cultural and historical sites. Last, but not least, Arizona is home to the Magnificent Saguaro Cactus.

This state is dotted with prior railroad towns, abandoned ghost towns, dude ranches, small historical towns, green spaces in which to relax, military outposts, areas in which to escape civilization for a while and beautiful places to enjoy the sound and beauty of water. In the fall, Arizona can also put on quite a display of color.

When you consider what this state contains, it is easy to understand why new residents become overwhelmed at first. There is always the question: where do I begin? We have been actively exploring this state for six years and we have collected several hundred dots: pieces of information that will complete a collage of this state.

Our goal, at first, was to explore every inch of Arizona. This lofty goal changed over time. There are some parts of this state that are beyond our hiking abilities and Gypsy's driving abilities. We will be content to explore all of the areas we can. At this point, most of the state is done and this has prompted one of our friends to offer us this advice: Now you need to meet Arizonans to gather some oral history. We started doing that when we visited Crown King and it was a successful trial.

In the process of learning, we were awed by the natural beauty of the volcanic past and amazed by the opportunity to experience history. Arizona is a baby state and pieces of history are still visible and tangible. Here, we can walk where Geronimo walked, we can visit a place where prehistoric man killed mammoths, we can visit incredible Indian ruins and can drive on stagecoach roads.

Four years ago, we met two cowgirls in Dragoon and had the opportunity to have lunch with them. In the conversation, the topic of Sonoran Hot Dogs came up and they were amazed that we had not eaten the local treat. We were informed that we could not become Arizonans unless we ate Sonoran Dogs. We searched a long time before finding our first one and, since then, we have located (and eaten) many more. One sad fact, however, is that we will never become Arizonans by eating Sonoran Dogs. We have decided, therefore, to make Arizona a part of us. We have successfully done that. This state has excited us, made us laugh, awed us, overwhelmed us, thrilled us, amazed us, made us sad, and has made us proud.

We hope that all fellow adventurers and explorers who come will have the same experience.

ACKNOWLEDGMENTS

Our thanks to our dear friends Sue Smith, Mary Newman, Irma Thibault, Bernadette Cardwell, Dotty Brack, Jacqui Harrold, and Betty Nolan for the great adventures, the hearty laughs and the memorable moments.

Our thanks to all family members and friends who have shared some Arizona adventures with us. Fun moments and wonderful memories.

Our thanks to Michael and Carolyn Flynn for their friendship since the day we arrived in Arizona. Thank you for your patience in dealing with our unending questions, for telling us not to eat the fruit of the Mountain Laurel and for joining us on Arizona adventures.

Our thanks to Ron and Vicki Sullivan for their friendship, advice and guidance when we needed it most.

Our thanks to Bruce and Kathleen MacLeod. Your assistance in proofreading our book was invaluable.

Our thanks to all of the wonderful people we have met in this state who have given us directions, offered their recommendations and gladly shared their knowledge. They assisted in making the exploration of this state more enjoyable.

Other Books by the Authors

One Mile at a Time

About the Authors

Marie J. Lemay (Midge) was born in New England. Mother of nine, grandmother of thirteen, and great-grandmother of three. Left Burlington Vermont to follow her dreams and currently resides in Green Valley, Arizona.

Suzanne T. Poirier (Sue) was born in New England and lived the majority of her life in New Hampshire. Currently resides in Green Valley, Arizona.

Made in the USA
Lexington, KY
15 May 2019